TROUBLE WITH THE LAW

Crimes and Trials from Ireland's Past

D1586187

Trouble with the Law

Crimes and Trials from Ireland's Past

EDITED BY

Liam Clare and Máire Ní Chearbhaill

THE WOODFIELD PRESS

This book was designed and typeset in Bembo 11pt on 14pt
by Carrigboy Typesetting Services for
THE WOODFIELD PRESS
17 Jamestown Square, Dublin 8
www.woodfield-press.com
e-mail: terri.mcdonnell@ireland.com

Publishing Editor
Helen Harnett

Publisher
Terri McDonnell

House Editor
Suzanna Henry

A catalogue record for this title
is available from the British Library.

ISBN 978–1–905094–02–8

Printed in England
by Cromwell Press, Trowbridge

Contents

Acknowledgements

Trouble with the law, a collection of essays on criminal cases and courtroom conflicts, is the latest in a series of local history studies prepared by a group of graduates of the MA course in Local History at NUI Maynooth. The group was established in 1994 to share ideas and to publish joint studies on local history themes. Previous publications in the series are *Irish townlands*, *Irish fairs and markets*, *Irish villages*, and *Hanging crimes*. The series aims to be of interest to practitioners and students of local history as well as to general readers who enjoy works of non-fiction.

The authors wish to thank Raymond Gillespie for writing the Introduction and for his support. Thanks are also due to the staff of the National Library of Ireland; Gilbert Library, Dublin; NUI Maynooth Library; University College Dublin Library; Westmeath County Library; National Archives of Ireland; Public Record Office of Northern Ireland; National Archives, Kew, London; Manx National Heritage Council; Hampshire Record Office, and BBC Written Archives Centre, for their assistance. The authors also wish to thank their families and friends for their patience and support.

The editors are most grateful to Terri McDonnell of The Woodfield Press for her confidence in this undertaking, and for her encouragement and sense of humour throughout the production process.

Abbreviations

CSOOP	Chief Secretary's Office, official papers
CSORP	Chief Secretary's Office, registered papers
JIHOC	*Journal of the Irish House of Commons*
NA	National Archives, Kew, London
NAI	National Archives of Ireland, Dublin
NLI	National Library of Ireland, Dublin
PRONI	Public Record Office of Northern Ireland, Belfast
RD	Registry of Deeds, Dublin

Illustrations

Contributors

Seán Bagnall is an accountant and lawyer and is a partner in an accountancy practice in Naas. He is also an historian and a keen gardener, with a major collection of over one hundred varieties of holly in his garden near Celbridge.

Liam Clare, now retired from local administration, is particularly interested in administrative history. He has written two books, *Victorian Bray* and *Enclosing the Commons*, has jointly edited *Irish villages*, and *Foxrock and Cabinteely memories*, and has written numerous articles and pamphlets on local historical subjects.

Paul Connell, a priest of the diocese of Meath, and president of St Finian's College, Mullingar, is the author of *Parson, priest and master*; *Cathedral of Christ the King, Mullingar* and *The Diocese of Meath under Bishop John Cantwell 1830–66*, and has edited and contributed to other books on local history.

Denis A. Cronin writes and teaches local history. A native of county Cork, he lives and works in Dublin. He is currently researching agrarian crime in early nineteenth-century Cork.

Karina Holton is a local historian whose research interests range from the medieval period to early nineteenth-century Ireland. She is co-editor of *Irish villages* and *Irish fairs and markets* and has contributed to a number of historical publications.

Tom Hunt comes from Clonea, Carrick-on-Suir, county Waterford and is a teacher in Mullingar. He is author of *Portlaw, county Waterford: portrait of an industrial village and its cotton industry*, and contributed a chapter to *Sport and the Irish: histories, identities and issues*. He has also contributed to *History Ireland*

and to various local history journals. His book, *Sport and society in Victorian Ireland: the case of Westmeath*, is due for publication in autumn 2007.

Máire Mhic Giobúin is a native of Kanturk, county Cork and now lives in Goatstown, county Dublin. A member of An Taisce, she is interested in local history, is an active environmentalist and has published a number of articles in these areas.

Maeve Mulryan-Moloney is a native of Williamstown, county Galway. She retains a keen interest in the history of her native place and regularly contributes to local publications. She taught in Rathcoole in west Dublin for twenty-five years. Her book, *A history of Saggart and Rathcoole parishes*, was published to coincide with the bicentenary of Father James Harold's arrest.

Máire Ní Chearbhaill lives in Cabinteely, county Dublin. She has been a free-lance editor for many years, and has a special interest in church history and in social studies. She has written numerous popular booklets and articles on religious topics.

Austin Stewart, a native of county Tyrone, is a teacher and author. His published works include *Coalisland, county Tyrone in the industrial revolution, 1800–1901*. He has also contributed to micro-studies in local history in the publications, *Irish villages* and *Hanging crimes*.

Introduction

RAYMOND GILLESPIE

Crime fascinates historians and exercises a morbid attraction that will not go away. At some levels, the reasons for the fascination are not difficult to find. High-profile murders and assaults contain all the elements of brutality and drama that were the staples of the popular press in the past, and because of this, evidence has survived to recreate the context and course of these events. In the past, moreover, mayhem had a habit of following murder and, thus, killings of landlords or their agents, policemen or family members, often sent shock waves through local communities that have persisted over long periods of time, especially in oral tradition. While murder may beguile and attract historians, it was not the only sort of crime that shaped local societies in the past. Breaking the law at any of its many weak points turned certain actions into special kinds of events. Whether the crime be embezzlement, extortion, rebellion or adultery, the interest of the historian is not in the questions of guilt and innocence (which are often impossible to determine at such a remove as we now are from these events) but rather what the breaking of the social rules tells us about the experience of those who lived in the past, particularly in their local contexts. The context is important for in most cases the result of a crime was that the small world of an individual, or a small group of individuals, challenged (however briefly) the large-scale social arrangements constructed to make the world manageable. The consequence was that the world was turned upside down; the powerless criminal was briefly powerful because he or she had evaded capture. Normal order was restored when the perpetrator of the crime was captured, convicted and punished. Thus the drama of the trial, well described in many of the essays in this volume, was deliberate. Trials were not simply technical events in which the law was applied and restitution made. They were events that returned the world to normal and the rituals of the courtroom were part of the affirmation of the prevailing social order.

Paradoxically, studying crime then tells us a great deal not about the deviant but about the law-abiding and illuminates details of everyday life by investigating how those came to be disregarded. The workings of crime, and hence the stories behind the essays in this volume, reflect social interactions in particular times and places. Thus, the essays reflect the relations between husbands and wives, between rulers and the ruled, and between buyers and sellers in the past. It is worth remembering that for every one of those encounters that broke down, thousands went unremarked by contemporaries. The debacle surrounding the break-up of the marriage of George Thomas Nugent, eighth earl and first marquis of Westmeath, examined in Paul Connell's essay, was one of the most sensational of the period simply because it was one of the most unusual. However, the issues that lay at its heart, the relations of husband and wife within the broader social context of the nineteenth century, were far from unusual.

Yet, trials such as this raise questions for those interested in forms of crime that lack the drama of murder or violent assault. Three questions, in particular, are significant. First, what was a crime? On the face of it this may seem to be a fairly simple question yet it is more complex than it first appears. Law, and attitudes to it, changed over time. New statutes were passed bringing within the ambit of the civil courts matters that previously had remained outside the law and judicial decisions altered and reshaped the nature of legal understanding. A case in point is the matter of marriage, which is crucial to some of the essays below. Before the middle of the nineteenth century, divorce (especially on the grounds of adultery) was not a matter for the civil courts but for their ecclesiastical equivalents. Adultery and divorce were not so much criminal matters as sins. The only legal remedy available for the aggrieved husband was that of 'criminal conversation', discussed in Karina Holton's essay. Even within the law, ambiguities about what was acceptable and what was not could lead to difficult and protracted legal wrangling, as Liam Clare's and Austin Stewart's essays reveal. Secondly, there is the problem of the enforcement of the law. As the understanding of law evolved so too did the mechanisms for enforcing that law. The replacement of the parish watch or the parish constable with a more professionalised police force during the early nineteenth century changed attitudes towards the application of law. The boundaries between what it was socially acceptable to ignore and what it was deemed necessary to clamp down on were often vague and ill-defined. As Tom Hunt's essay shows, members of the police themselves were among the participants in some of the legally dubious practices associated with sporting meetings. Policing styles, and the bureaucratic structures that surrounded them, evolved only slowly and Seán Bagnall's essay captures this process in the case of one police inspector in Tallaght in the early nineteenth century. Finally, there is the problem of analysing the criminal experience itself. Crime, by its very nature was secretive. Some sorts of political crime, such as those dealt with in the essays by Denis Cronin and Maeve Mulryan Moloney, were positively conspiratorial. The view that we have of these crimes is usually not through the eyes of the perpetrator but rather from the perspective of those in authority concerned with punishing the offender. If anything, that problem of perspective is compounded by that most Irish of complaints: the destruction of sources. The loss of the court of King's Bench records in the eighteenth century and many of the nineteenth-century criminal trial transcripts in the 1922 Public Record Office fire means that it is difficult to reconstruct patterns of crime. Abduction cases such as that dealt with by Máire Mhic Giobúin, can only be pieced together from surviving fragments on a case-by-case basis. It is, therefore, very difficult to understand whether the cases being reconstructed are typical of criminal experience as a whole or exhibit unusual or aberrant features.

Despite the problems of defining the nature of crime, understanding the enforcement of the law, and contextualising the criminal experience, the study of crime on a case-by-case basis can reveal a great deal about the workings of past worlds. The law, with all its ambiguities and changing enforcement practices, provides a yardstick against which it is possible to measure patterns of social behaviour in the past. The trial of the accused laid bare a set of relationships not only between victim and accused but also between the accused and the entire community within which he or she lived. Breaches of the law were not discrete events involving merely the accused and the victim; they were social crimes, and, as such, they reflected not only the dominant value systems of the court but also those of the criminal world. These wider attitudes on display as part of the criminal process were sometimes motivated by naked greed associated with theft or extortion, as is made clear in the essay by Liam Clare. In other cases, less obvious value systems came into play. The essays by Denis Cronin and Maeve Mulryan Moloney reveal that one man's criminal was often another's hero, reflecting a mismatch between the dominant value systems of the law and the more popular ones of political protest. Again Tom Hunt's essay embeds the apparently criminal world of drunkenness and dubious gambling practices in the context of a popular culture of commercialised sport. Finally, the complexities of the cases analysed by Máire Mhic Giobúin, Máire Ní Chearbhaill, Karina Holton and Paul Connell can best be understood by reference to the dominant value systems of honour and the position of a man in the eyes of his neighbours that dominated the aristocratic worlds of eighteenth- and nineteenth-century Ireland.

Taken together, these essays allow us to see something of the local, public and private worlds of Ireland in the past. Crime touched every level of society, often on a daily basis. For all our eagerness to measure the typicality or otherwise of particular types of crime the reality was that every break of the law was different although many had common features. Motives and contexts changed from event to event and by dissecting those motives and contexts, as these essays do, it is possible to understand something of the social dynamics of past worlds, and, in particular, the inner workings of local societies. These insights are often very different from what contemporaries thought, but by analysing crime in this way, we are better placed to understand how people in their own worlds of the past chose to live their lives. That is one of the real achievements of the essays that follow in this volume.

Extortion at the Treasury, Dublin Castle

George Roe's twenty-year struggle for justice

LIAM CLARE

George Roe was not a man to accept defeat. He would not, and could not, give up. As one of the many victims of a crime of extortion perpetrated by officialdom in Dublin Castle, he fought a twenty-year battle for redress, initially as one of a large group, but later as a single-handed campaigner. This campaign involved two sworn inquiries, three parliamentary bills, as well as four appeals to Queen Anne and her successors.

A native of London, George had migrated to Dublin in the late 1600s, and had participated in various camps and sieges during the conquest of Ireland by the army of William of Orange. He settled in Dublin and became a merchant shoemaker, employing numerous out-workers and agents. In his own words, he had enjoyed a plentiful fortune until he became impoverished as a result of advancing credit to facilitate the furnishing and clothing of the army in Ireland for expeditionary regiments to Flanders.[1]

His troubles began in September 1705, when three suppliers of military uniforms for King William's – and subsequently Queen Anne's – armies in Ireland, ran out of funds. Their insolvency brought financial ruin to hundreds of families – not just to the dependants of the clothing and footwear merchants like George Roe, to whom the suppliers owed large

---

Some events were recorded many times in the various sources; references below have been simplified.

1   Undated petition (c. 1724), of George Roe to King George I, NA, SP63/382, (26).

sums of money, but also to the weavers and their families labouring in their workrooms, the needlewomen sewing in their cabins, and the shoemakers working in their homes. These unfortunate people were left unpaid by the impoverished merchants.[2] The resultant furore uncovered an extortion fraud of gigantic proportions which forced the two leading officers of the Irish treasury to flee the country, leaving behind a financial mess which was never fully sorted out, despite Roe's dogged twenty-year campaign for compensation.

The chain of events which caused the financial collapse had started around 1698, when James Leathly, Benjamin Taylor and James Duggan, three clothing merchants, were engaged as suppliers of uniforms and footwear, of stockings, belts and ancillary articles to the Irish regiments of the army. These three main suppliers had recruited some eighty sub-contractors, woollen manufacturers, shoe-makers, stocking-makers, cutlers, saddlers and so on, creating an interdependent economic network of rich and poor. When the 'big three' at the top became insolvent, the repercussions echoed throughout the clothing industry. The trio will be referred to throughout the story as 'the partners' or 'the three partners'.[3]

To comprehend fully the impact of the subsequent financial collapse on the lives of those affected, it is necessary to take a look at the clothing industry in Dublin at the time. There were no large factories in the year 1700, as there would have been a century or so later when steam- or water-powered machinery was pushing out large quantities of finished products; the collapse occurred a generation or two prior to the start of the industrial revolution. With no large plants or machinery, the industry was dispersed into the houses and cabins of the workers not only in the towns, but also in the surrounding rural hinterland.[4] In Dublin the domestic clothing industry was centred in the Liberties; the names 'Weavers' Square' and 'Tenter-fields' remind us of this. However, much processing was also done outside the city walls.[5]

The clothing merchant typically marketed the products, secured the orders and contracts, purchased the materials and engaged sub-agents. These

2   Undated petition of George Roe to King George I, NA, SP63/382, (26); *JIHOC*, ii, (1692–1713), appendix, pp. clxxii–clxxvi, *passim* (henceforth appendix 1707); *JIHOC*, iii, (1715–1730), appendix, pp. ccxxxi–ccxxxiii, *passim* (henceforth appendix 1721).
3   *JIHOC*, appendices 1707 and 1721.
4   Duncan Bythell, *The sweated trades* (London, 1978), pp. 9–24; T.S. Aston (ed.), *An economic history of England: the eighteenth century* (London, 1969 reprint), pp. 97–104.
5   C.T. M'Cready, *Dublin street names dated and explained* (Blackrock, 1987 edition), pp. 140, 133; J.J. Webb, *Industrial Dublin since 1698* (Dublin, 1913), pp. 6–7, 58; Art Cosgrove (ed.), *Dublin through the ages* (Dublin, 1988), pp. 68–71.

sub-agents, in turn, recruited the workers, lent them the raw materials, carried out any troubleshooting necessary to drive production, paid the wages, wrote up the accounts, and collected back the completed work. The workers – men, women and children – mainly laboured in their cabins using their own or rented implements like spinning wheels or small hand looms which were the tools of their trade. They sold only their labour and that of their families, spinning or weaving, knitting stockings, running up garments, making shoes or even parts thereof, and being remunerated for their efforts with very low piece-rates. It is easy to understand how this entire economic community would be pushed over the edge by the collapse of the three partners, the merchant capitalists at the top of the pile, who were financing the production.[6]

George Roe, who employed twenty, forty, sixty, or even a hundred men at different times, was just one of the sub-contractors impoverished by the collapse. There was also John Throke, a stocking-maker, who employed three or four hundred families in the making-up of his products, and Richard Maguire, a woollen sub-contractor, who claimed that he kept about a hundred people in work. Other out-of-pocket creditors had employed ten, twelve or maybe twenty men, so that the total number of families benefiting from the contracts had been very considerable.[7]

On delivery of uniforms or boots to the quarter-masters of the various regiments, the suppliers received dockets authorising payment out of the national treasury in Dublin, or occasionally from the treasury in Great Britain. The man in charge of the Irish treasury was Sir William Robinson, then Deputy Vice-Treasurer of Ireland, and he was assisted by Thomas Putland, his cashier, who, in turn, employed Joseph Nuttall as his clerk. These three men were later accused of causing the financial ruin of the suppliers through extortion.[8]

It is necessary to explain at this point the situation of banking and currency in Ireland at the time of the events being described. It was not simply a case of a contractor lodging a treasury payment cheque to his bank account. In the late 1600s in Ireland there were no banks and no currency notes; there was total financial chaos. There were gold and silver coins in circulation – English or sterling coins, French coins and Portuguese coins – but no Irish money of any kind, except coppers. Most large transactions were arranged in Irish currency, but settled in English money. Somebody had to

6   Duncan Bythell, *The sweated trades*, pp. 9–24.
7   *JIHOC*, appendix 1707.
8   *JIHOC*, appendices 1707 and 1721.

facilitate trade by filling the vacuum. Consequently, in the late 1600s, receipts for bullion lodged with goldsmiths and other merchants for safe keeping, began to be traded by other merchants as if they were official currency.

Soon receipts for non-existent gold lodgements were being issued by astute merchants and used as currency, relying on the financial security of the individual issuing them. Such receipts developed into bank notes, similar to those still being issued by banks in Northern Ireland. In addition to foreign coins, therefore, there was a wide variety of paper currency – cashable receipts, promissory notes (IOUs), 'accepted bills of exchange' (agreements to pay money on demand or at some future date), and so on.[9] But a supplier could reasonably expect payment in gold or silver coins, albeit in sterling, on presenting a payment warrant or authorisation docket to the treasury.

The first recorded problem for the three partners occurred in 1698, soon after the contracts had been signed and the first deliveries made, when they failed to receive the full amounts shown on their payment dockets. This practice of underpayment persisted and every additional deduction increased the financial pressures on the suppliers. A vicious circle of ever-increasing debt was established, which grew in intensity until the bubble finally burst on 12 September 1705, when the three partners ran out of cash and were forced to cease trading.[10] By then, out of the total payment of £86,640–10s. –4½d. due to them, some £9,417 remained outstanding.[11] The sheer extent of the money withheld can be appreciated best by noting that it was the equivalent of 40 per cent of the total cost (£24,000) of building the newly completed, extensive, Royal Hospital at Kilmainham![12]

In the aftermath of the collapse, at the very time that the partners were looking into the financial abyss, Putland was moving to a more upmarket residence, being one of the first to leave the over-crowded, disease-ridden, medieval inner city, in favour of the fashionable, new, private, green-field estate being laid out by Henry Jervis, north of the river Liffey. Here he built

9 Pádraig McGowan, *Money and banking in Ireland* (Dublin, 1990), pp. 3–9; Eoin O'Kelly, *The old private banks and bankers of Munster* (Cork, 1959), pp. 2–3; F. G. Hall, *The Bank of Ireland* (Dublin, 1949), pp. 1–4; Bernard Share (ed.), *Root and Branch – Allied Irish Banks, yesterday, today and to-morrow* (Dublin, 1979), pp. 15, 23; Cosgrove, *Dublin through the ages,* p. 70.
10 *JIHOC,* Appendices 1707 and 1721.
11 Somewhat different figures were quoted from time to time, sometimes rounded and sometimes including interest. The 'total payable' is taken from the table in NLI, Ms 2487, pp. 422–5, prepared *circa* 1721; the 'amounts outstanding' are the sum of Nuttall's refund of £1,206, Putlands's refund of £3,472 plus earlier payments of £205, and the amount claimed from Robinson of £4,534 – total £9,417.
12 Maurice Craig, *Dublin 1660–1860* (Dublin, 1980), p. 59.

a large mansion on the site now occupied by the Parnell Centre. He was obviously confident of a sound economic future.[13]

Initially, he continued in his role of cashier – very officiously – as if nothing was amiss. For example, he was complained about for 'scrupling' about paying a retired officer's pension out of the treasury funds. But he gradually became more worried, and in the following year, 1706, he sent Nuttall to the partners to deliver £100 to each of them, to help support their families at home, or to take them abroad. The partners thanked Putland in writing for these payments, despite his previous treatment of them. Perhaps he had forced them to do so in anticipation of an investigation, as their letters of thanks were later produced on his behalf. Presumably he also hoped to buy their silence. In this he may have been successful as it was their sub-contractors rather than the partners themselves who eventually took action against the officials. On the other hand, perhaps it was their fear of being formally bankrupted that ensured their initial silence. There was no general law of bankruptcy or bankruptcy courts at the time, and an insolvent debtor might have his entire assets seized to pay the very considerable costs of a special act of parliament as well as the total sum owed, if the creditors went down that road.[14]

Dublin was a small city in the early eighteenth century and despite Putland's precautions, word began to circulate that the collapse had been directly triggered through extortion by the treasury officials. Putland later blamed Nuttall for making his involvement 'known to the world' by his indiscriminate gossiping. The public reaction to the rumours soon led to the holding of a public inquiry. By then his former boss and friend, Sir William Robinson, had described Putland as 'almost frightened out of his life'.[15]

* * *

Although initially only Putland and Nuttall were accused of the extortion, Robinson was also implicated at a later stage. Sir William Robinson, the most senior of the trio, was born in England around 1643 and came to Ireland in 1670, apparently under the patronage of the then lord lieutenant.

---

13 Craig, *Dublin 1660–1860*, p. 27; Marriage settlement re Thomas Putland Junior, 11 August 1708, p. 13, (manuscript copy held by Ms Toler-Aylward, Paulstown, Co. Kilkenny, photocopy held by author).

14 Historical manuscripts commission, *Calendar of the manuscripts of the Marquess of Ormond deeds* (new series, viii) (London, 1920), p. 253; *JIHOC*, appendix 1707; Malcolm Dillon, *The history and development of banking in Ireland* (Dublin, 1889), p. 19.

15 *JIHOC*, appendix 1707; index to British departmental correspondence 1683–1740, letter, 23 July 1707, Sir William Robinson to Joshua Dawson NAI, 1A 52/142.

1 Portrait of Sir
William Robinson by
Godfrey Kneller.
Courtesy of The
Huntington Library,
Art Collections, and
Botanical Gardens, San
Marino, California

He soon became engineer and surveyor-general of military buildings, and
was responsible for the building of the Royal Hospital, Kilmainham and of
Charles's Fort, Kinsale, among other public buildings. He also redesigned
Dublin Castle after a disastrous fire. His career pattern had its ups and
downs. He had to flee to England when James II came to power but he
returned with the Williamite army in 1690, and resumed his engineering
and architectural posts. He was a jack-of-all-professions, however, and soon
took on additional positions like auditor, attorney and administrator, as well
as Deputy Vice-Treasurer of Ireland. He was also a knight, a member of the
Irish parliament and of the Irish privy council.

In 1703, having submitted a report on the national debt, Robinson was
accused of misrepresentation, a charge which he strenuously denied.
However, he was declared 'unfit for public employment in this kingdom'
and imprisoned by the Irish house of commons. After a month he was
released and fled to England to carry out further work on the accounts. He

returned after a year or so, but fled again around the time that the extortion scandal broke. He never again ventured back to Ireland.[16]

The next most senior alleged offender, Thomas Putland, was a self-made man. As a twenty-six-year-old blacksmith in 1677, the king had granted him a pardon for all his past 'felonies and offences'. Why an ordinary blacksmith's situation should be put before the king of England is not known, but it indicates that Putland had already got good friends in high places. And he was already spreading his ambitions beyond metal working. Like other shrewd merchants of the time, Putland had become a *de facto* banker. As early as 1683, Putland the blacksmith had been accepting bills of exchange, that is giving undertakings to pay cash at a fixed date, for hundreds, even thousands of pounds, to finance importers and exporters of goods. And in 1693 he was among sixty investors led by the Duke of Ormond, and three earls, who were granted the patent to operate the Royal Fisheries of Ireland.

Putland was also into property speculation. He purchased many landed estates on offer by those who had received grants of confiscated property. Many grantees wished to liquidate their land allocations for cash by unloading them on to some entrepreneur like Thomas Putland, who was willing to take the risks of investing in real estate in those disturbed times. By 1708 Putland owned lands in Dublin and Cork cities, as well as counties Cork, Wicklow, Kilkenny, Queen's County, Kildare, Meath, Westmeath, Roscommon and Clare.

Putland's association with his boss, Sir William Robinson, went back at least to the Royal Fishery Company of 1693, in which they were fellow investors; indeed, it is possible that it was Robinson who had secured for him his Royal pardon in 1677. In any event, Putland became Robinson's cashier, as well as his life-long colleague and confidant, and ultimately executor of his will. After the extortion scandal had become public, and as soon as he was able to extricate himself, Putland fled to England, bringing his wife and some of his ten children with him. He settled in London at the fashionable Paradise Row, in the then suburban Chelsea. He died there a wealthy man in 1723.[17]

The background of Joseph Nuttall, Putland's clerk, much younger and only a minor figure in the events, is more difficult to tie down. There is

16 Rolf Loeber, 'Sir William Robinson' in *Quarterly bulletin of the Irish Georgian Society*, xvii, nos 1 & 2 (January–June 1974), pp. 3–9; Rolf Loeber, *A biographical dictionary of architects in Ireland, 1600–1720* (London, 1981), pp. 88–97.
17 Liam Clare 'The Putland family of Dublin and Bray' in *Dublin Historical Record,* liv, no. 2 (autumn 2001), pp. 183–8.

some circumstantial evidence that he was the same Joseph Nuttall[18] who became Sheriff of Dublin city in 1721, Lord Mayor in 1731 and a partner in Nuttall and McGuire's bank which was established in 1721 and went broke in 1735.[19]

* * *

On 9 August, 1707, nearly two years after the financial melt-down of the three partners, a petition was lodged at the Irish house of commons on behalf of some sixty sub-contractors injured by the insolvency. They claimed that the partners were owed £10,000 by the treasury, resulting from extortion by its officers. They sought relief from parliament. The sub-contractors involved included George Roe. A committee of parliamentarians was established with powers to summon and examine witnesses, to requisition documents and to report their findings. Witnesses could be represented by counsel.[20]

At the committee, the petitioners alleged that payments, already overdue to the partners from the treasury, were refused on the false grounds of there being no public money available. The partners were then offered 'loans', allegedly from Putland's and Nuttall's own funds (though actually out of treasury moneys). The amounts due to be paid were reduced by a deduction for 'interest on the loan'. The partners had no option but to accept the 'loans', having been backed into a corner by the withholding of money already overdue and urgently needed. In contrast, the British treasury always paid its debts promptly.[21]

Benjamin Taylor, the partners' accountant, listed in evidence many transactions where the partners had to pay interest to Putland and Nuttall, ranging from 2½ per cent to 20 per cent, for securing the payments already overdue in respect of goods supplied. This levy had cost them about £9,000 out of the £100,000 due. The partners were currently in debt to the sum of £14,000. Taylor was later cross-examined on each of twenty-three notes which he had produced to document his transactions with Nuttall. These indicated that even if the deductions had not been fraudulent, the interest

---

18 Same name, similar age, similar profession, absence of any evidence of the existence of a namesake.

19 R. W. Smith Jnr, 'The Nuttalls of County Kildare' in *County Kildare archaeological society journal*, viii (1915–1917), pp. 180–81; C. M. Tenison 'The old Dublin bankers' in *JCHAS,* series 1, iii, no. 27 (March 1894), p. 55.

20 *JIHOC*, ii, p. 529.

21 Ibid.

rate charged was more than twice the legal maximum. Taylor also then alleged a second rip-off: they had to pay six pence in the pound (2½ per cent) as 'currency exchange' for converting payments into Irish from English currency, even though payments in Irish currency had been specified in their contracts.[22]

James Duggan, a tailor and another of the partners, described the case of Pallin, a cutler, and the partners' sub-contractor for swords. For lack of cash, they had paid an instalment to him with a treasury IOU for £272. But Nuttall, when cashing it, deducted £65 for 'advance payment' and only gave him £207. To recover his loss, Pallin absconded without delivering the swords, thereby causing a further loss of £101 to the contractors. To support his statement, Duggan produced the record of this payment of £207 endorsed 'burn this' in Nuttall's handwriting.[23]

Some witnesses, including George Roe, described the misery caused to themselves and to their employees by the fraud at the treasury. George was at a loss of £500. But his resultant impoverishment was increased by a knock-on loss of other business, and by the need to borrow money. John Throke, the stocking-maker, said that he personally would have had to leave town only for a loan from a gentleman.[24]

The next witness described the cash records of the treasury which detailed all payments to contractors. These would, when produced, resolve many of the questions raised. Thomas Putland was, therefore, called in and ordered to produce the cash books. He admitted that he had them in his possession, but pleaded that as both treasury transactions and his own business transactions were entered side-by-side throughout the books, it would be wrong to produce them publicly, for fear of exposing the private circumstances of his business associates. As the house was going into the summer recess, Putland was given until the autumn session to produce the treasury cash books.[25]

At the autumn session Taylor described an additional form of extortion. Instead of cashing payment dockets on the spot, the officials had sometimes offered as payment, 'exchequer acquittances' similar to cheques, but cashable only in Cork or Foxford. The officials would then offer to buy them back for actual cash in Dublin – at a discount.[26] Whatever about Cork, the offering of payments in Foxford, 'a very remote part of the Kingdom' was totally impracticable and unrealistic, because of the impossibility of safely transporting a quantity of gold and silver coins through the

22 Ibid.   23 Ibid.   24 Ibid.   25 Ibid.   26 Ibid.

intervening trackless and lawless territory. Another new allegation to emerge at this session was that Mr Putland's money, Mr Nuttall's money and the money of the crown, was all kept in the same box or treasure chest, and that both treasury payments and personal 'loans' by the officials were paid out of it.[27]

Putland and Nuttall produced a clothier, Robert Chetham, to state that he had always been properly treated by the treasury, but other suppliers contradicted this evidence. Asked what he had to say in his own defence, Joseph Nuttall submitted the names of seven members of parliament as character references.[28]

Putland disobeyed the summons to attend but sent along his counsel to say that he was much indisposed in his health. This excuse did not go down well at all. He also informed the committee that the treasury cash books were his private property, not the treasury's and argued that if he had deducted the amounts as alleged, to produce the books would in fact be admitting the criminal offence of charging an illegally high interest rate. He would thereby be incriminating himself and he had the right in common law to refrain from self-incrimination. He was, therefore, withholding the records. Putland later happily recovered his health and survived for a further sixteen years.[29]

Putland may have anticipated that the examining committee was going to cite him for contempt over the withholding of the books. He appealed over their heads, unsuccessfully, for a hearing before the entire house of commons – to be deferred pending the recovery from his illness.[30]

Monday 6 October 1707 was the agreed date for the committee's final report to the full house of commons. Joseph Nuttall, Putland's clerk, no doubt fearing the outcome, lodged a petition affirming that the sum of £1,206 was the full amount for which he was responsible and offering to refund this amount to the three partners. He also begged the house to take his 'misfortunes' into consideration. The partners, sensing that at least some money was within their grasp, issued a statement urging that as Nuttall had made full satisfaction and, because he was still a young man and a 'true penitent', the extenuating circumstances should be considered by the committee.[31]

The report of inquiry contained bad news for both Nuttall and Putland. The committee had resolved, among other things, that the allegations were proved, that both Thomas Putland and Joseph Nuttall had unjustly taken and illegally extorted great sums of money payable by the treasury on clothing

27 Ibid.   28 Ibid.   29 Ibid.   30 Ibid., ii, p. 535.   31 Ibid., ii, p. 537.

payment warrants to the ruin of many poor families, that these acts were a breach of the trust and a high misdemeanour, and that Thomas Putland having notoriously betrayed the trust placed in him, was unfit to serve in any public employment in the kingdom.

With the inquiry closed and the report studied, the full house of commons passed a resolution that Putland had obstructed the inquiry and was in contempt, through failing to produce his account books. They ordered that he be taken into custody and he was immediately landed in jail at Dublin Castle. Unfortunately, no records remain of the length or conditions of Putland's detention.[32]

2 Putland family arms with crest. The motto proclaims '*Deus astra regit* – God rules the heavens'.

* * *

The full house, having endorsed each of its committee's resolutions, passed a bill within three days, for the relief of the partners' creditors at the expense of Thomas Putland. It went straight to Lord Pembroke, the lord lieutenant, who, within a further week, had met with his privy council and drafted a letter to Queen Anne's secretariat seeking her signature for its enactment. This indicates the determination of all concerned. Robert Johnson, baron of the exchequer, remarked, 'Mr Putland has the misfortune to have the whole house against him, however much they differ [among themselves] in other matters.' Putland fought on, as George Roe observed, 'justly apprehending that justice was overtaking him'. Through the lobbying of friends he had the bill referred back for further consideration by two prominent members of the house of commons.[33]

32 *JIHOC*, appendix 1707 and ii, p. 537.
33 Ibid., ii, pp. 540–44 and appendix 1721; NA, SP63/382 (26); *Calendar of the manuscripts of Ormond,* p. 311; undated petition of George Roe to King George I: NA, SP63/382, (26).

Meanwhile, the petitioners had engaged a go-between with Putland, who had recently sworn an affidavit stating that he had received only £3,472 0s. 4d. out of the money extorted. The affidavit also implicated his boss, Sir William Robinson, in the sum of £4,667 14s. 10d. He had by then fled the country. The two MPs appointed to review the case ordered Putland to pay the £3,472 to the creditors and recommended the prosecution of Robinson for the balance. The parliamentary bill making Putland responsible for the entire amount extorted was abandoned.[34]

Having been declared unfit to serve in any public employment in Ireland, and having paid over his £3,472, Putland fled to England. There he renewed his close friendship with Robinson. He also kept in touch with events in Ireland. He remained in regular correspondence with Sir Joshua Dawson, secretary to the lords justices of Ireland, about business conditions, investments, requests for favours, personal medical treatments, Robinson's health, his own domestic affairs and so on. This correspondence indicates that despite his extortion, he had not been completely ostracised by society in Dublin. Moreover, his eldest son, Thomas junior, made a good marriage in 1708. These things are not surprising having regard to the prevailing attitude not only to fraud, but also to the principle of *caveat emptor* (let the buyer beware), and to what would today be regarded as 'sharp practice'. At that time if you 'got away with it', well and good! Nevertheless, Thomas senior dared not return to Ireland, and his wife Merial travelled alone on the long journey from London via Chester, to visit her father in Dublin.[35]

* * *

The repayments of moneys extorted by Putland and Nuttall did not end the story, as a new campaign commenced aimed at Sir William Robinson. By now, George Roe had assumed the high-profile role of chief campaigner for the creditors. Having squeezed all they could out of Putland and Nuttall, they turned on Robinson for the balance outstanding. Roe engaged an agent in England to present a petition for redress to Queen Anne. But soon a new and unforeseen obstacle to their campaign became apparent.[36]

34 *JIHOC*, appendix 1721.
35 Index to British departmental correspondence 1683–1740, various items, NAI, 1A 52/142; Clare, 'Putland family' p. 188; John Carswell, *The South Sea bubble* (London, 1961), pp. 13–14.
36 *JIHOC*, appendix 1721.

Robinson had died in 1712, widowed and with no children. Litigation over his will led to further complications for the creditors. As he lay dying, his existing will was allegedly torn up and a new one forced on him by Putland and Luke King, two of his executors. The question of whether this will (partially to Putland's and King's benefit) was valid, was litigated over for twelve years until 1724. The first ruling on its validity was negative which resulted in two successive husbands of one Sarah Wren, later Sarah Cutler, later Sarah Bonsey, later Sarah Palmer, appearing on the scene claiming to be the next-of-kin and entitled to the estate in the absence of a will. And the crown also entered the legal battle, because in the absence of both a valid will and of heirs, the estate would become its property.[37] The delay was not helping the creditors. On 27 January 1716, James Duggan, the tailor and one of the three main contractors, petitioned the Irish parliament for relief – from his cell in the Marshalsea debtors' prison.[38]

By 1719, George Roe had employed another lobbyist to try to tap Robinson's estate in England through the British parliament. However, in a new twist to the story, it came to light that property belonging to Robinson, at Carlow and Roscrea, had been misappropriated by Thomas Putland senior and assigned by him to Thomas junior, who still lived in Dublin. So Robinson's estate had property in Ireland after all.[39] This Irish property was targeted when, in September 1721, George Roe and other creditors of the three partners petitioned the Irish house of commons to place Robinson's Irish estate with trustees who would use it to pay off the balance of £4,667 due from the moneys extorted. A second inquiry was established by the parliament.[40]

* * *

Although both inquiries examined precisely the same events, Robinson was hardly mentioned in the earlier inquiry, and Nuttall was totally ignored in the later investigation. This indicates that on each occasion the best potential source for compensation was targeted rather than the objectively-perceived

---

37 Loeber, *Biographical directory*, pp. 91–3; index to British departmental correspondence 1683–1740, various items, particularly vol. 1, pp. 260, 270, 284 NAI, 1A 52/142; William A. Shaw (ed.), *Calendar of Treasury Books* xxviii, part 2 (London, 1955), p. 416.

38 *JIHOC*, iii, p. 72.

39 *JIHOC*, appendix 1721; undated petition of George Roe to King George I, NA, SP63/382, (26).

40 *JIHOC*, iii, p. 254.

culprits. In this later inquiry, the theme was that Sir William Robinson and Thomas Putland had mutually shared the proceeds of their illegal 'loans'. Although much of the evidence from 1707 was repeated in 1721, other allegations were new. It was claimed that Robinson had on one occasion charged the contractors without their consent some £36 for procuring 'the queen's letter', that is, the document needed to authorise payments, that Putland had then refused to honour this authority alleging that it contained an error, and that Robinson had then charged another £36 for a second letter.[41]

Benjamin Taylor, one of the three partners, claimed that he had never once received a payment without signing a blank receipt, which could be subsequently filled in by Putland as he thought fit, perhaps entering the amounts which *should* have been paid rather than the amounts actually handed over. James Duggan alleged that in a conversation, Robinson had admitted his collaboration with Putland, but had dismissed the taking of a cut from the payments due as 'a small matter', given the size of the partners' profits.[42]

A late witness, Richard Edwards, a member of the Irish house of commons with no vested interests, gave new, independent and important evidence. He was intimately acquainted with both parties to the disputes. At an early stage, Robinson had urged Edwards to influence the partners into accepting him as a partner or, alternatively, to pay him some commission or 'return'. In turn the partners, when things had turned sour, had asked Edwards to beg Robinson not to oppress or to ruin them.[43] Edwards himself had been exploited by Robinson. Promissory notes, that is, IOUs of the treasury, which he had held personally, had been cashed by Robinson subject to a deduction for alleged interest. And Edwards too had paid a fee to avoid being sent to Foxford or Derry to collect his money. He believed that Robinson had falsified his office records.[44]

The committee rather naively summoned Mr Putland from London to produce his cash books, which he had previously refused to do some fourteen years earlier. Putland did not attend, but sent along his agent, as well as his counsel. No new information emerged at the inquiry and no books were produced.[45]

An undated, unfinished and unsigned advice by an anonymous lawyer still survives. This raised the difficulty of pinning the entire sum outstanding on Robinson, given that the inquiry had identified only two payments (of £636 and £72) as actually coming into his hands. The lawyer advised that

---

41 *JIHOC*, appendix 1721.   42 Ibid.   43 Ibid.   44 Ibid.   45 Ibid.

Robinson might be successfully linked to the extortion by emphasising Mr Edward's independent evidence that he too had been a victim of Robinson, as well as the inference to be drawn from Putland's withholding of the treasury records which could have cleared Robinson, if he had been innocent.[46] The report of this committee to parliament, when published, merely recounted the proceedings of its 1707 predecessor and added the new evidence, without any incisive comments or recommendations.[47]

A schedule was drawn up at this stage, giving an analysis down to the last farthing for each army regiment of the moneys withheld or still due out of the total contract price of £86,640 10s. 4½d. It also analysed the sums due to the creditors by Putland and Robinson. Curiously, the sums listed do not include the £1,206 extorted by Joseph Nuttall. Had Nuttall been running a separate scam? Was his share a payment by Putland out of the latter's own illegal income? Coincidentally, Nuttall's and Putland's admitted profits together virtually equalled Robinson's.[48]

A bill to confiscate funds from Sir William Robinson's estate in Ireland to pay off the creditors was introduced and passed in the Irish parliament, was considered by the privy council, was signed by the lord lieutenant and was sent to London, all within a period of three weeks in November 1721, despite strenuous opposition from London by Putland, who was still expecting to benefit under Robinson's will.[49]

On its arrival in Britain, the bill was considered by the 'board of treasury'. The board also received a petition from Francis Annesley, one of the litigants over Sir William Robinson's will, claiming an altruistic interest on behalf of the charities named as beneficiaries from Robinson's estate, and opposing the bill on the grounds that it had been promoted by people solely to secure a benefit from the estate by raising new allegations against Robinson after twenty years had passed, and nine years after Robinson's death, allegations which had never been prosecuted in his lifetime.[50] While the bill was being processed, some official noticed that the documents had omitted to certify that the facts had been proved to the Irish privy council as well as to the Irish house of commons. The papers were, therefore, rejected with 'the loss of much time and large expenses' for the petitioners and their political

---

46 Ormond manuscript vol. 187, pp. 429–34, NLI, Ms 2487.
47 *JIHOC*, appendix 1721.
48 Ormond manuscript vol. 187, pp. 422–5, NLI, Ms 2487.
49 *JIHOC*, iii, pp. 282–7; letter dated 12 December 1721 from lord lieutenant and privy council to London forwarding certified bill for the king's signature, NA, SP63/382 (29); undated petition of George Roe to King George I, NA, SP63/382 (26).
50 Undated petition from Francis Annesley, filed as 1721, NA, SP 35/77 (188).

T O T H E
King's Moſt Excellent Majeſty,
The Humble Petition and Caſe of George Roe:

Moſt humbly Sheweth ,

H A'T *James Leathley, Benjamine Taylor* and *James Duson* in the Reign of His late Majeſty King *William* (of *ever bleſſd Memory*) and for ſeveral Years ſince, were Concern'd as Parteners in Cloathing the Army of *Ireland*, upon which Account there became due to Them Eighty-ſix Thouſand ſix Hundred and forty Pounds, ten Shillings and nine Pence Farthing, which they from time to time had Warrents on

3 Opening lines of George Roe's petition to King George I, *circa* 1724

lobbyists.[51] Following the inquiry and the bill of 1707, which was with-drawn when Putland had paid up his share, and the further 1721 inquiry and bill which was found to be defective, a third round of the campaign commenced.

A further petition, in similar terms to that which had been submitted two years previously, was again lodged in the Irish house of commons in September 1723 by George Roe, Simon Sherlock and sixty others. The MPs worked quickly. A committee considered the petition; a bill was introduced, discussed and passed; it was sent to the lord lieutenant who considered it with his privy council; he forwarded it to England. All this happened within two months. This time there was a clear certificate that the case had been fully proved and that the bill was reasonable and necessary. A prompt endorsement with the king's signature and seal was requested, so the bill could be implemented quickly.[52]

But this was wishful thinking. This bill, instead of being laid before the king, was referred to the attorney general of Great Britain, who was still in

51 Undated petition of George Roe to King George I, NA, SP63/382, (26).
52 *JIHOC*, iii, various pages between 320 and 348; undated petition of George Roe to King George I, NA, SP63/382 (26); letter dated 17 November, 1723 from lord lieutenant and privy council to London forwarding certified bill, and – on same page – resolution of Irish house of commons, dated 7 February 1724, endorsing this resolution, SP63/382, (28).

litigation on behalf of the crown over Robinson's estate. The referral was because the approval of the bill to compensate the petitioners out of Robinson's estate could mean in effect paying the money out of crown coffers, if the pending litigation ended in judgments both voiding Robinson's will, and recognising no heirs. This outcome would have resulted in the lands passing to the crown. The desire to avoid a loss to the crown exceeded the desire to compensate the petitioners so this bill also was laid aside with much further loss of time and expense and even greater frustration to the petitioners.[53]

George Roe returned to Ireland after a period of unsuccessful lobbying of the administration as well as attending at the law courts which were trying the Robinson will case in England. He went back with the other creditors to the Irish house of commons yet again.[54] The house of commons couldn't pass yet another bill, as their previous bill had not been rejected, but had been merely shelved away, in England. Instead, they passed a resolution urging the lord lieutenant to lay a petition before His Majesty, and instructed the members of the house, who were also privy council members, to lobby the lord lieutenant in support. That was early in 1724, twenty-six years after illegal deductions were first made by the treasury officials.[55]

Roe, growing desperate, drafted a detailed personal petition to the king in the customary grovelling language of that time, seeking some relief. Having summarised his previous attempts to achieve redress, he complained, though in cautious and respectful terms, that in addition to the large sum he had lost through the extortion itself, he had spent much further money pursuing his previous petitions, in both Ireland and Britain. He supported his claim by stressing his lifelong loyalty to the crown, from way back in King William's time, and stressing the fact that he was 'a good subject and had a plentiful fortune' until he was impoverished by advancing credit towards clothing the king's army.[56]

In July of the same year, the courts in England ruled that Robinson's deathbed will, previously declared null and void, was in fact valid. But Sarah

---

53 Undated petition of George Roe to King George I, NA, SP63/382 (26); petition of George Roe and Simon Sherlock, c. 24 November 1723, letter from lord lieutenant to lords of the treasury 24 November 1723, NA, T 244/43.
54 Undated petition of George Roe to King George I, NA SP63/382, (26); *JIHOC*, iii, 387; letter dated 17 November, 1723 from lord lieutenant and privy council to London forwarding certified bill, and – on same page – resolution of Irish house of commons, dated 7 February 1724, endorsing this resolution, SP63/382, (28).
55 *JIHOC*, iii, p. 387.
56 Undated petition of George Roe to King George I, NA, SP63/382 (26).

Wren and one other relation appear to have succeeded to at least some of Robinson's property. In any event, the estate was no longer potentially crown property, and there was no longer any financial reason why the bill to pay the claimants out of the Robinson estate, could not be endorsed by the king. Robinson's Irish estate was probated in January 1725. And still there was no royal response to the petition.[57]

George Roe's personal petition appears to have reached the king's desk in June 1727. George must have thought that things were finally, finally, falling into place. The king, George I, was to leave in four days' time to visit his German relatives at his family home in Hanover, north-west Germany. He promised that he would deal with the petition on his return from his holidays.[58]

George I crossed the channel on 16 June 1727, landing a few days later at Schoonhaven, a river port upstream from Rotterdam, and he set off immediately by carriage for Osnabrück, his family's home town, staying in hostelries overnight and rising at dawn in good humour and spirits and eager to continue his journey towards his ancestral home. On 21 June, his party again set off early, but half-an-hour along the road, when George was returning to his carriage after alighting for a comfort stop, his party noticed that his face had become distorted. He fainted and his travelling surgeon diagnosed a stroke. They pushed on towards Osnabrück where high-quality medical treatment would be available. They arrived at 10.30 p.m. but George died soon after midnight without regaining consciousness.[59]

It was back to square one for George Roe after a saga lasting twenty-nine years and spanning the reigns of four British monarchs. He must have pondered the despairing words of Hamlet's soliloquy: 'who would bear … the law's delay, the insolence of office and the spurns …'. Yet George resolved, to try again, to 'catch the conscience of the King'.[60]

Roe petitioned the new king, George II, attaching copies of previous correspondence and 'humbly praying his majesty's great condescension in perusing his case and doing therein, as his majesty in his royal and undoubted goodness and princely bounty should think most proper towards

---

57   Loeber, *Biographical directory,* p. 92; Betham abstracts, NAI, I, 57, p. 149.
58   Undated petition (post June 1727), of George Roe to King George II, NA, SP63/382, (25).
59   R.M. Hatton, *George I, elector and king* (London, 1978), pp. 280–3.
60   William Shakespeare, *Hamlet,* Act III, scene 1, lines 70–73; *Hamlet,* Act II, scene 2, line 603.

the support of his petitioner and his large family'. His petition was hardly oozing of confidence in a successful outcome![61]

Was he being over-pessimistic? Whatever happened to this last petition? The Irish parliament had made all the right noises throughout, as lobbying politicians who are not making the decisions are wont to do, but the administration in England, the decision-making agents, had been legalistic, ungenerous and dismissive in their responses. Roe's final petition, post-1727, was eventually filed away under '1723', with no evidence of any royal reaction. So we must conclude that there was no response by George II the law-maker, to George Roe the shoe-maker. It appears that George Roe's dogged efforts to achieve justice merely added expense to loss, disappointment to frustration, and insult to injury.[62]

61 Undated petition (post June 1727 – possibly as late as November 1729 – see date on back of SP63/382 (28), of George Roe to King George II, NA, SP63/382 (25).
62 Typescript calendar made by PRO Belfast of the state papers Ireland in the PRO London, (1720–1724), Ms 9610, NLI; undated letter, necessarily post June 1727, filed with 1723–4, SP63, Item 847A.

The Knife, the Card and the Trick-of-the-Loop

Crime and sport in county Westmeath

TOM HUNT

S port spectating was an important social outlet during the 1890s and early 1900s in Westmeath. The sporting occasion provided a multi-entertainment package, attracting a variety of ancillary activities to the main event, which added to the festivities of the occasion. It has been suggested that crowds assembled at an event were of two types: those who were spectators of an event and those who were participants in an event.[1] Spectators at a sports gathering embraced both these dimensions, participating in many of the ancillary events, both formal and informal – and some of dubious legality – that were a by-product of the core business of the occasion.

The Crookedwood sports during the period from 1893 to 1905 provided some of the most serious examples of crime associated with a sporting occasion but there are also examples here from other events in Westmeath. Crookedwood is located about five miles from Mullingar, county Westmeath. From 1893 it was the location for aquatic, athletic, equestrian and cycling events. The venue for the meet was one of extraordinary natural splendour. The u-shaped natural valley with steep sides provided ideal viewing platforms, while a flat bottom, dominated by Lough Derravaragh provided the perfect arena for the aquatic events. This was fronted by a large expanse of flat ground where the athletic, equestrian and cycling contests took place.

---

1 Peter Jupp and Eoin Magennis, 'Introduction: crowds in Ireland, c.1720–1920', in Peter Jupp and Eoin Magennis (eds), *Crowds in Ireland, c.1720–1920* (Basingston, 2000), p. 30.

CROOKEDWOOD
Athletic and Cycling Sports
AND REGATTA,
On Tuesday, 21st June, 1904.
Commencing at One o'clock sharp.

Handicappers, Starters and General Managers
Messrs FRITH and MURPHY.
Hon. Sec.—WILLIAM GIBSON,
Crookedwood.
ENTRIES CLOSE with the Hon. Sec.—
Wm Gibson, Martinstown, Crookedwood,
Mullingar, on June 14th, and must be on
Standard Entry Form, and accompanied with
the Entry Fee, without which they will not
be received No late entries wil be accepted.

PROGRAMME.

ATHLETIC AND CYCLING EVENTS'
Boys'. Race, confined
440 Yards   do.
100 Yards (open)
120 Yards Hurdle
Half Mile Flat
Siamese Race
Sack Race
One Mile Cycle
Two Miles Cycle (confined to a radius of
3 miles of Crookedwood)
Three Miles Cycle
Donkey Race (to be run in heats if
necessary). 1s entrance.

ACQUATIC EVENTS.
Three-Oar Boat Race for amateurs
3s entrance.
Two-Oar Boat Race for amateurs,
2s entrance.
Boats to be classed by the Committee.

4 Notice in the *Westmeath Examiner*, 1904 of forthcoming
Crookedwood sporting events

The first sporting event held at Crookedwood in October 1893 included a two-mile bicycle race that attracted only two competitors. The organisers may have been a bit premature in including cycling at this stage but a decade later cycling had become popular enough to warrant the inclusion of four bicycle races.[2] An attempt to encourage lady cyclists into the competitive loop was equally premature in 1899 as an advertised half-mile ladies' open event attracted no competitors and 'as a consequence the meeting was robbed of one of its best attractions. Six entered but when it came to fulfil their liabilities, they fought shy of the engagement.'[3]

As Crookedwood expanded over the years, it attracted competitors from throughout Leinster and Connacht. Dublin-based Walter Newburn, arguably the greatest-ever Westmeath athlete, won the Amateur Athletic Association's (AAA) long-jump title in 1898 and 1899. Newburn, the first athlete in history to long-jump over twenty-four feet, had represented Ireland in an international match against Scotland at Ballsbridge in 1898.[4] Another great long jumper of the era, Peter O'Connor, also competed successfully at Crookedwood in 1898 where he won his favourite event with a jump of twenty-two feet, two-and-a-half inches.[5]

* * *

Attendance at a sports event provided the chief reason for the assembly of large crowds of people in Westmeath in the 1890s and 1900s. Approximately fifteen events were annually organised within the county, where the reported attendance was numbered in the thousands. The racecourse, the makeshift athletic arena and the football field was a cross-class, multi-dimensional entertainment venue that offered the additional advantage of granting free entry to the majority of spectators throughout the nineteenth century.

Spectators were drawn from all sections of the local community, from the aristocracy to the landless labourer, from the industrial proprietor to the factory worker, 'from the blue blood aristocrat to the thread-bare men-dicant. The upper ten and the lower five, with the intermediate numbers'

2   *Westmeath Examiner*, 4 November 1893; 23 May 1903.
3   *Westmeath Examiner*, 12 July 1899.
4   Tom Hunt, 'Mullingar sport in the 1890s: communities at play', in Mary Farrell (ed.), *Mullingar: essays on the history of a midlands town in the 19th century* (Mullingar, 2002), pp. 18–19.
5   *Westmeath Examiner*, 25 June 1898.

were all assembled at the sports venue as the century ended.[6] Those who worked regular hours for a living, especially in the urban centres of Mullingar and Athlone, were facilitated in their desire to attend sporting occasions as their places of employment normally closed for business at mid-day.

Despite the cross-class appeal of sporting events and the claim that the racecourse was a place 'where the beggar man often rubs skirts with him who holds a title', spectators were heavily segregated, an aspect of course management that helped to reinforce social hierarchies.[7] Throughout much of the century the use of a grandstand, a reserved enclosure and a carriage enclosure were the chief means of segregation. Musical entertainment was included specifically to entertain those who frequented the reserved enclosure. For most of the Victorian period, music was provided by the Athlone or Mullingar-based military bands. In 1903, the band of the sixth Battalion Rifle Brigade entertained.

The core business of the sports ground supported an ancillary range of activities, both formal and informal, that provided much of the attraction of the event for the masses. It was this range of activities that encouraged newspaper reporters to refer frequently to the carnival nature of the day's activities. Even the small country meets featured the full range of carnival attractions. At Kilbeggan racecourse in 1903, for instance, 'the tents, shooting galleries, roulette tables, card tables, and all the other integral portions of a racecourse ensemble were in evidence and the variety of colour obtained from these several attractions as well as from the costumes of the ladies produced a pleasing effect.'[8]

At the 1888 Castlepollard meet, the range of attractions included 'Aunt Sally', the swing boats 'patronised on a large scale by those who wished to enjoy the sensation of flying through the air for a short space of time', roulette and the penny show with its 'usual concomitant of burlesque'.[9] In 1895 at Athlone, 'gipsy girls hooded in showy handkerchiefs issued forth to tell fortunes and ventriloquists and conjurers counted the likely sixpences long before they were earned.'[10]

The inaugural Moate meet of 1889 also drew the full complement of attractions. The unenclosed area was occupied by the 'stalls of the itinerant vendors of oranges, cakes and sweets', as well as:

6   *Westmeath Independent*, 17 June 1899.
7   *Westmeath Independent*, 4 May 1901.
8   *Westmeath Examiner*, 2 May 1903.
9   *Westmeath Examiner*, 25 August 1888.
10 *Westmeath Independent*, 4 May 1895.

… the knife, the card, the trick-of-the-loop, and the gun-men also managed, unobserved by the police to trade a little in their peculiar lines and as to musicians they were also in abundance and between the races played for the accommodation of lads and lassies who beguiled away the time by the exercise of the light fantastic.[11]

The three-card-trick operator set up his stall using a makeshift table that might have been no more substantial than a cardboard box. Passers-by were invited to find the 'lady card' from the three cards that were shuffled and placed downwards on the table. Those who decided they could find the lady, bet a sum of money and if successful, won a sum the equivalent of the amount that was invested in the gamble. The operator was accompanied by a number of associates who successfully gambled in order to tempt the innocent and uninitiated in the ways of the scam. A member of this group would also offer to share an investment in finding the queen card. The skilful sleight of hand of the trickster made it almost impossible for the gullible gamblers to win at this game.

The trick-of-the-loop was a totally fraudulent game. A leather strap or belt was used to make a figure of eight and the participant was required to find the centre of one of the loops. Properly set up, it was impossible to find the centre and the victim always lost. Thimble-riggers invited people to identify which of three thimbles contained a hidden pea. The thimble-rigger used trickery to conceal the pea under a thumbnail or in finger joints and ensured that the pea was always under an unexpected thimble when the gambler made his choice. As with the three-card-trick, operators of these games also used accomplices to attract interest and display how easy it was to win. Aunt Sally was a game in which the head of an old woman was set up with a clay pipe in her mouth and players threw sticks at it to try to break the pipe. Advertisements for sports meetings regularly included a notice banning Aunt Sally. This may have been a general ban on all dubious gaming operators.

Illegal gaming activities were not always confined to the unreserved sections, nor was the appeal of these activities confined to the unsophisticated masses. In Moate, in 1889 for instance, 'some of the extensive gamblers, the wheel of fortune and *rouge et noire* people' paid for admission and gained access to the private enclosure in front of the grandstand. Their presence in the area provided an additional opportunity for the wealthy

11 *Westmeath Independent*, 6 April 1889.

patrons to engage in gambling activities and in a form of conspicuous consumption to the benefit of the games promoters who, according to the *Westmeath Independent* reporter, 'literally coined during the day, their tables bending down with gold, silver and copper won from the unlucky gamesters'.[12]

In 1890, also at Moate, 'betting men and roulette men were present in the reserved enclosure in the same numbers as are present at the Curragh and other principal races.' There, 'the itinerant gamesters made large odds on the speculation of their dupes.' And to prove that the appeal of the gamesters was universal, and that their presence met with the tacit approval of the authorities on occasions, those gambling included 'the son of a lord, a D.I. of the Constabulary and many members of the RIC'.[13] At the 1891 meet it seemed that the band of professional betters and roulette table-owners appeared on the occasion to have combined and succeeded in 'filching from the pockets of the gilded every spare sovereign, shilling or half-penny'.[14] Again, 'the son of a lord … and the male and female gentry of the district were engaged at playing and they left behind them all their cash and patience.'[15]

At the revived Athlone meeting of 1899 the roulette promoters were also present in the 'sacred precinct' of the grand stand. Here, the roulette provided entertainment at the intervals between the races and 'around the tables were seen many of the smart set'.[16] The list of fairground-type attractions available at the 1899 Athlone meet was extensive and exotic. As well as the standard roulette and thimble-riggers there was 'the figure of a soldier attired somewhat after the fashion of a Turkish Bashi bazank', to which spectators invested the sum of one penny for the opportunity to throw three balls at 'his much abused head'. Behind another screen of canvas were figures in male and female guise 'deriving melancholy consolation from two short pipes and apparently sympathising with each other on the ill-treatment of fate'.

There was also the representation of 'some birds of foreign plume, one of which presented the investor of a penny with his or her fortune, or an outline of his or her future life'. Most novel of all was a line of 'instantaneous photography' by means of which, on putting a penny in the slot the investor received a portrait of his or her 'future husband, wife or mother-in-law',

12 Ibid.
13 *Westmeath Independent*, 12 April 1890.
14 *Westmeath Independent*, 18 April 1891.
15 Ibid.
16 *Westmeath Independent*, 17 June 1899.

according to the slot selected. Letters from sweethearts were also supplied for the same moderate contribution.[17] The Crookedwood sports also experienced this phenomenon and in 1902 the venue was 'dotted over with tents, roulette tables, and other accessories of all sporting events held in the open'.[18] These cardsharpers of all kinds and the thimble-riggers with their tin cups, dried peas and horny thumbnails, found racecourses, especially the local rural ones, an ideal venue for their trade where they could take advantage of the country people who probably only attended a few local meets and were easily duped by the slickness of the promoters of these games and their accomplices.[19]

Illegal gambling opportunities were not confined to the course. Gambling games were also promoted at Mullingar railway station. The commentator of the national journal, *Sport*, considered it his duty to support the comments of a 'morning contemporary', on the 'scandalous manner in which the railway platform at Mullingar was allowed to be crowded with roulette tables and the like', making the platform both difficult and dangerous to cross.[20]

Welching bookmakers were also part of the racing scene: 'an ever-recurring nuisance' according to the *Midland Reporter*, and instances of duped punters were reported in the contemporary press.[21] These were bookmakers who disappeared without paying out on winning bets. Two such instances occurred in Athlone in 1901. A bookmaker, operating within the enclosure, absconded after the end of the third race with fifteen guineas of the punters' cash. 'The man in the crowd' who reported for the *Westmeath Independent*, invested a winning but modest sum in the first race but when he returned to collect his winnings all that remained of the 'refinedly-cruel bookie was a tattered account-book, a square yard of green baize and a mineral water case'.[22]

John Garland, a bookmaker from Manchester, who attended the Westmeath Polo Club races in September 1899, was not as lucky and failed to make his escape from Mullingar. Garland had miscalculated the odds on one of the winning horses at the races and in 'a fit of temporary absent-mindedness was leaving the course without fulfilling his engagements' when

17   Ibid.
18   *Westmeath Examiner*, 28 June 1902.
19   Wray Vamplew, *The Turf: a social and economic history of horse racing* (London, 2002), p. 137.
20   *Sport*, 10 June 1893.
21   *Midland Reporter*, 31 March 1900.
22   *Westmeath Independent*, 4 May 1901.

'some parties interested, doubted the purity of his intentions and forcefully detained him'. Saved by the intervention of the police, Garland later turned up at Mullingar railway station where he was detained for assaulting a railway official and being drunk and disorderly.[23] The former offence earned him a sentence of one month in prison with hard labour and for being drunk and disorderly he was fined five shillings, or five days in jail on default. For the obstruction of a railway officer a fine of £1 was imposed, with fourteen days' imprisonment in default of payment.[24]

Racing meant crowds, and crowds presented pickpockets with an ideal opportunity to practice their skills; if spectators did not gather in sufficient numbers, decoys would be employed to attract them.[25] Pickpockets relieved Mullingar publican John Rainey of his gold watch and chain at the summer meet at the Newbrook course in 1905.[26] The robbery was a classic of the pickpockets' trade. A suspicious Rainey, conscious of the intentions of the two Dubliners in his vicinity, was still not vigilant enough to prevent the theft when the appropriate diversion was created. Crowds also provided business opportunities for prostitutes. At least one woman was convicted of 'loitering in the streets of Mullingar for purposes of prostitution' on the evening of a race meet.[27]

The availability of alcohol was an attractive part of the day's events and the granting of space to a publican at the event was an important source of finance for the meet organisers. Eight publicans sought permission to erect tents to sell liquor at the Athlone races of 1899 but magisterial exactitude reduced the number to four, with hours of business confined to between twelve and six-o-clock, and accompanied by the warning that:

> Those who have these licences should be very careful as to whom they serve drink, as if there is any drunkenness in future I would be opposed to the granting of any licences at all.[28]

Drunkenness associated with sporting occasions encouraged the morally outraged to vent their disapproval in the local press. A letter writer to the *Westmeath Guardian* in September 1899 objected strongly to the hosting of

23 *Westmeath Guardian*, 22 September 1899, 29 September 1899.
24 *Westmeath Examiner*, 30 September 1899.
25 Vamplew, *The Turf*, p. 136.
26 *Westmeath Examiner*, 8 August 1905.
27 *Westmeath Guardian*, 16 June 1899.
28 *Westmeath Independent*, 3 June 1899.

5 Cartoon with the caption 'reasoning with a welcher' which
appeared in the *Midland Reporter* in the early 1900s

sports events on the Sabbath Day and the associated heavy consumption of
alcohol. The writer felt that it was time that public opinion was brought to
bear before it was too late:

> to stamp out such desecration on the Sabbath as is barefacedly carried on
> Sunday after Sunday in several villages in Westmeath, or else we may
> expect before long to have a 'Paris at Home' ... It is a well-known fact
> that these sports are got up for a purpose in nearly all cases by the propri-
> etors of country public-houses, not to encourage sports, but to encourage
> a horrible 'tap-room traffic' and increase the sale of porter ... How they
> must chuckle with delight when they know how successful they have

been in grabbing the surplus of Saturday night's pay, heedless of the cries
of starving children and the wants of a poor care worn mother.[29]

Some sense of the indulgence of race-goers is captured by the *Westmeath
Independent's* 'man in the crowd' who encountered drinking tents around the
course at the 1899 meet 'each choke-full of customers, all of whom seemed
to be excessively thirsty, judging from the avidity with which they
consumed porter, ale, whiskey and other inebriating fluids, and the eagerness
with which more was demanded and consumed'.[30]

Violence in the streets and roads at the conclusion of a day's races was
one of the problems posed by a race meet which presented challenges to
those responsible for maintaining law and order. According to the report on
the Westmeath Hunt races of 1892, drunkenness on the course was
conspicuous by its absence but 'the same could not be said of the streets, as
great numbers displayed unmistakable signs of having imbibed "not freely
but too well" the majority being of the class who travel from one racing
meeting to another'.[31] Included in the range of actions reported before the
courts were stabbings, assault on policemen, robbery, pickpocketing, drunk
and disorderly offences, prostitution, civilian assault, and as described earlier,
welching bookmakers.

The 1894 Athlone race meet provided a large number of candidates for
the local petty sessions court, although the *Westmeath Independent* reporter
drew consolation from the fact that the twenty-seven who were arrested
were 'not in any way identified with our town or its surroundings. The
offenders were for the most part tramps or suspected pickpockets, who got
drunk out of spite for losing their expected profits on drink.' So many were
arrested for drunk and disorderly offences and 'undecent [sic] language' that
the cell accommodation in the local Brawney barracks was inadequate to
cater for the offenders so that 'the bedrooms of the RIC, the kitchen and
other available locked up apartments, were utilised'.[32]

Some of the itinerant vendors and gamesters found themselves arrested
for practising their trades on the streets on race evening. In 1889 at Athlone,
Peter Doyle was arrested for playing the three-card-trick outside the
Palace bar on the night of the races and was sentenced to fourteen days'
imprisonment. James Dinnegan from Mullingar and a trick-of-the-loop

29 *Westmeath Guardian*, 21 September 1899.
30 *Westmeath Independent*, 17 June 1899.
31 *Westmeath Guardian*, 8 April 1892.
32 *Westmeath Independent*, 21 April 1894.

exponent had a very successful day at the races and celebrated his day with too much alcohol and by attacking the arresting constable, earning himself six months' imprisonment.[33]

The Crookedwood sports were the occasion of the two most serious incidents of crime associated with a recreational event within the county. The indulgences associated with the 1898 event ended before the grand jury at Mullingar with the charging of John Gaffney for having 'unlawfully, feloniously, wilfully and with malice afterthought killed and murdered Daniel McKeown'. The charge followed the death of McKeown as a result of a stabbing incident on the road outside the sports venue on the evening of 21 June 1898 after both men had spent several hours consuming alcohol on the day. Gaffney, in evidence to the magisterial inquiry, explained that he was attacked as a result of his friendship with a water bailiff and produced the knife to defend himself as he was assaulted several times by McKeown. Gaffney pleaded not guilty but in the course of the trial changed the plea to manslaughter. The mitigating circumstances impressed the presiding judge to the extent that he imposed a particularly lenient sentence of twelve months' imprisonment.[34]

A similar stabbing incident with far less serious consequences happened at the 1899 sports, which resulted in a magisterial investigation. Michael Connor, Kiltoom was charged with 'unlawfully and maliciously wounding with a knife, one Thomas Delamere, residing at Lacken, Multyfarnham, on 27th June at Crookedwood'.[35] This incident happened following an evening spent drinking at the tent of John Gaynor. A row that involved 'eight or twelve people' ended with the stabbing of Delamere. Connor was a gardener employed by Lord Longford. Both parties made their escape in two separate boats before they were ordered to return to shore by the policemen present. Medical evidence described Delamere's wound as 'a clean cut wound on the head about an inch long', that didn't present any great threat to his future welfare. The resident magistrate, Mr P. D. Sullivan, returned Connor for trial to the quarter sessions despite the fact that the case was 'clearly one of circumstantial evidence'.[36]

Management committees and the forces of law and order adopted various approaches to improve the conduct of the sport and its spectators.

33 *Westmeath Independent*, 17 June 1889.
34 *Westmeath Examiner*, 2 July 1898.
35 *Midland Reporter*, 18 July 1899.
36 Ibid.; *Westmeath Guardian*, 30 June 1899.

According to the writer, Wray Vamplew, by the end of the nineteenth
century, five major methods of crowd control had been devised: improvements in the conduct of the sport, improvement in the organisation of the
events, segregation within the crowd, control of ancillary activities and the
use of control agents.[37] Although Vamplew's research was confined to British
sport, Irish committees adopted similar strategies to manage their events.

Of the measures outlined, the control of ancillary activities was the most
important restriction. In particular, restrictions that regulated the consumption
of alcohol were introduced. Measures to control drinking varied over the
course of the half-century. The individual initiative of the most powerful
power-broker in the Moate district, Canon Kearney, led to a total ban on
the sale of intoxicating liquor at the short-lived Moate meeting. This
impacted on attendance, with contemporary reports attributing the reduced
attendance at the 1890 meet to the ban. This had a positive impact and the
good order displayed during the day was attributed to the fact that 'no
refreshment tents were allowed on, even for the sale of mineral water'.[38] The
importance of drink to the carnival of racing was evident in the town of
Moate as Canon Kearney's ban extended to the sale of alcohol in the town
on race morning. The town 'appeared to be in mourning and not rejoicing
over the races', when 'publicans and other establishments had their shutters
up and strangers asked who of importance is dead'.[39] The reporter commented, oblivious to the irony involved, that 'the course and its surroundings,
crowded with spectators had no excitement thanks to Canon Kearney'.[40]

Race committees accepted the problems of alcohol sale and the necessity
for its control by approving the establishment of temperance booths on the
course. In the 1890s, in Athlone and Mullingar, temperance clubs were active
in providing an alternative to the beer- and spirit-selling booths. In Athlone,
the Fr Mathew Club established a booth where 'a bottle of lemonade and
cup of tea and a sandwich', were available. This served the needs of those
who objected to the sale of strong liquor and those who refused to
'consume the minerals and cakes vended by the nomadic tribes'.[41]

In Mullingar, following the commercialisation of the sport, it was the
National Workingmen's Club, prompted by Catholic curate, Revd P. Barry,
that intervened to provide a temperance marquee at Newbrook. Fr Barry

---

37 Wray Vamplew, 'Sports crowd disorder in Britain, 1870–1914: Causes and controls' in
    Journal of Sport History, vii, no.1 (Spring, 1980), p. 11.
38 *Westmeath Independent*, 12 April 1890.
39 Ibid.   40 Ibid.
41 *Westmeath Independent*, 17 June 1899.

proposed that a marquee that supplied a 'good drink of spring water made palatable by an ingredient' such as 'limejuice syrup' would provide a viable alternative to the places where 'spirituous liquors were sold' and patrons were 'exposed to grave temptations'.[42] The intervention was later reported to have been a total success and was continued at later events. At the Mullingar autumn meeting the temperance tent, manned by volunteers from the Workingmen's club, was reported to have done a roaring trade and 'supplied a want that was long felt'.[43]

Magisterial intervention was also an important control measure. On occasion, magistrates handed down exemplary sentences in an attempt to send a message that future examples of misbehaviour would not be tolerated. As the voluminous consumption of alcohol was identified as the chief problem by the authorities, magistrates and police combined to regulate the number of drinking booth licences issued, to limit the hours when the booths were opened, and to refuse licences to those who had been convicted of breaches of the licensing laws.

Police maintained vigilance on race day and ensured that the temporary licence-holders did not abuse their privilege.[44] The rigorous control of the issuing of licences to sell alcohol had its impact on the good order and control at the Athlone races. The 1902 meeting was distinguished by 'practically the entire absence of disorderliness'. 'There was not a single unseemly incident to interrupt the harmony and good-fellowship that prevailed amongst the crowd.'[45] An incident at the Mullingar races in 1902 became somewhat of a local *cause célèbre* when the publican Gonoud was charged with serving alcohol to an already intoxicated person.[46]

The numerical strength of the forces of law and order ensured that much of the disorder and trouble had been eliminated by the end of the century, especially in Mullingar. From 1890 onwards, when the Mullingar races were promoted by a limited company specifically incorporated for the purpose, the maintenance of good order at the racecourse became a commercial imperative. This company had invested all profits up to 1903 in ground and course infrastructure and once enclosure had been achieved there was a threat to gate receipts if crowd disorder and on-course annoyance deterred paying customers from attending. Prior to enclosure the company increased

42 *Westmeath Guardian*, 30 May 1890.
43 *Westmeath Guardian*, 5 September 1890.
44 *Westmeath Examiner*, 13 June 1905.
45 *Westmeath Independent*, 31 May 1902.
46 *Westmeath Guardian*, 19 September 1902.

police presence by organising a battalion of the Dublin Metropolitan Police to maintain order inside the course. This was a relatively inexpensive means of managing law and order as the cost of hiring the police and military band for 1890 amounted to only £11 19s. 7d., or 1.4 per cent of the total expenditure.[47] The local RIC were responsible for maintaining order outside the racecourse and on race days they maintained a high profile presence on the road from the railway station to the racecourse. This policy not surprisingly met with the approval of the local press. The *Westmeath Examiner* commenting on the 1898 summer meet stated that:

> Under the supervision of a large contingent of the Metropolitan Police the order of the course was well maintained not a hitch occurring to mar the harmony or enjoyment of the occasion whilst the RIC as regulators of the heavy traffic on the road to the course could not be excelled.[48]

Into the new century, evidence from the newspapers strongly suggests that the racecourse behaviour of the 'general public' had improved considerably. According to reports, 'drunkenness seemed to be scarcely present at all, clamour and fights and indifferent language were also entirely absent on the [Mullingar] course'. The good order and decorum evident in the ring was replicated 'in the betting and other pursuits of the public outside'.[49] The final stage in the modernisation of racing in the county was achieved in Mullingar in 1903 when work on the boundary wall was completed and from the spring meet of April 1903 an entry fee of 6d. was charged with 'no change given at the turnstile'.[50]

The relationship between spectators and the Mullingar race company was now fundamentally changed. As paying customers, spectators now expected minimum standards of comfort when attending a race meet. Enclosure enabled the most extreme form of segregation to be introduced, that is, the exclusion of undesirables from the venue. The impact was immediate. At the summer meet of 1903 spectators were relieved of 'the torment of tramps and others begging on the course'.[51] This had a significant impact on the behaviour of the racecourse crowd and received

---

47 *Westmeath Guardian*, 9 January 1891.
48 *Westmeath Examiner*, 11 September 1898, 23 September 1899.
49 *Westmeath Examiner*, 7 June 1902.
50 *Westmeath Examiner*, 11 April 1903.
51 *Westmeath Examiner*, 13 June 1903.

the approval of the local press, the *Westmeath Examiner* commenting that at the 1905 summer meet there 'was not one row or sign of disorder, and the conduct of the thousands of people assembled was highly credible in every way'. Enclosure, according to the report, aided 'good order and real enjoyment of sport and has helped to bring about a vast change from what was experienced previously, when brawls and the annoyance of all sorts of nomads were naturally to be faced, as on other open courses and were unpleasant experiences of the day's outing'.[52] 'The enjoyable character of a day at the races on any part of the course is now clearly realised whilst rows, riots, bad language and drunken brawls are practically a thing of the past on such occasions.'[53]

The racecourse-fuelled violence wasn't a particularly local or Irish phenomenon. Wray Vamplew has documented the extent to which British race meetings and other sporting events were frequently scenes of violence. Vamplew exonerated the criminal element for much of this violence and considered that the British working classes were notoriously rowdy and aggressive. 'Violence seemed to be an inevitable accompaniment of any event attended by the less respectable of working men.' He believed that the ready availability of sex, alcohol, gambling and the activities of the criminal fraternity served to aggravate the situation.[54] In Ireland, intervention by church authorities and guardians of law and order had combined to sanitise the festivals of popular culture such as fairs, patterns, weddings and wakes. The sporting occasion provided a carnivalesque alternative to these occasions.

52   *Westmeath Examiner*, 10 June 1905.
53   *Westmeath Examiner*, 5 April 1905.
54   Vamplew, *The Turf*, pp. 138–9.

Sir Henry Brown Hayes, Abductor

A Corkman's crime and the aftermath

MÁIRE MHIC GIOBÚIN

News of the abduction of Mary Pike in the early hours of Saturday 22 July 1797 broke in Cork city later that day. A native of the city, Mary was the daughter of a deceased principal of Pike's bank, and it was well known in Cork that she was an heiress to a sizeable fortune. The news of the abduction would have spread with great rapidity among the dwellers of the close-knit maritime community and the whole area would have been seething with rumour and wild speculation. The high profile of the families involved added an extra dimension to the incident.

Abduction of unmarried young women possessing a fortune or the prospect of an inheritance was a crime still reported in Ireland in the latter half of the eighteenth century. Many of these incidents aroused no more than a short-term local interest but several became notorious, as much for the factors that surrounded the abduction as for its aftermath.[1] The abduction of Miss Pike in Cork ranks among those infamous eighteenth-century abductions. Many elements connected to the Pike abduction border on the bizarre. Later events associated with the story took place well beyond the boundaries of Cork and far removed from Ireland.

Abduction was defined by law, as 'an outrageous act of violence, the taking away for motives of lucre of a woman to detain her against her will

---

1   See, for instance, the abduction the Kennedy sisters of Rathmaiden, county Kilkenny in 1779, PRONI, The Abercorn Papers, D.623/A/35, 1 December 1761, and of Mary Anne Knox of Prehen in county Derry in 1781, cited in Margery Weiner, *Matters of Felony* (London, 1967).

with intent to marry or carnally know her'.[2] Money, land, property and lifestyle, all or some of these factors were linked to abduction. Barnard, writing in recent times, sums it up: 'What was at stake when a young woman was snatched was property. With the abduction of an heiress, even to a modest inheritance, came the prospect of commanding her goods.'[3]

In the higher echelons of society, families depended on suitable marriage arrangements to maintain their status and lifestyle. Marriage alliances were often of a diplomatic or political nature, while in the lesser-established circles, abductions were frequently viewed as a short-cut to a better life. Writing in 1847, John Edward Walsh, master of the rolls in Ireland, describes how:

> an association was formed in the south of Ireland, which could not have existed in any other country. The association was known as an 'abductors club', the members of which bound themselves by an oath to assist in carrying off such young women as were fixed upon by any members.[4]

Walsh contended that no class of society was exempt from this behaviour; 'the daughters of opulent farmers as well as the gentry could be victims.'[5] He described the activities of a category of abductors known as 'squireens', a term which was often applied to the younger sons or connections of respectable families having little or no patrimony of their own.[6] The perpetrators tended to follow a like pattern, where a group of men, as a rule masked and led by the abductor, carried out the crime. A female relative or friend of the abductor was often involved, possibly to provide a sense of comfort or, more likely, to lessen suspicion on the part of the victim.

Mary Pike, described as 'daughter of Samuel Pike, Esq., of the city of Cork, banker',[7] was twenty-one years old in 1797. She was of the Quaker community, an only daughter, and believed to be heiress to a fortune in the region of twenty thousand pounds. Pike's banking business had traded in Cork for many years and Mary's father, a man well advanced in years at the time of his death in 1796, would have ensured that his daughter was well

2 Cited in Weiner, *Felony,* pp. 80–81.
3 Toby Barnard, *The abduction of a Limerick heiress: social and political relations in mid-eighteenth century Ireland* (Dublin, 1998), p. 8.
4 John Walsh, *Ireland sixty years ago* (Dublin, 1847), p. 34.
5 Ibid.
6 Ibid.
7 Reward notice (Richard Pike), *Hibernian Chronicle,* 24 July 1779.

provided for. In July 1797, Miss Pike was staying at Wood Hill, the residence of her uncle, Cooper Penrose,[8] as her mother was in poor health. The Penrose family, also Quakers, were a well-established mercantile family engaged in multiple business pursuits in Cork. The Cooper Penrose residence was in the North Liberties, in the area now known as Montenotte, overlooking the river, about one-and-a-half-miles from the city.

Sir Henry Brown Hayes was a 35-year-old widower with four children in 1797. He resided at Vernon Mount in the South Liberties. Coming from a mercantile family, he was well connected in local business circles and was a member of many organisations and associations. His late wife, a Miss Smith, had been an heiress from Ballinatray estate on the Blackwater, near Youghal and had died in 1794.[9] Henry was the son of Attwell (Attiwell) Hayes, a Cork businessman,[10] whose enterprises had provided much of the Hayes family's wealth. A comment in 1837 on Henry Brown Hayes, said: 'He, as well as his father, Attwell Hayes, were noted for their flamboyance and attention seeking.'[11] Records show that on the occasion of a masquerade ball in Cork, Attwell Hayes 'drove into the ball-room in a small state chariot to which was yoked a very fine goat.'[12] This incident caused great excitement among the attendance. Resulting from this escapade – and also the fact that the same goat lived to a great age – a popular saying evolved in Cork that anyone living to a very advanced age was referred to as being 'as old as Atty Hayes's goat'.[13]

Henry Brown Hayes was admitted a freeman of Cork city on 12 November 1782.[14] He was appointed sheriff of the city in 1790, and in the same year received a knighthood from the lord lieutenant.[15] He also had held a captain's commission in the South Cork militia;[16] he was described as arrogant and overbearing, 'haughty in manner, over-dressed and very proud of being a captain in the militia'.[17] He is alleged to have had his tent

---

8   Richard S. Harrison, *Cork city Quakers, 1655–1939* (Dublin, 1991), p. 10.
9   Entry in register of deaths, Christchurch, Cork, certified by C.V. Moore, Hon. Secretary, 1976.
10 Thomas Davis, *The speeches of the Right Hon. John Philpot Curran* (Dublin, 1855), p. 350.
11 W. Roe, *Sketches of Cork* (Cork 1837–9).
12 Charles H. Bertie, *The story of Vaucluse house and Sir Henry Brown Hayes* (Sydney, c. 1913), p. 3.
13 Ibid.
14 [?] McMahon, 'Sir Henry Brown Hayes Knight', *JCHAS*, vol. xx, second series (1914), p. 74.
15 *Dublin Chronicle*, 30 October 1790.
16 Bernard Caillard, 'Sir Henry Brown Hayes', in *The Victorian Mason* (autumn 1992), p. 4.
17 Caillard, *Victorian Mason*, p. 4.

covered with silk rather than with the canvas traditionally used by the soldiery. Another source declared, 'he lived extravagantly, was fond of display, had a fine suburban mansion, surrounded by beautiful grounds and kept a retinue of servants.'[18] He was also a freemason, having been initiated into lodge number 71 in Cork in 1796, 'and crafted on the same night'.[19]

* * *

The evidence would suggest that the abduction of Mary Pike was well planned. The Cooper Penrose property at Wood Hill was one of the show places of Cork in 1797, and the family had established the custom of allowing visitors to view their gardens and walk in the grounds. From evidence at his subsequent trial, it seems that Sir Henry presented himself as a visitor there some time in July of 1797 and that Mr Penrose, on hearing of his presence, personally conducted him on a tour of the grounds. It would seem that Sir Henry ingratiated himself with his host and stayed for so long that Penrose felt obligated to invite him to dine with the family that evening. The invitation was accepted by Sir Henry, and as Penrose's niece, Mary Pike, was staying at the house, he would have made her acquaintance in the course of that day. At his trial, it would be alleged that Sir Henry intentionally used the occasion to meet Miss Pike. Within days of this visit, in the very early morning of Saturday 22 July, a messenger arrived at the Cooper Penrose residence with a letter which read:

> Dear Sir,
> Our friend Mrs Pike is taken suddenly ill. She wishes to see Miss Pike. We would recommend dispatch, as she may not have many hours to live. Yours,
> Robert Gibbings[20]

Gibbings was the medical doctor who attended the Pike family. The tone of the letter suggests that Mr Penrose was acquainted with the doctor. This letter was later proved to be a bogus message.[21] On foot of the note, a carriage was immediately prepared to carry Mary Pike to the bedside of her

18   McMahon, 'Sir Henry Brown Hayes', *JCHAS*, p. 74.
19   Caillard, 'Brown Hayes', *Victorian Mason*, p. 4.
20   Davis, *Speeches of J.P. Curran*, p. 374.
21   R.E. Parkinson, *History of the grand lodge of free and accepted masons, Ireland* (Dublin, 1957), ii, p. 306.

sick mother. She was accompanied by her cousin, Miss Mary Penrose, and another female passenger, possibly her uncle's wife. The carriage left Wood Hill to take the party to the Pike residence. As they neared the city centre, close to the Brickfields (now Kent Station), the carriage was suddenly halted and surrounded by a masked group. Some one of the group 'thereupon cut the traces of the horses, letting them go free'.[22]

Mary was the only one of the three passengers to be taken from the carriage and was conducted to another carriage waiting nearby, where a woman was seated. When one of the men joined them, he removed his mask, showing himself to be Sir Henry Brown Hayes. It was later established that the woman accompanying him was his sister. The carriage then 'drove off with her to the house of the said Sir H. Brown Hayes, at Vernon Mount in the South Liberties of Cork.'[23]

The events that took place at Vernon Mount have been widely written about and attested to at the trial. On arrival, Sir Henry lost little time in declaring his devotion to Mary Pike and in proposing marriage to her. His sister adopted the role of promoting his cause. Mary Pike was 'informed that she was under the roof of one of the best and most generous of men, who was head over heels in love with her and whose heart would be broken if you would not consent to be his wife.'[24] It is said that Attwell Hayes was also present in Vernon Mount.

From the beginning, Mary Pike unwaveringly refused to consider his proposal. At some later time Sir Henry absented himself, and when he returned, he was accompanied by a man. Trial evidence held that the 'man dressed in the habit of a clergyman read some ceremony partly in English and partly in a language unknown to Mary Pike but which she presumed to be French.'[25] Sir Henry declared the reading to be a marriage service and stated that they were lawfully wed. It is said that he forced a ring onto her finger but she resisted robustly, throwing the ring on the floor and refusing to recognise the so-called marriage ceremony. Mary Pike was apparently not as compliant as had been anticipated, and whatever expectations Sir Henry may have had, it must have become clear to him by then that his plans had gone awry.

Accounts of what followed are somewhat confused. Mary Pike was deeply distressed immediately following her ordeal and when recalling the

22 Reward notice (Richard Pike) in *Hibernian Chronicle,* 24 July 1797.
23 Ibid.
24 Anon., 'Sir Henry Brown Hayes Knight, in *JCHAS*, vol. xx (1914), p. 77.
25 W. S. Hill-Reid, *John Grant's journey, a convict's story* (London, 1957), p. 56.

events later. Following the so-called ceremony, she was placed or held in a room alone. After a period of time – perhaps later that day or next day – she found a means of sending a message to her relatives. She was quickly located and reunited with her family. By this time, Sir Henry had departed, and it would seem that his sister and his father had also left Vernon Mount. It is believed that Sir Henry left Cork without delay and that he stayed away for up to two years.

* * *

Following the abduction, the lord lieutenant and council posted a proclamation in the national newspapers. The *Hibernian Chronicle* on the following Monday morning, 24 July, stated that there was a reward of £200 posted for 'apprehending the said Sir Henry Brown Hayes and fifty pounds for each and every person aiding and assisting the said Sir Henry Brown Hayes'.[26] This edition also carried a reward notice inserted by Richard Pike, who offered the sum of 500 guineas 'to any person or persons that shall lodge the same Sir Henry Brown Hayes, within six calendar months in any of his Majesty's Gaols in the Kingdom'.[27] The notice described Sir Henry as being 'straight-made, rather fresh-coloured, a little pock-marked and has brown hair, with remarkable whiskers, about five feet seven inches high'.[28] Richard Pike described himself as 'uncle to Mary Pike and executor to her father'.[29] Cooper Penrose also offered a large reward for the capture of her abductor and his accomplices.[30] These same proclamation and reward notices continued to appear in national newspapers from July 1797 for the next several years. Sir Henry Brown Hayes, knight, was now officially a wanted man, carrying a price on his head.

Following the abduction, Mary Pike is said to have gone to Bath in an effort to recover from her distressing experience.[31] Despite the absence of both herself and of Hayes from Cork following the abduction, curiosity and rumour in the city was rife. Salacious and ribald comment was widespread, and rhymers and songwriters engaged in producing popular verse and story about the event. The following was among ditties that 'already children were singing in the city streets'.[32] It was sung to the tune of 'Merrily danced the Quaker' and went:

26 *Hibernian Chronicle*, 24 July 1797.
27 Ibid.   28 Ibid.   29 Ibid.
30 Harrison, *Cork city Quakers*, p. 10.
31 Bertie, *Story of Vaucluse house and Sir Henry Brown Hayes*, p. 7.
32 John O' Mahoney, 'Great Irish trials' in *The Irish Packet,* ii (February 1904), p. 456.

Sir Henry kissed behind the bush,
Sir Henry kissed the Quaker,
And if he did and if he did,
He surely did not ate her.[33]

In due course, Sir Henry returned to Cork, where he was apparently able to outwit those who sought him and to move freely around the city notwithstanding his 'wanted' status. There is no evidence of efforts being made to claim any of the rewards offered or to hand him over to the authorities. At his trial in 1801, John Philpot Curran put forward the opinion that Sir Henry had lived openly in Cork during this time, 'basking in the favour of numerous kindred and acquaintances in a widely extended city'.[34] The logic of Curran's argument possibly alluded to his significant number of influential friends, allies and followers. On foot of his connections with commerce, the militia, the corporation and the masonic brethren, they all seemed to have supported him despite the price on his head. As his closest family members had actively aided him in the carrying out of the crime, it is likely that they continued to do so.

In 1800 a new reward notice appeared in the papers, this time in the name of Mary Pike herself. A 500 guineas reward was again offered for information, Sir Henry Brown Hayes being described as 'now and for sometime past an outlaw'.[35] In that same year, Sir Henry decided to hand himself in and 'he wrote to Miss Pike offering to stand his trial before a jury of his country.'[36] The manner in which he went about the process was undeniably unusual. He arranged with a Mr Coughlan, an old friend of the Hayes family, who ran a hairdressing and perfumery business on the Grand Parade, to take part in an elaborate charade. Sir Henry suggested to Coughlan 'that he might file the necessary information to claim the reward, which he did, and Sir Henry was duly taken into custody'.[37]

By the time preparations for the trial began in 1801, nearly three years had elapsed since the abduction of Mary Pike. There were further delaying tactics when the matter of the venue for the trial came under review. The Pike family requested that the trial be held in Dublin as they were of the opinion that they would get a fairer hearing there. Sir Henry, however, would not agree, convinced that the jury in Cork would not convict him.

33 Ibid.
34 Davis, *Speeches of Philpot Curran.*
35 Reward notice, *Hibernian Chronicle,* 31 July 1800.
36 Bertie, *The story of Vaucluse house and Sir Henry Brown Hayes*, p. 6.
37 Ibid.

Finally, agreement was reached and the trial of Sir Henry Brown Hayes was set for the spring assizes on 13 April 1801 in Cork, before Mr Justice Day.

John Philpot Curran, counsellor for the Pike family, was a hugely popular figure, who was appreciated both for his sharp mind and for his sharp wit. The story is told that on the day of the trial as he made his way into court, a member of the gathered spectators called out: 'Counsellor, we hope you will gain the day!', and, to the delight of the crowd, his reply was: 'If I do, take care you don't lose the knight!'[38]

Once the jury was chosen, the trial got quickly underway. By virtue of his high profile, Curran, who was the chief prosecutor, got the main attention from those in attendance in court as well as those waiting outside. One writer who had read the transcript of the trial described his address to the jury as 'one of the finest efforts of that very able man'.[39] Curran presented his case with great adroitness and effect.[40] Commenting on Hayes's first encounter with Mary Pike in the home of her uncle, Cooper Penrose, he declared:

> It will appear that his first approach to her was meanly and perfidiously contrived, with the single purpose of identifying her person, in order that he might feloniously steal it, as the title deed to her estate.[41]

At the end of the day, and after retiring for an hour or thereabouts, the jury returned a verdict of guilty. However, Judge Day referred the case to the opinion of twelve other judges as he had a doubt as to whether the evidence supported the indictment. The opinion of these judges was that the evidence did support the indictment.[42] The original deliberation of the jury was that he was guilty. The mandatory sentence for abduction was death but there was a recommendation that the case be referred to Dublin for a judicial review. In August 1801 the twelve judges upheld the guilty verdict; Sir Henry was condemned to death but on a plea for leniency the sentence was commuted to transportation for life.

Apart from the local interest in the abduction, the case of Mary Pike and Henry Brown Hayes was discussed and evaluated at government and administrative levels in Dublin, as this correspondence concerning Brown Hayes and an abductor in another case known as 'Mappy' Murphy shows:

38 McMahon, *JCHAS,* vol. xx, second series, p. 75.
39 Bertie, *The story of Vaucluse house and Sir Henry Brown Hayes*, p. 7.
40 *Hearing transcript, genuine edition of the trial* (Cork, 1801). Hereafter *Trial.*
41 *Trial.*   42 *Trial.*

… on 3rd September 1801, Lord Hardwick wrote to Abbot on the subject of the commutation of the sentence; he justifies the reprieve of Hayes but will not reprieve Mappy [Murphy] guilty of abduction and rape. Having carried off Miss Pike, introduced a person dressed up as a clergyman who rattled off a service, a ring was forced on her finger which she flung off and would have nothing to say; next day Hayes brought her pen and ink; she wrote to her friends and was taken back; he offered no violence.[43]

The same source states that letters in respect of the case were sent to the lord chancellor, the lord lieutenant and Lord Kilwarden. A letter to John Fitzgibbon, first earl of Clare, then lord chancellor of Ireland, from Lord William Auckland, joint postmaster general in Ireland, dated 19 September 1801 and covering numerous issues, acknowledges that Lord Hardwick had sent correspondences to him upon the fate of Sir Henry, on which he said:

Sir Henry Hayes and Murphy were indicted and tried on the same statute, each for carrying off a woman with intent to marry her. Murphy succeeded in ravishing his lady. Sir Henry attempted to ravish his but did not succeed because the cock would not fight, and after standing out all legal process for five years and bidding defiance to two proclamations offering a reward of five hundred pounds for apprehending him, he was brought to trial, found guilty and respited by Mr. Day, upon a silly doubt in his mind on a point of law.[44]

Another reference to Sir Henry is found in the masonic records of the county of Cork, dated 9 July 1801, stating that lodge no. 71, 'authorised the Worshipful Master and Wardens to act for the Lodge in signing a Memorial or Petition … in favour of our esteemed but unfortunate Brother, Sir Henry Brown Hayes.'[45] Ironically, Mary Pike 'had consented to take an oath concerning her evidence, resulting from this she was disunited from the Society [of Friends]'.[46] It would appear that no chorus of disapproval or support for her has ever been documented.

* * *

43 Colchester Mss, *Historical Manuscript Commission*, appendix to fourth report 1874, p.345, NLI.
44 *Sneyd Papers*, PRONI, T/3220/1 (original papers at Keele University).
45 Cork Minute/Record Book, Masonic Lodge, no. 71, 1801, p. 119.
46 Harrison, *Cork city Quakers*, p. 10.

In September 1801, Sir Henry, holding the status of convict, set sail for Botany Bay on the sailing ship, the *Atlas*, under the command of Captain Richard Brooks. She 'embarked her first prisoners in Dublin ... and completed her complement of convicts at Cork.'[47] Many of those aboard were already suffering from typhus and dysentery.[48] The ship ran into heavy weather shortly after leaving Cork port and conditions on board became disordered. By the time the *Atlas* arrived at Rio de Janeiro, on 2 February 1802, fifteen prisoners had died since embarkation and many more were ill.[49] One prisoner on board suffered no privations; this passenger was named as 'the privileged Sir Henry Brown Hayes'.[50]

Thomas Jamison, also on board, was returning to Australia from England to take up the position of principal surgeon in the colony. Jamison was particularly aggrieved at the preferential treatment accorded to Sir Henry, and had had words with both Captain Brooks and Sir Henry on the subject. Allegedly, 'Hayes assaulted Jamison during a quarrel in Brazil.'[51] Highly affronted, Jamison left the ship there, taking another to Australia. On arrival of the *Atlas* in Sydney, on 6 July 1802,[52] Governor King instituted an inquiry into the conduct of Captain Brooks on the voyage, as there had been a death toll of twenty-five passengers en route. The appalling condition of the convicts was also questioned.

Dr Jamison, already arrived, and by now chief surgeon of the colony and additionally a magistrate, pressed charges against Sir Henry. In the course of his trial evidence, Sir Henry explained that 'in order to secure myself a respectful treatment and decent accommodation on board, I had paid a considerable sum to Captain Brooks.'[53] Hayes was sentenced to six months' hard labour in Van Diemen's Land[54] on foot of the assault. This was his introduction to his new life in Australia and was to be the first of many clashes with the law.

Sir Henry Brown Hayes would have been categorised as a 'special' convict in 1802. 'Specials were gentlemen by birth and education, who had been convicted for offences which, however, from a legal point of view, did not involve any degree of baseness.'[55] John Lang, writing later in the nineteenth century, at a time when many of the older residents of the

47   Charles Bateson, *The convict ships* (Library of Australian History, 1988), p. 182.
48   Ibid.   49 Ibid., p. 183.   50 Ibid.   51 Ibid.   52 Ibid.
53   Bertie, *The story of Vaucluse house and Sir Henry Brown Hayes*, p. 8.
54   Yvonne Cramer, *This beauteous and wicked place: letters of John Grant, gentlemen convict* (Canberra, 2000), p. 97.
55   John Lang, *Botany Bay: true tales of early Australia* (London, 1890, this edition, Sydney 2004), p. 77.

colony were still alive, says that convicts coming from this background were 'treated rather as prisoners of war on their parole than as prisoners'.[56] By law, they were not allowed to buy land nor were they given grants of land but were allowed to locate themselves on any unoccupied piece of land around Sydney Harbour. Sir Henry came from such a background and it was said that in his new setting 'he was surrounded by every comfort that money could purchase ... the only defect in his character was, that he was too patronising.'[57]

As was his wont, Sir Henry found a way to circumvent the rules on acquiring land. A certificate of an auction sale, dated 1803, records:

> Certain farms situate near South Head, in this territory, were purchased by Sir Henry Browne Hayes ... 22nd Day of August 1803 ... signed in the presence of Robt. Rhodes and Saml. Breakwell.[58]

This sale related to about 105 acres of land near the mouth of Sydney Harbour. Samuel Breakwell from Cork city, was a former employee of Sir Henry or of the Hayes family. As a freeman, he had legal status in Australia. There is no valid explanation as to how Sir Henry was able to purchase the land, as this concession was not legally his. Not only did he acquire the land but later he also had a house built on it. He named his house 'Vaucluse'; it appears he compared the area – and possibly his situation – to the valley in France where the Italian poet, Petrarch, had retired in self-exile for a period. The valley was known as 'Vallis Clausus', hence the name 'Vaucluse'. The immediate area and the house on it are still identified by that name, in Sydney.

In December 1804, Sir Henry leased Vaucluse to Samuel Breakwell for a term of seven years at a rental of £27 per annum.[59] Hayes executed another lease to Breakwell 'on January 1812 of 99 years at a rental yearly of one peppercorn'.[60] The first of these leases was considered to be only a device to help Sir Henry out of his troubles. The second lease was a gift of the property to Breakwell, probably as an expression of Hayes's gratitude to the man who was his friend during those troubled years.[61]

Another example of Sir Henry's controversial activities took place in 1803 when freemasonry was deemed illegal in Australia. This was respected by the British grand lodges, which did not grant Australian warrants.[62]

56 Ibid.   57 Ibid.
58 Cited in Bertie, *Vaucluse house and Sir Henry Brown Hayes*, p. 11.
59 Ibid., p. 14.   60 Ibid.   61 Ibid.
62 Caillard, 'Sir Henry Brown Hayes', *The Victorian Mason*, p. 4.

Although refused permission to form a lodge in Australia, this in no way deterred Hayes, who boldly claimed to have a warrant, procured 'from a French ship'.[63] He determined to go ahead with this venture and held a meeting in his house. The *Sydney Gazette* of 22 May 1803 reported:

> Henry Brown Hayes, in contempt of that injunction, was found with several others assembling as Free Masons … His Excellency has judged it expedient to order the said Sir Henry Brown Hayes to hard labour to be served at Van Diemen's land.[64]

There is no evidence, however, that Sir Henry ever served this sentence.

In March 1804, there was a so-called 'Irish rebellion' by the convicts in the colony. It was widely suspected by the authorities that Hayes was involved in the rising, and on foot of this, he was sentenced to exile on Norfolk Island. With his usual resourcefulness, Sir Henry found a method of having the originally-nominated destination of his exile changed from Norfolk Island to that of Tasmania. But fate intervened in a kindly way, in the guise of bad weather, which delayed the sailing of the prisoners' vessel for a period.[65]

His second reprieve came when 'his friend Captain Bligh became Governor and quashed the entire sentence'.[66] In 1804 William Bligh – remembered especially for his role on the *Bounty* – was appointed governor of New South Wales. Once again, Sir Henry could reside at Vaucluse house and tend to his lands. Now free and safe from harassment for the next three years, he would seem to have lived peacefully, pursuing the development of his land, selling his produce and socialising with Bligh and other friends. A recollection of a resident of that time was that he was surrounded by every comfort that money could purchase, and he was always glad to see persons of whom he was in the habit of speaking as 'those of my own order'. According to another observation, 'he lived in remarkable style and freedom for a convict'.[67]

However, this period of peace and tranquillity for Sir Henry was about to come to an end. William Bligh was a staunch disciplinarian; his firmness is well documented in the *Bounty* episode.[68] By 1808, not alone had the

63 Ibid.
64 *Sydney Gazette*, 22 May 1803.
65 Caillard, 'Sir Henry Brown Hayes', *The Victorian Mason*, p. 4.
66 Ibid., p. 5.
67 *Australian dictionary of biography*, 'Journal of Proceedings of the Royal Australian Historical Society (1788–1850)', vol. i, p. 526.
68 Caroline Alexander, *The Bounty: the true story of the mutiny on the Bounty* (London, 2003).

6 William Bligh of *Mutiny on the Bounty* fame. Brown Hayes and Bligh became friends and allies in Australia. Image courtesy of Gutenburg Project

convicts become mutinous but his subordinates also found it difficult to work with him. Governor Bligh would seem to have come to an impasse in the colony; he had become generally unpopular and, consequently, his support dwindled. A mutiny occurred when Major George Johnston took a decision in January 1808 to assume lieutenant governorship and arrest Bligh.[69] William Bligh was ousted and held prisoner by Johnston and his associates, following which they took charge of the colony. This mutiny is referred to historically, as the 'rum rebellion'. It would seem that Sir Henry was among the few who continued to support Bligh but he paid a price for this loyalty. The rebel administration twice sent him to work in the dreaded Newcastle coal mines for long periods of hard labour.[70]

At the penal colony on Norfolk Island, Sir Henry formed a deep friendship with another 'gentleman' prisoner, a highly-educated scholar from Buckinghamshire. His new friend, John Grant, was a writer and recorded events that were significant, both to him and Sir Henry. His journal, dated 5 February 1809, notes that Bligh was liberated on Saturday 'but after

---

69 *Australian dictionary of biography*, vol. ii, p. 20.
70 Caillard, 'Sir Henry Brown Hayes', *The Victorian Mason*, p. 5.

signing that he will embark for England by the twentieth of the month in the HMS Porpoise'.[71] William Bligh did not forget his erstwhile friend, nor the support he gave him during the period of the mutiny. It gained Sir Henry 'the favour of that governor, who recommended that he be pardoned'.[72] However, the mutineers did not honour the pardon and Sir Henry continued to serve his sentence of hard labour in the Newcastle coalmines. After an inquiry had exonerated William Bligh on his return to London and he had been promoted to admiral, he did not forget his faithful ally, Sir Henry. In a letter from Bligh to the earl of Liverpool in August 1811, he attached the facts of the pardon and enclosed a copy of it, saying:

> ... after Governor Macquarie's arrival I could not succeed in getting this effected, being not formally reinstated according to his Majesty's commands and therefore I determined after all the public trials should be over, to earnestly solicit his Majesty's Government to realize my intentions so justly advocated on all occasions.[73]

The earl of Liverpool wrote to Governor Macquarie, transmitting a copy of this letter and said:

> I have appraised you of the circumstances in order that you may be enabled now to extend the indulgence then intended to have been granted to this individual by Admiral Bligh ... in case his conduct should have been such as to entitle you, with a due regard to the ends of justice, to remit the punishment to which he has been condemned ... On his case, however, I most respectfully solicit your lordship to allow this pardon to take effect, that Sir Henry Browne Hayes may be restored to his liberty and respectable family in this country.[74]

Eventually, the pardon came into effect under Governor Macquarie in 1812. Ten years after his transportation to Botany Bay, Sir Henry Brown Hayes regained his freedom and set sail for Ireland, on the *Isabella*, on 4 December 1812. The captain of the ship was none other than his old friend, Richard Brooks, the master of the *Atlas* that had carried him to Australia in 1801. He

---

71 Cramer, *This beauteous and wicked place*, p. 178.
72 Extract from press release on the opening of a history museum at Vaucluse House, 26 July 1978.
73 Cited in Bertie, *The Story of Vaucluse house and Sir Henry Brown Hayes*, p. 21.
74 Ibid., p. 22 Australia (Historical Records), vol. 7.

was accompanied by the faithful Samuel Breakwell. Also on the ship was Joseph Holt, one of the leaders of the 1798 rebellion in Wexford, who had also been transported to Botany Bay and was now free and returning to Ireland.

The following snippet from the *Watty Cox Magazine* records the arrival of the travellers in Dublin:

> General Holt and Sir H.B. Hayes. These two eminent gentlemen have arrived from Botany Bay. The General has commenced to trade in Kevin Street; the knight lives on his money at 35 Dawson Street. It is singular enough that the two were transported for the Pike business. Sir Henry was transported for stealing a Pike and the General for bestowing Pikes.[75]

* * *

Sir Henry stayed in Dublin for a period before returning to Cork to live out his last years. He was a familiar sight in Cork city, where he lived on Grattan Hill in the North Liberties until his death, on 13 April 1832. He was entombed at Holy Trinity (Christchurch) on 16 April.[76] The following notice appeared in the *Cork Constitution or Cork Advertiser* on 19 April 1832.

> On Friday last at his residence, Grattan Hill, most sincerely and universally regretted, Sir Henry Brown Hayes, Knt. Aged 70 years. He sustained a very severe and painful illness for many months with pious resignation; he was a kind and indulgent parent, and a truly adherent friend. The suavity and gentlemanly manner he possessed made him endeared to every person who had the happiness of his acquaintance.[77]

Sir Henry was a complex and impetuous man who had his admirers and detractors. Evidence given at his trial in Cork in 1801 clearly demonstrated that he had no previous acquaintance with Mary Pike prior to meeting her at her uncle's home in July 1797, shortly before the abduction. Young,

---

75 *Watty Cox's Magazine*, July 1814, cited in Bertie, *The story of Vaucluse house and Sir Henry Brown Hayes*, p. 23.

76 Register of burial records, Christchurch/Holy Trinity, Cork 1832, p. 110, Representative Church Body Archives.

77 *Cork Constitution or Cork Advertiser*, 19 April 1832.

7 Holy Trinity (Christchurch), Cork, burial place of Henry Brown Hayes in 1832.
Photograph by author

unmarried, Quaker women were carefully chaperoned and led a sheltered life in that period. She and Sir Henry moved in different circles and it would seem that his visit to Wood Hill was a deliberate ploy to make her acquaintance. Mary Pike became the tragic victim of events outside the control of herself and her family; she had no hand in the ill-fated events that overtook her and blighted the rest of her life. She descended into madness; 'only a few years later it became necessary to confine her to Bloomfield Retreat in Dublin, a mental institution run by Friends on principles of kindness and care.'[78] Her death notice as follows appeared in May 1832:

> On the 6th inst. at the Society of Friends, Bloomfield near Dublin Mary Pike aged 56, daughter of Samuel Pike, formerly of the City of Cork, Banker.[79]

78   Harrison, *Cork Quakers*, p. 10.
79   *Constitution or Cork Advertiser*, 12 May 1832.

The varied details from Sir Henry's life show him to have been an entre-preneur and adventurer who constantly embroiled himself in controversy. Despite his many self-created misfortunes it is difficult to imagine that he would have chosen another path. In the transcript from his trial and in the subsequent writings and books that his story spawned, there is no indication that he expressed remorse for his crime.

An elderly widow, whose husband was an army officer during Hayes's early years in Australia, gives an insight into how Henry Brown Hayes himself felt about the crime he had been convicted of in Ireland – and of his feelings for Philpot Curran, the chief prosecutor in the abduction trial.

> … that Hayes was perfectly mad on the crime that led to his banishment there could not be the slightest question; but upon all other points no one could be more rational. That his statements to his case were untrue, no one who read the reports of his trial could doubt for a single moment; but that Hayes himself believed his own version to be the correct one, was equally certain … By the way, he did say once in my presence, on the occasion of his killing a fly with the handle of a carving-fork, 'that's how I would like to crush John Philpot Curran!'[80]

The motives for his crime remain unclear; the acquisition of Mary Pike's fortune was probably his prime objective. Contrary to contemporary reports, he had no apparent shortage of funds and his lifestyle in Australia was a comparatively comfortable one, which, initially at least, must have been funded from Irish resources. Of the variety of opinions about Sir Henry that have been expressed, the following are widely at variance in content.

A Mr McMahon, in an account on Sir Henry that became part of an article in the *Cork Journal* of 1914, had the following opinion:

> Hayes must get the credit for having behaved with a certain amount of courtesy to his captive. At all events, in the very tempest and whirlwind of his passion for Miss Pike – or at least for her fortune – he preserved some discretion.[81]

---

80 Quoted in Lang, *True tales*, p. 78
81 [?] McMahon, 'Sir Henry Hayes of Cork', *Cork Journal*, vol. xx (1914), p. 78.

In 1929, Philip Morton wrote:

> Sir Henry Browne Hayes paid the full price for his indiscretion: eleven
> years of degradation, in which he tries to play the three-in-one role of
> knight, gentleman and convict. His path would have been easier if he
> had not the impetuousness of the Irishman, but also had the courage
> of that race and the heavy hand of officialdom was powerless to
> subdue him.[82]

Finally, the opinion John O'Mahoney, writing in the *Irish Packet*, in 1904:

> Reading the cold print of his trial today, one finds it hard to have
> sympathy for the old blackguard.[83]

82 Philip Morton, 'Vaucluse estate from 1793–1829'. Paper read to Australian Historical
    Society, 1929.
83 John O'Mahoney, *The Irish Packet* (1904), p. 456.

Pursuit of the Criminal in Nineteenth-century Tallaght

Sub-inspector Burke investigates

SEÁN BAGNALL

Sub-inspector William Burke rode his fine bay gelding from the constabulary barracks in Tallaght towards the crossroads at Killininney on 11 November 1839. He considered himself lucky with his appointment to Tallaght. This was a quiet part of the country and this year so far, he had dealt with only eight outrages in the parish of Tallaght. His remit covered much of the barony of Uppercross but other sub-inspectors had busier beats. In common with all other officers of the constabulary at this time, William Burke had a military background.[1]

The road to Old Bawn and Killininney passed over the Watergate Bridge just outside the village of Tallaght and then climbed to that point where the millrace passed under the road on its way from McDonnell's large paper mill at Oldbawn to Neal's mills at Harlem. The road then fell gently, passing the gate to Old Bawn House on the right. It fell more steeply as it passed the gate to Dr Burkett's residence at Mountain View on the left and then levelled out as it crossed the Dodder before arriving at the crossroads at Killininney. Here, Burke stopped his horse just outside McCoy's public house to his right and the prosperous farm of Nicholas Read to his left.

His duties as sub-inspector involved his travelling on a regular basis to such rendezvous points in his area to meet with the constables from other barracks. At this crossroads today he was to have his regular meeting with

---

1 Donal J. O'Sullivan, *The Irish Constabularies 1822–1922* (Dingle, 1999), p. 175.

the constable from the barracks at Ballinascorney. He would listen to that constable's report of the state of affairs in the uplands of Ballinascorney and Glenasmole. This report may have recounted some cases of animal trespass, boundary disputes and other possible causes of breaches of the peace in the Glenasmole valley. In this way information was passed among the various constables while their network of frequent patrols and scheduled meetings with other constables ensured that the police force was always well informed of goings-on in the parish. The stated purpose of the police force was the prevention of crime[2] and this method of frequent patrols by officers on foot or on horseback made the force highly visible to the population.

This locally-circulated detail, together with the information circulated nationally in *Hue and Cry*, formed the basis of much police detection work at the time. *Hue and Cry* was the original police gazette and was first published in London in 1786. It arose out of an earlier periodical issued by Henry Fielding, the novelist, shortly after 1751, and over time it evolved into *The Police Gazette*, which is still published today. An Irish *Hue and Cry* was being published by 1822 and appeared continuously from then until 1922.[3] It contained reports of crimes, descriptions of stolen property and animals, of persons sought in connection with crimes, details of rewards offered and other information to be circulated to local constables. The expression 'hue and cry' dates back to the Statute of Winchester, 1285. Under this act a night watchman had to raise a 'hue and cry' if a stranger or suspicious person failed to stop on being challenged. All able-bodied men were obliged to join in the chase.[4]

Having received his reports, Burke made his way back to Tallaght. Policing as now practised was a new profession. Nineteenth-century policing evolved out of a number of different services and statutes. During the eighteenth century constables were appointed by the grand juries, were few in number and were poorly paid out of county funds.[5] Thus, the quality of policing varied greatly from county to county, with some areas only putting together a police force as a reaction to immediate threat of disturbance. Dublin city was more organised, with lay magistrates and up to four hundred constables.[6] Constables appointed under the policing acts of 1787 and 1792 were not distinguished from civilians. They wore no uniforms.

2   Ibid., p. 24.
3   Jim Herlihy, *The Royal Irish Constabulary* (Dublin, 1997), p. 73.
4   O'Sullivan, *Irish Constabularies*, p. 8.
5   Herlihy, *Royal Irish Constabulary*, p. 27.
6   Ibid., p. 27.

8 Irish constabulary on patrol, from an engraving of 1834.
From Jim Herlihy, *The Royal Irish Constabulary* (1997), reproduced
with permission of Four Courts Press

They were under no effective supervision and were not disciplined. They also continued to follow their usual occupations.[7]

Under an act 'to provide for the better execution of the laws in Ireland',[8] Robert Peel formed the Peace Preservation Force (PPF).[9] Resident magistrates were appointed under this act together with chief constables and sub-constables. But this Peace Preservation Force was formed in response to disturbances and could be withdrawn or disbanded when tranquillity was restored. This flexibility also enabled the grand juries to minimise the cost of maintaining the PPF.

The Constabulary Act of 1822[10] provided for a county constabulary, with each barony to have sixteen sub-constables appointed by the magistrates.

7   Ibid., p. 28.
9   Herlihy, *Royal Irish Constabulary*, p. 29.
8   54 George III, *c.*131.
10 Ibid., p. 39.

The quality of policing gradually improved, and in 1835 Thomas Drummond was appointed under-secretary for Ireland. He had been involved in the ordnance survey and also in applying the poor law to Ireland. He was a reforming under-secretary and among other achievements he organised and improved policing in Ireland.

Shortly after his appointment, the Constabulary (Ireland) Act 1836[11] – 'The Drummond Act' – was passed. This act repealed and consolidated all preceding legislation relating to policing. The act dealt with recruitment, training, educational standards and substantial organisational matters relating to the police force. Drummond also introduced a code of conduct for the police in 1837 and under a further act of 1839 a training depot was to be established in the Phoenix Park. Drummond died in 1840 but the improvements initiated by him continued, and training commenced at the new depot in 1842.[12] Under Drummond's system, sub-inspectors such as Burke were paid £250 per annum, but the lowest grade, a sub-constable, was paid £25 per annum.[13] These salaries were further regulated by amending legislation passed in 1846. The reforms were affecting everyday policing and so had a real impact on the working life of Burke.

The 'Outrage Papers' for county Dublin are available for the years 1836 to 1850. They contain correspondence between the various police stations and Dublin Castle on all serious crime in the county and city along with some witness statements, known as informations, various other correspondence and some copies of reward notices. Up to 1840 the reports were written out in longhand on blank paper. Depending on the officer who wrote them they could be colourful, descriptive reports or terse and to the point. The reports varied greatly and even the paper on which they were written varied. Sub-inspector Burke could source his paper locally and this gave him an excuse to visit and establish contact with Michael McDonnell and his workers at the Oldbawn paper mills. Burke regarded these contacts as an integral part of his policing function.

But in 1838, pre-printed report forms first appeared. These forms were supplied centrally and so disturbed Burke's contact with his local supplier. The first forms had a basic heading on them with spaces for filling in a reference number, county, barony, parish, townland, distance from the nearest police station, whether a reward was considered expedient, the date and time of the most recent patrol at the crime scene before the outrage took

11 6 William IV, c.13.
12 Herlihy, *Royal Irish Constabulary*, p. 50.
13 O'Sullivan, *Irish Constabularies*, p. 43.

place, and when and by whom it was reported to the police. The rest of the form was left blank, allowing for a description of the outrage and for a record of the reaction of the superiors in the office of the inspector general to the report. So, until 1840 the reports retain their colourful descriptions and speculations. A new form headed: 'Abstract report of outrage' appeared in 1841 and the reports from then on lose much of the narrative and insight of the earlier reports. Burke had mixed feelings about such centralisation and wondered where it would all lead.

Other areas of his job were affected by local politics and local inter-ference. This bothered him. He saw his duties as falling into four categories: chase and apprehension, assistance in prosecution, prevention of crime, and interference in civil processes.[14] But magistrates and others regularly put police officers under pressure to carry out what were properly the duties of the local sheriff or the local magistrate. Police officers had been drafted in as clerks at petty sessions and to help at hangings and at the subsequent disposal of the bodies.[15] These pressures put a conscientious officer in conflict with his superiors in Dublin Castle, who regularly reminded officers such as Burke, that their primary function was the preservation of the peace and the prevention of crime. In Tallaght, Burke avoided becoming involved in the collection of tithes, rents or fines, as police in many other areas regularly did.

As faction-fighting was a serious problem in other parts of the country Burke would have considered himself lucky that such outrages did not occur in his area and among his people. At a faction-fight at Ballybunion in June 1834 at least twenty men had been killed in a fight involving over two thousand participants.[16] But today he was about to find himself confronted with the outcome of a fight which broke out three days previously, following the fair day at Saggart.

When Burke got back to his barracks in Tallaght there was a man waiting to see him. The man identified himself as Thomas Lennon and he proceeded to tell Burke about an attack on him at the Saggart fair. He told how on 8 November, he attended the fair at Saggart with his brother, Michael. On their way home they were attacked and beaten by two men whom he named as John Brady and John Reynolds of Slademore. In the course of this attack, John Reynolds had caused a serious wound to his

---

14 Stanley H. Palmer, *Policing and protest in England and Ireland 1780–1850* (Cambridge, 1988), p. 262.
15 Ibid., p. 263.
16 O'Sullivan, *Irish Constabularies*, p. 55.

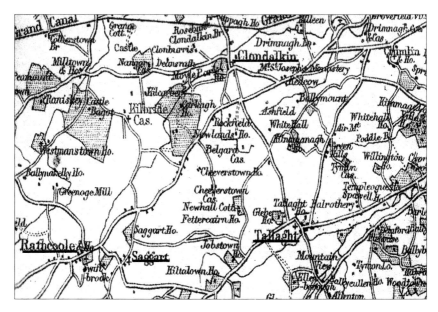

9 Map of Tallaght and district where Sub-inspector Burke was
responsible for law and order in the nineteenth century.
Source: based on map by Edward Weller, 1890

head, with the head of a churn dash. Burke could clearly see the wound
inflicted with this common household implement and he wondered at
Lennon's ability to carry on working and travelling in spite of it. At this stage
Burke apparently regarded the incident as no more than an assault and
battery. Not quite a faction-fight, but the nearest substitute for one in this
part of the country. In the course of telling his story, Lennon also told Burke
that he would summon Brady and Reynolds to the next petty sessions and
get his satisfaction there in a civil action. Burke decided to keep in touch
with Lennon and when his health began to deteriorate on the following
day, Burke got a magistrate to take a deposition from him and issued a
warrant on foot of it. Subsequent events proved this to be a wise move.

Burke made a report of the outrage to Dublin Castle on 15 November.[17]
He went on to report that Brady held a farm at Slademore and was at a
funeral in county Meath. Reynolds was described in the report as a wander-
ing labourer who was at present digging potatoes in county Wicklow. In this
report, Burke stated as the cause of the dispute, that Brady suspected the
Lennons of taking some of his turf from an adjoining bog.[18] Brady's holding

17 Burke to Inspector General, 15 November 1839, NAI, Outrage Papers, county Dublin, 1839.
18 Ibid.

at Slademore was located in the high hills between the villages of Brittas and Rathcoole. While Burke enclosed the descriptions of the wanted men with his report, he pointed out that as the men were expected home in the next few days, there was no need to put the descriptions in *Hue and Cry* just yet. It appears that Lennon himself identified and named the two men who assaulted him and named Reynolds as the man who inflicted the blow. Burke did not think that a reward was necessary in this, his first report of this outrage.

In a further report dated 18 November 1839, Burke was getting more anxious. He had by now tried to execute a warrant on the two wanted men on three separate occasions and failed 'in consequence of the offenders having fled'.[19] At this stage Burke also reported that Lennon had become extremely ill and Burke recommended a £20 reward for their apprehension. He also asked that a full description be included in *Hue and Cry*. The next report from Burke is dated 20 November, in which he stated that Lennon had died the previous night of the injuries he had received. This had now become a murder hunt. The extent of the hunt for the fugitives and the difficulties encountered by the police were briefly described in this report:

> The police parties were again in search of the offenders last night without success, but I received information while out last night that they were still hiding in the neighbourhood, and that a subscription was on foot to enable them to leave the country immediately. It is very difficult to discover them as they have so many relations on the mountains who secret them – a person we can rely on has promised to give the police the earliest information of the offenders, and I have circulated numerous descriptions of the two men, and also sent to the neighbouring seaports. I beg leave to suggest that the reward be increased from £20 to £50. I have written to the coroner to hold an inquest.[20]

Just over one week later, on 28 November, Burke set out the verdict of the coroner's inquest in his next report in the case:

> That Thomas Lennon died of a beating which he received at the fair of Saggart on the 8 November from John Brady and John Reynolds who have fled and absconded for [illegible]

This report goes on to state:

19 Burke to Inspector General, 18 November 1839, NAI, Outrage Papers, county Dublin, 1839.
20 Burke to Inspector General, 20 November 1839, NAI, Outrage Papers, county Dublin, 1839.

> The offenders are still in the country and have as yet succeeded in
> evading the watchfulness of the police. I am informed through their
> counsel, that it is their intention to offer bail.[21]

It appears from this report that some sort of negotiation was going on and
that a counsel had been appointed to represent the men. It might be
expected that a negotiated surrender was about to happen. Burke was
dithering and continued to dither for almost three weeks. During this
period there is no indication in the reports as to what efforts Burke was
making to further negotiations with Brady and Reynolds, or whether he
was attempting to apprehend them at all. It appears he was content to wait
until the reward being offered enticed an informer to give information and
so relieve the police of the need for diligent work and extensive enquiries.

But Sub-inspector Burke had another new case on his desk, and he was
about to learn that the new standards of policing were to be taken most
seriously, and applied rigorously by the inspector general and the staff at
Dublin Castle. On 7 December, John Quin entered the police barracks in
Tallaght and reported the disappearance of his father, one Edward Quin.
Quin had been an overseer of bricklayers and had travelled to Clondalkin to
purchase bricks on 27 November 1839. This business was transacted with
James Singleton in the vicinity of William Carmichael's public house at the
Ninth Lock. At the conclusion of business, Quin and Singleton drank some
whiskey there.[22] After his drink Quin was seen proceeding along the bank
of the canal towards Dublin where his home was at Mountjoy Court in the
north inner city. He was never heard from afterwards.

A number of assumptions and speculations were set out in the first report
of 16 December 1839, from Burke at Tallaght police station to the inspector
general at Dublin Castle. This report was made three weeks after Quin had
disappeared and nine days after John Quin had reported his father missing.
It was thought by his family that if Quin had accidentally fallen into the
canal, then his body or some part of his property such as his hat or walking
stick, would have been found. His family thought that he must have been
intentionally injured in some manner or his body concealed, as no account
of him could be had.

21 Burke to Inspector General, 28 November, 1839, NAI, Outrage Papers, county Dublin,
   1839.
22 Burke to Inspector General, 16 December, 1839, NAI, Outrage Papers, county Dublin,
   1839.

Sub-inspector Burke also set out that Quin was looked on as a 'colt', a nickname given to persons who were not regular tradesmen. He had enemies in consequence, and some time previously he had received severe beatings in Dublin. Burke then reported that the constable in charge in Clondalkin had told him he would find out nothing more on the subject by visiting the place, as he 'has made enquiries and saw Quin's friends who live in Dublin'. Finally, Burke included a description of Quin and recommended that it be included in *Hue and Cry*.

It was a strict requirement that each outrage be reported to the office of the inspector general immediately and where this did not happen, explanations were always required. Burke's initial report, apart from being tardy, contained a number of items of information setting out police and family speculation as to what might have happened to Quin, but reported none of the facts surrounding his disappearance.

The subsequent papers set out the reaction of those at the inspector general's office in Dublin Castle. Drummond's improved organisation of the police was about to be visited on the Tallaght outpost and Sub-inspector Burke would be informed of new standards and new expectations. Subsequent correspondence between Burke at Tallaght and his superiors in Dublin Castle in relation to this case illustrate this pressure to raise standards in policing. The reaction to Sub-inspector Burke's initial report was not what he expected.

An instruction was issued at the inspector general's office in very precise terms, setting out the faults in the report submitted in relation to Quin's disappearance:

> [...] inform the sub-inspector that he takes a very mistaken view of his duty by neglecting the regulations of the establishment on such grounds. If an officer is to take for granted that his researches, in any particular case, must prove unavailing, he may excuse himself from all exertions, and leave the constables to perform the work which the Inspector General expects him to attend to in person. Instruct him now to make all possible enquiry respecting the disappearance of Edward Quin. At whose public house had he been drinking – who was in his company, or in the house at the same time with him – who last saw him – was he alone at the time – was he perfectly sober & etc. Information is required on all these points & such information should have been acquired, in the first instance by Mr Burke himself & should have been embodied in this report. Let him also account for the delay

which has occurred in reporting to headquarters what has been known to the constabulary since the 7th instant.[23]

This reaction expressed considerable dissatisfaction with Burke's initial handling of Quin's disappearance. It also outlined what was considered a basic level of investigation and emphasised the promptness with which information should have been submitted to head office. A letter in just these terms, signed by W. Miller, was dispatched to Sub-inspector Burke on 17 December. In a subsequent reply, Burke refers to this man by his rank as Colonel Miller.

Burke replied to this letter on 18 December and set out a much more systematic account of the disappearance than was in his initial report:

> Referring to my report of the 16th instant and in reply to Colonel Miller's communication of the 17th relative to the mysterious disappearance of Edward Quin; I have further to state that I proceeded to the public house of Wm Carmichel at the 9th Lock and ascertained there that Edward Quin and James Singleton (the person to whom he came to purchase bricks from) both entered Carmichel's public house where they remained about five minutes while they drank of whiskey each previously to parting – they then left the house and went over the canal bridge about 20 yards off where they parted: Quin going towards Dublin by himself, & Singleton returned the same way they went, it being then between 4 & 5 o'clock P.M.
>
> From the time that Quin and Singleton entered the public house until they separated at the bridge, it was not more than a quarter of an hour, and all were good friends – Singleton was the last person who saw Quin, and states he was not drunk, but rather jocular in his manner and well capable of taking care of himself. I also saw Quin's sons in Dublin who could give me no information but what I stated in my first report, which I could have made sooner to the Inspector General had the circumstances of the case permitted me, as I felt myself obliged to wait to know the result of the various searches and enquiries which were being made, it being at first supposed that the man had accidentally been drowned. I shall of course report any further information I may be able to collect.
>
> W.B. Burke.
> Sub Inspector.

23 Miller to Burke, 17 December 1839, NAI, Outrage Papers, county Dublin, 1839.

[PS] I think there was a report today, that the body of Edward Quin was found.[24]

Burke replied very much in the format laid out by his superiors and this report sets out a clear picture of the events leading up to Quin's disappearance. Burke's first report did not contain this information, but contained several speculations reported from Quin's family and also outlined his past reputation. By comparison, the second report clearly sets out the purpose and events of his visit to Clondalkin. This new report has also added to it the news that Quin's body had been found. This may have been added subsequently by somebody in Colonel Miller's office and is not in Burke's handwriting. A further report from Burke dated 20 December, sets out that Quin's body was found in the canal about a mile-and-a-half from Clondalkin that morning with marks of violence on his face.

There is one further report dated 23 December 1839, setting out the verdict of the inquest jury as follows: 'Edward Quin found dead in the water of the Grand Canal at 7th Lock – but whether said Quin came to his death by violence, or by falling accidentally, or in a state of intoxication, or thrown in by some person or persons unknown, said jury cannot say.' The inquest was held on 21 December at the Seventh Lock, Grand Canal.[25] The Seventh Lock was, and still is, located as the Grand Canal passes by the townland of Ballyfermot.

A number of issues arise from this series of reports. For all the urgency in Colonel Miller's letter of 17 December, there were lengthy delays at every stage of this incident. Quin's meeting with Singleton was on 27 November. His son, John Quin, did not report his disappearance until 7 December. And Burke did not first report the incident to head office in Dublin Castle until 16 December. At that stage, Quin was missing for almost three weeks. By the time the body was found, Quin had been missing for three weeks and two days. If the body was in the canal for all of that time, even allowing for December's cold weather, it cannot have been a pleasant sight for the boatmen who found him. There is no further information in the papers dealing with Quin which would give any indication of the cause of death or of any further investigation. A mystery remains as to why this man died, and there are some intriguing details of his life.

24 Burke to Inspector General, 18 December 1839, NAI, Outrage Papers, county Dublin, 1839.
25 Burke to Inspector General, 23 December 1839, NAI, Outrage Papers, county Dublin, 1839.

He lived in Mountjoy Court, a short street described in 1850 as having eight houses in tenements.[26] This street was just off Mountjoy Square and even taking the more direct line along the Grand Canal bank was quite a walk from there to Clondalkin. Quin appears to have set out to walk this distance in both directions in the one day. It also appears he set out to return to Dublin just as it was getting dark.

From Burke's first report, it appears that Quin was not a regular tradesman and had made enemies in consequence. While the cause of his death and any possible motive for his suspected murder is speculative, there had previously been trouble at the Ninth Lock in Clondalkin between local workers and competing workers from Dublin. A report dated 3 August 1836 of William Harpur, chief constable at Lucan, states that Mr Stokes, the engineer of the Grand Canal Company, had occasion to employ a number of men at the Ninth Lock. It appears from the report that this work was carried out on 2 and 3 August 1836. The report goes on to state that some labourers who came down from Dublin to be employed, threatened destruction to those allotted to the water department of the work, if they took less wages than two shillings per day.[27] William Colback, the magistrate of Clondalkin, was called in with the small force of police available to him and they 'happily succeeded in suppressing the riotous disposition until the work was completed'. Quin might have been among the labourers who came from Dublin on this occasion and may have made enemies among the labourers of Clondalkin well before his own demise in November 1839.

But what effect did the criticism of Burke's competence have on the conduct of his investigation in the Saggart murder? The letter of criticism of 17 December in connection with Quin's case, prompted immediate action in the pursuit of Brady and Reynolds. Burke was under pressure and reacted by becoming more effective. By 20 December Burke could report that John Brady had been arrested the previous night concealed in a hayloft in the townland of Gollarstown [sic] near Rathcoole, by constable William Lodge and his party of the Rathcoole station.[28] An individual gave information to the police leading to the location and arrest of Brady, and Burke recommended that some reward be given as the individual promised to find out where Reynolds was hiding. The informer was named in this report as James Malone of Slademore and it was pointed out by Burke that Malone

26 *Dublin pictorial guide and directory*, 1850.
27 Harpur to Miller, 5 August 1836, NAI, Outrage Papers, county Dublin, 1836.
28 Burke to Inspector General, 20 December 1839, NAI, Outrage Papers, county Dublin, 1839.

requested his name be kept private 'as danger to his life would ensue were it known.'[29]

On 28 December a further report from Burke informed the inspector general that John Reynolds was arrested on the previous night by the police from Brittas, on private information given to them by Michael Hodgens of Tallaght Hill.[30] In this report Burke recommended that Malone and Hodgens be paid the reward of £20 each. To this end he forwarded the names and addresses of the two men to Dublin Castle. However, in Dublin Castle, Colonel Miller submitted the reward request to the inspector general who added the comment that 'the sum recommended, £20, seems rather too large at the present stage of the case' and he authorised the payment of £10 to each of the informers. Miller, on instruction, added the comment that 'the decision of the government in this case should guide him in future instances of like nature'.

Brady and Reynolds were brought to trial on 13 January 1840. The *Dublin Evening Post* for the following day contained this report:

> Yesterday, John Reynolds and John Brady were indicted for the murder of Thomas Lennon. The deceased was engaged in a quarrel at the Fair of Saggart and his death was caused by a beating he received. The prisoners were acquitted.[31]

There is no further or deeper report of the conduct of the trial, so it can only be speculated as to why these men were acquitted. It appears from the facts of the case that Lennon was struck in some sort of affray and the reports set out no evidence of premeditation. Premeditation was a necessary prerequisite for murder and if it could not be proven, then the men charged could not be found guilty of murder. The discretion allowing a jury to bring in a verdict of guilty on a lesser charge such as manslaughter, is a recent development and was not available to a jury in 1839.

It turned out to be a busy Christmas for William Burke. In addition to the apprehension of Brady and Reynolds he had a case of sheep-stealing to deal with on 21 December. On that day some sheep were stolen from the farm of Nicholas Roe at Johnville, just beside Jobstown. Nobody was ever caught for this outrage but the Roes were a prominent family, and their case warranted full attention.

29 Ibid.
30 Burke to Inspector General, 28 December 1839, NAI, Outrage Papers, county Dublin, 1839.
31 *Dublin Evening Post*, 14 January 1840.

So ended the year 1839. Sub-inspector William Burke dealt with a total of nine outrages in the parish of Tallaght alone. An agrarian problem in the townland of Kiltalown accounted for three of these. In January 1839, Michael and William Carroll resisted legal proceedings when the sheriff and bailiffs tried to evict them. In June of the same year, John Carroll of the same family tried to take forcible possession of the holding and issued a threatening letter. In July, cattle belonging to James Loughlin at Kiltalown were maimed. It was alleged in the outrage report that this was done by sympathisers of the Carroll family.

Two of the reported outrages concerned bodies found. In March, the body of James McKenna was found on the edge of the river Dodder at Oldbawn. He was thought to have died accidentally. The following month, the body of Daniel Rooney was found in Firhouse, where he had fallen drunk. An incident common in many parts of the country happened at Tallaght in June when Michael Fitzwilliam tried forcibly to release animals from the 'pound' in an outrage described as a 'pound breach'. The cattle had been impounded by Benjamin Bradley for rent and the report states that Michael Fitzwilliam, the owner of the cattle, was supposed to have taken possession of them. Searches for the cattle, however, were not successful. A further case of cattle-stealing happened in August in Ballyroan when cattle belonging to Edward Nolan were taken. No perpetrator was apprehended. Then in October, two threatening letters were sent to Mrs Digges La Touche in Templeogue. The report indicates that a former tenant of the house rented by her wanted to regain possession. While the offence could not be fixed on that former tenant, one John Keenan, no further action was taken in this case.[32]

Other outrages were committed in other parts of the barony of Uppercross and were dealt with by Burke during the year. He smarted for a while from the criticism in the Quin case but recovered – and resolved to improve his policing duties. He worked fairly with the population and was regarded with some affection by them. Twenty-eight years later he was referred to familiarly as 'Chief Burke', when he dealt courageously with the Fenian marchers and prevented an attack on Tallaght police barracks on 6 March 1867.[33]

32 Burke to Inspector General, 16 October 1839, NAI, Outrage Papers, county Dublin, 1839.
33 William Domville Handcock, *The history and antiquities of Tallaght* (Cork, 1976), p. 142.

The Bigamist of Ballinavin

A tale of charity betrayed

MÁIRE NÍ CHEARBHAILL

Charles Berry, attorney, had offices at 28 Arran Quay, Dublin, in the early years of the nineteenth century.[1] He was one of several attorneys who practised along the Liffey quays at the time, in the massive shadow of the new Four Courts building. On a summer's morning in 1810, there was an unexpected knock at his door. A run-down and poorly dressed individual stood before him, bearing letters of introduction. Why he singled out Berry from the other legal men in the district remains a mystery, and why Berry responded in the way that he did is an even greater mystery. This first encounter saw the beginnings of a tale of charity and intrigue that would ultimately end in betrayal and take both men to court in a celebrated trial for bigamy.[2]

But these events were still in the future in 1810. The stranger was more interested in telling the attorney about his past. In the manner of the prodigal son, he began to pour out the story of his misspent youth and the loss of his fortune. He gave his name as Robert Robinson, the grand-nephew and heir of Lieutenant General Robert Robinson who had died in 1793.[3] Robert senior held property in both Ireland and England. His ancestral home, Ballinavin Castle, was near Borrisokane in north Tipperary but he had lived at Marlborough Street in London and owned other

---

1 *Wilson's Dublin Directory 1810*, p. 118.

2 *Report of the trial of Robert Robinson for bigamy* [The king at the suit of Charles Berry versus Robert Robinson] (Dublin, 1812), p. 2. Hereafter *Trial*.

3 Robert Robinson is recorded as a Lieutenant General in *A list of the officers of the army and marines* (War Office, 1 January 1792), p. 2, published annually, but is no longer listed for 1793.

property in fashionable parts of the city.[4] The younger Robert was a boy of thirteen when the general died, leaving him with £500 per year and £100,000 in government funds.[5] As a young man, this large inheritance had enabled him to buy himself into the cavalry, and he was quartered at Clonmel in the years immediately after the rebellion of 1798.[6]

Robinson went on to tell Charles Berry of his acceptance into the family of Thomas Stoney, landowner and deputy governor of Tipperary, grand juror and farmer. A history of the Stoney family gives a colourful picture of the man who was to become Robinson's father-in-law. Thomas Stoney was described as a gregarious, outgoing man with a large family and extensive lands in Tipperary. He kept a pack of hounds for the amusement of his friends. In his blue cutaway coat, red waistcoat, frilled shirt and white cravat, topped by a powdered wig with a pigtail in the style of George III, he cut a dash when he swept into a room. His family of twelve sons and daughters were expected to stand and to remain standing until he was seated.[7] Stoney entertained lavishly and open house was a feature of life at his home at Arran Hill, near Borrisokane. He was also a shrewd man. Meals were served at two dining tables: one for the married and one for the unmarried guests. It is likely that it was at the singles table that his third daughter, Ruth, met the young cavalryman, Robert Robinson. A mutual attachment followed. Ruth and Robert were distant cousins – the first Stoney to arrive in Tipperary from Yorkshire in the late seventeenth century had married a Robinson in 1712.[8]

Although he was under twenty-one, Robert assured the attorney that Thomas Stoney had encouraged the alliance, and even made arrangements for their wedding in Scotland. He had also pressed him to buy his way out of the army.[9] Because Robert was still a minor, and his guardian was dead, a wedding in Scotland was considered a less complicated option.[10] English marriage law was more restrictive, and many couples found it easier to cross the border to Scotland for their weddings at Gretna Green or other centres.[11] Portpatrick, on the west coast of Scotland, was popular with Irish couples in the eighteenth and nineteenth centuries as it was just a short boat trip from the seaside port of Donaghadee in county Down.[12] It was to this

4 R.A. Stoney, *Some old annals of the Stoney family* (London, 1879), p. 8. Hereafter *Stoney annals.*
5 *Trial*, p. 3.   6 Ibid.   7 *Stoney annals*, p. 66.
8 Ibid.   9 *Trial*, p. 5.   10 *Trial*, p. 23.
11 Colin Chapman, *Marriage laws, rites, records and customs* (Dursey, 1966), p. 70.
12 A.P.W. Malcolmson, *The pursuit of the heiress: aristocratic marriage in Ireland, 1750–1820* (Ulster, 1982), p. 38.

destination that the Robinson–Stoney wedding party made its way in December 1801.[13] The distance from Dublin to Donaghadee was about ninety-five Irish miles, along good roads, and there was an ample supply of coaches running north at that time. A packet sailed from Donaghadee to Portpatrick, a distance of about twenty miles.[14]

Charles Berry listened as Robert Robinson revealed all the details of his inheritance, courtship and marriage. But there was more to tell. In the years following his marriage, Robinson described how he had settled in England and acquired both a town and a country house; he became the father of four children and purchased seven racehorses; he had even made an unsuccessful bid for parliament. His extravagance, he admitted, led to huge debts and he was forced to flee to Ireland with his wife and family and to throw himself at the mercy of his father-in-law, Thomas Stoney.[15]

Stoney had agreed to help his daughter and son-in-law, and to work out a strategy to keep the creditors at bay. He invested in a small piece of land on behalf of Robinson in the district, which was yielding some rental income. Robert owed his wife maintenance (pin money), and Ruth agreed to take an amicable action against him for its recovery. The effect of filing this suit against her husband would lead to a receiver being appointed to the land and other creditors being excluded. Robert had expected that the rental income would then come to him, but the plan didn't materialise in this way. Stoney, Robinson declared, had pocketed the lot and he received not a penny. Ruth, too, apparently had had enough. With her four small sons she returned to her father's house, leaving her husband penniless, in poor health and ostracised.[16]

By the time that Robert Robinson's long story of misfortune had come to an end, Charles Berry was drawn into the sorry tale. In addition to his financial troubles, Robinson suffered from a serious ailment that affected his limbs and his ability to walk.[17] In spite of never having set eyes on the man before, the Dublin attorney took it upon himself to try and rehabilitate the unfortunate man. His first step was to get him lodgings, which he did, on his own security. He then put him in touch with an apothecary and a physician to care for his health problems. Then he began the slow work of disentangling his financial affairs, as Robinson was both a debtor and a creditor.[18]

13   *Trial*, p. 4.
14   Nathaniel Jefferys, *An Englishman's descriptive account of Dublin … and … the road from Dublin to Donaghadee* (London, 1810), p. 116.
15   *Trial*, pp. 5–6.   16   *Trial*, pp. 5–6.
17   Ibid., p. 20. Described as a rheumatic condition by his doctor in court.
18   Ibid., pp. 3–6.

One of the suits that Berry filed on his behalf was to reverse his wife's earlier suit for maintenance. Neither men was to know it at the time, but this document would be used as vital evidence at the later trial for bigamy.

After he had settled into his new lodging place, bailiffs continued to cause Robinson considerable inconvenience. Bailiffs could make arrests by day but not by night, so if Robinson needed to discuss his financial matters with the attorney, he was forced to slip out under cover of darkness to make his way to the Berry home. Again, the generous Berry came to the rescue: he invited Robinson to share his home with his wife and his two young daughters while his affairs were being dealt with.[19]

Robert Robinson settled in well with the Berry family, which included Charles's wife, a delicate and highly-strung woman in need of constant medical care, and the Berry girls, Ismenia and Maria, who were then aged about thirteen and ten. He was with the family for some time when Mrs Berry became ill and her doctor advised an extended trip to the spa waters at Cheltenham. Charles Berry was too busy with legal matters to accompany his wife, but it happened that Robinson was planning a trip to England to collect some moneys owing to him. Berry requested that Robinson escort his wife and the older daughter, Ismenia, to Cheltenham. Robinson was only too happy to oblige. Long the recipient of the charity of Charles Berry, he declared himself well pleased to be of some practical assistance to the family. In addition, he purchased a few small gifts for Ismenia as a token of his gratitude. The trio set out and remained in England for a number of months, returning to Dublin in the spring of 1811.[20]

Summer and autumn rolled uneventfully by and Robert Robinson continued to be part of the Berry household. All was about to change. On a November afternoon, Ismenia and Maria were getting ready for a piano recital in rooms over Vigne's jeweller shop in fashionable Nassau Street. Robinson, who had a taste for music, had suggested the outing: the jeweller's sister was giving the recital and the girls would benefit from hearing such a proficient lady play. The girls' father agreed. Still afflicted by his rheumatic condition, Robinson announced that he would be going to the hot baths, but offered to get the valet to drop the girls off in Nassau Street on the way. The three set off together in the Berry carriage.[21]

The Richmond baths in Temple Street – called after the Lord Lieutenant and his Duchess wife – were open every day from seven in the morning until ten in the evening. Considered essential for health, they offered hot,

---

19 Ibid., p. 37.   20 Ibid., pp. 8–10.   21 Ibid., p. 12.

salt-water baths for 4*s*. 2*d*., and in case there was any doubt as to the cleanliness of the water, the visiting ladies and gentlemen could observe the baths being filled and emptied.[22]

But Robert Robinson did not make the journey to the Richmond baths on that day in November, nor to any other baths. Instead, he, too, paid a visit to Vigne's jewellers in Nassau Street. His interest, however, was not in the piano recital. In a room above the jeweller's, a clergyman awaited to officiate at his marriage to fourteen-year-old Ismenia Berry. A ring was purchased on the spot, and young Maria Berry acted as witness. This was not a runaway marriage in the literal sense: the groom's physical ailments forced him to be carried back to the coach by the valet after the wedding ceremony.

Where did the newly-weds go? It would appear that both returned to the Berry home, but their secret alliance initially remained intact. Her parents, however, were quick to observe that young Ismenia was pale-faced and tight-lipped. Not a word did she utter, however, even as her demeanour and loss of appetite began to arouse further suspicion in the following days. Eventually, she could hold her secret no longer and declared her new status as the wife of Robert Robinson! There was consternation in the Berry household. Mr Berry, who knew so much of the circumstances of Robinson's life – including the existence of a wife and family in Tipperary – was stunned and outraged. The delicate Mrs Berry went into hysterics and there were fears for her life. Aunt Hetherington – whose property Ismenia was expected to inherit – suffered an apopleptic fit.[23]

What was Charles Berry to do? At the subsequent trial, his lawyer, Peter Burrowes, would raise the options that were available to the grief-stricken father. Mr Berry, he explained, had three possible courses of action. First, he could have connived at the improper connection between the pair, 'choosing between exposure and vice'. Secondly, he could have tried to hush the whole business, but this was not an option as Robinson continued to openly claim Ismenia as his wife. Berry chose the third course: to take Robinson to court, so that he might 'derive consolation from the recollection of his having brought a delinquent of his atrocious guilt to punishment, and in having provided that this man shall not repeat his crimes, and bring sorrow into the bosom of other families …'[24] Robinson was arrested and charged with bigamy.

22 *Freeman's Journal*, 7 July 1812, advertisement.
23 *Trial*, pp. 12–14.
24 Ibid., p. 14.

TRIAL

OF

ROBERT ROBINSON,

FOR

B I G A M Y;

TRIED IN THE SESSIONS HOUSE, GREEN-STREET,

AT THE

COMMISSION OF *OYER* AND *TERMINER,*

BEFORE THE

Hon. JUSTICES MAYNE AND FLETCHER,

On WEDNESDAY *the* 24*th of* JUNE, 1812.

---

10 Detail from title page of pamphlet recording the trial of Robert Robinson for bigamy

'*Bigami*', as far back as the thirteenth century, described those who had married a second time, their first spouses having died. The meaning subsequently narrowed to refer to those who had more than one spouse at the same time, and under the Bigamy Act 1603, this became a felony punishable by death.[25] An Irish act of parliament of 1725–6 decreed that those guilty of bigamy be 'transported to some of his majesty's plantations in America'.[26] At the time of Robinson's trial, capital punishment was no longer being enforced for bigamy, and as the American colonies had been closed off following their War of Independence, the sentence handed down for bigamy was usually seven years' transportation to Australia.

The trial of Berry versus Robinson was held in Green Street courthouse in Dublin on 24 June 1812 amid great public interest. Anticipating this

25 1 James I, *c.*11.
26 12 Geo I, *c.*3.

interest, the *Freeman's Journal* promised to give extensive coverage following the trial.[27] Less than a decade earlier, Robert Emmet had stood in the same court. The two Roberts shared the expertise of several of the eminent legal men of the time. Edward Mayne, a member of the prosecution team in the Emmet trial, had been appointed a judge in 1806[28] and now sat on the bench with Judge William Fletcher at the bigamy trial. Leonard McNally, barrister and informer, he who had kissed the doomed Robert Emmet on the forehead after his guilty verdict was pronounced in 1803,[29] was Robert Robinson's defender in court.

But it was Peter Burrowes, chief advocate for Emmet, but now on the prosecution side in the Robinson trial, who was the outstanding voice among the legal men. Described as an 'honest but eccentric genius,'[30] as a student in Trinity College, he had become acquainted with Wolfe Tone, with the Emmet family and with other revolutionary thinkers of the time. Although a zealous supporter of constitutional and parliamentary reform he was no advocate of physical force against the crown. He had been elected MP for Enniscorthy in 1800, but with the fall of the Irish parliament, his term as a politician was short-lived.[31] At the time of the trial of Berry versus Robinson, he was an established barrister in the city, possessing in abundance that florid style of delivery in court that was characteristic of the times. While forced to remain silent for most of the trial of Robert Emmet, he had no such restraints in the trial of Robert Robinson.

The court heard the charge against the accused:

> … that on the 8th day of December in the 42nd year of the King's reign, at Portpatrick in Scotland [he] … did marry one Ruth Stoney, spinster, and had her for wife; and afterwards on 20th November in the 52nd of the King … feloniously did marry, and to wife did take, one Ismenia Berry, spinster, and to her was married (the said Ruth, his former wife, being then alive) …[32]

The jury of twelve were sworn in, and the eloquent Burrowes began with his opening address.

27 *Freeman's Journal,* 25 June 1812.
28 *Annual Register,* 1810.
29 Patrick Geoghegan, *Robert Emmet: a life* (Dublin, 2003), pp. 227–39.
30 D. R. Plunket, *The life, letters and speeches of D. R. Plunket,* i, 1867, cited in Marianne Elliot, *Wolfe Tone, prophet of Irish independence* (New Haven and London, 1989), p. 36.
31 *Oxford dictionary of national biography* (Oxford, 2004), vol. viii, pp. 1018–19.
32 *Trial,* p. 1.

> My Lords and Gentlemen of the Jury, it falls to my lot … to state to
> you a case as pregnant with circumstances of human woe, as strongly
> appealing to the feelings of humanity, as ever appeared in a court of
> justice. The prisoner at the bar stands indicted for a crime too often
> committed yet seldom prosecuted in this country – a crime which I
> think you will agree with me, stands pre-eminently high in the scale
> of offences – a crime at once preying upon the best interests of society,
> and annihilating the happiness of the individual who chances to be its
> victim.[33]

Peter Burrowes went on to set the scene for the jury, urging them to
consider the plight of the unfortunate, kindly Mr Berry who had taken pity
on the accused, and had been rewarded by this shocking assault on the
honour of his impressionable young daughter. He had but one piece of
consolation for the jury: 'I am happy, Gentlemen, to say that he [Robinson]
did not, he could not, render his crime perfect and complete.'

He explained in great detail the circumstances that had reduced Robert
Robinson from his status as a wealthy young heir to that of a penniless
debtor without friend or family. All the detail about his life that Robinson
himself had originally poured out to Berry at their first meeting in Arran
Quay was now being used against him. Painting a vivid picture of extravagance and recklessness, Burrowes told of Robinson's fashionable house and
country villa acquired just after his marriage; his carriages and his race
horses. 'He flourished at all places of public resort; at Newmarket and at
Epsom. He shot like a meteor across public observation. He dazzled for a
week; he was recollected for a month.'[34]

The business of the court, however, was to establish whether or not the
man at the bar was guilty of bigamy, so the line of questioning centred both
on the validity of the first marriage in Scotland and of the second ceremony
in Nassau Street. Samuel Barry, attorney, with offices at 58 Cuffe Street,
Dublin[35] was married to Elizabeth, Ruth Stoney's sister.[36] When called as a
witness, he was able to tell the court that he had travelled to Scotland with
the wedding party in December 1801, that the banns had been read and the
bells rung in Portpatrick; the ceremony of marriage had taken place before
a Dr McKenzie, clergyman of the Church of Scotland, and a congregation

---

33 Ibid., pp. 1–2.
34 Ibid., p. 4.
35 *Wilson's Dublin Directory 1810*, p. 117.
36 *Stoney annals*, p. 74.

11 Peter Burrowes, counsel for Robert Emmet in 1803 and chief prosecutor in the trial of Robert Robinson in 1812. Courtesy of the National Library of Ireland

of fifty to a hundred people. He had a certificate to prove it.[37] With such strong evidence from a reliable witness, there was little impact that defence lawyer, Leonard McNally, could have in cross-examination.

Attention now turned to the circumstances of the second ceremony in Nassau Street, especially to the credentials of the Revd Mathew Harris who had performed the ceremony. Could a marriage between two Protestants by a Roman clergyman be considered valid? The same Act of Parliament of 1725–6 that had meted out capital punishment for bigamists also contained provision for the prevention of marriages by degraded clergyman and Popish priests, imposing the death penalty for the felony.[38]

As this act might have relevance to the current trial, the judge cautioned Harris that he could well expose himself to a penalty if he were a clergyman of the church of Rome. Harris admitted that he had been ordained a Catholic priest in Douai but, he said, he had conformed to the established church long ago. He had printed evidence specifying his conformity.[39] The French town of Douai had several colleges for the education of priests during penal times, including an Irish college.[40]

Matthew Harris's flippant and evasive manner under questioning did little to endear him to the court. He admitted that he had performed the marriage ceremony in a drawing room over the jeweller's shop in Nassau Street but said he didn't know the girl's age – he would think it impertinent to look into any lady's face. She might be a hundred for all he knew. He thought her name was Emilia, not Ismenia and he wasn't certain whether her surname was Berry or Barry. He was only in the room about three minutes. No, he did not bring the marriage certificate to court because he was not desired to do so.[41]

Young Maria Berry was then summoned to give evidence. She wept bitterly throughout the ordeal, was unable to say what age she was, and could not identify Harris as the clergyman who had performed her sister's wedding. What she did tell the court was that Robert Robinson had persuaded herself and her sister to go to Vigne's, the jewellers, and that she

---

37 Family Search International Geological Index, www.familysearch.org, viewed September 2003. This source records the marriage details of 7 December 1801, and lists Thomas Stoney as the father of the bride.

38 12 Geo I, c.3.

39 *Trial*, p. 19. The *Convert rolls,* ed. Eileen O'Byrne, Irish Manuscripts Commission (Dublin, 1981), pp. 299–301, does not include a Mathew Harris in its list of convert priests for the years 1703 to 1838.

40 Douai', www.newadvent.org, p. 1, viewed 17 November 2003.

41 *Trial*, p. 19.

was present when the marriage ceremony was performed.[42] A further vital piece of evidence was the bill filed in chancery by Charles Berry to try and reverse Ruth Stoney's earlier attempt to sue her husband for maintenance. The court accepted that the existence of this legal document was proof that Robert and Ruth were man and wife.[43]

In summing up the case, Judge Fletcher instructed the jury that to return a guilty verdict, they must be satisfied in their consciences that two marriages had taken place, solemnised according to all the legal formalities. He reminded them that Harris had admitted conforming to the established church, and being formerly a Catholic priest, he became entitled to perform the sacraments as a Protestant clergyman without further ordination. They were not, he cautioned them, to be persuaded by the emotional and eloquent advocacy of Peter Burrowes but by the facts of the case. If they had any doubts they should acquit the accused. The jury had no such doubts. Without leaving the dock, they returned a unanimous guilty verdict. Robert Robinson was sentenced to seven years' transportation.[44]

* * *

Although thousands of Irish men and women made the long journey to Australia from the 1790s as transportees, convictions for bigamy were rare. Peter Burrowes had stated at the Robinson trial that bigamy was a crime 'too often committed, too seldom brought to justice'. A cursory examination of the surviving transportee records from 1836 to the 1850s would suggest that he was right. Of the 116 John Murphys, 119 John Ryans and 71 John Reillys, sentenced for various crimes, there was not a bigamist among them.[45]

However, in spite of his conviction, Robert Robinson never sailed into the southern hemisphere. Instead, the jailer carried him the few short steps from the courthouse in Green Street to Newgate prison to serve his sentence, and there he remained. A petition was the only hope for convicts of having their sentence reviewed. Petitions were sent in the first instance to the lord lieutenant, who then referred them to the trial judge, the local constabulary and sometimes to the jail governor to confirm statements made by the convict on his state of health. Although it was very difficult to receive

42 Ibid., p. 20.
43 Ibid., p. 25.   44 Ibid., pp. 22–26.
45 www.nationalarchives.ie/transp3.html, viewed 2 November 2003.

a mitigation of sentence on health grounds,[46] Robinson in fact succeeded.[47] The recommendation of a physician had saved him from transportation, and his sentence was changed to seven years' imprisonment in Newgate.[48]

Dublin's Newgate prison in the early nineteenth century was a gloomy, black-stoned building. The hangman's equipment permanently dangled over the main door. Although 'old' Newgate had moved from Thomas Street in 1781, it continued to be called the 'new' prison, even in Robinson's time. All manner of prisoners were housed there, including some awaiting transportation and some awaiting execution.[49] The fate of United Irishmen, Lord Edward Fitzgerald and Oliver Bond, who both died within its walls in 1798, was still fresh in the public mind. The prison had a dreadful reputation for neglect and vice. At the time of Robinson's incarceration, small gestures towards prison reform were getting underway, with William Wellesley-Pole, Chief Secretary, frequently visiting and inspecting the prison.[50]

In spite of his reprieve from transportation and the efforts of prison reformers, Robinson bitterly resented being locked up in Newgate. And he did not appear to be in the least remorseful for his crime. In July 1814, he appealed for his release to William Gregory, Under-Secretary for Ireland:

> Sir,
> During the administration of his Grace, the Duke of Richmond, I had a memorial presented stating the very great hardships and privations I had suffered from imprisonment and ill health, and for an error of the head more than the heart. You, Sir, must be informed that the charge against me was bigamy, a charge which could not have been substantiated had I made any defence ... My fortune, my life, my character depends on your interference, for after near three years imprisonment I can scarcely hope to be able to bear four more, which was my sentence.
>
> I have the honour to be your most obedient servant,
> Robert Robinson[51]

46 Ibid.
47 Reference to Judge Fletcher's Report, 5 June 1813 and the Lord Lieutenant's decision on application, 16 March 1814, NAI, PPC/4065.
48 NAI, PPC/4065.
49 Bernadette Doorley, 'Newgate prison' in David Dickson (ed.), *The gorgeous mask: Dublin 1700–1850* (Dublin, 1987), pp. 122–4.
50 J. Warbuton et al., *A history of the city of Dublin* (Dublin 1818, ii, p. 1049), cited in Bernadette Doorley, 'Newgate Prison' in David Dickson (ed.), *The gorgeous mask*, p. 130.
51 Robert Robinson to William Gregory, July 1814, NAI, PPC/4065.

His appeal did not have the desired effect. A wry comment on the back of his letter – initialled 'W.G.' – reads.

> If he had said that it was an error of the heart and not of the head, I should have thought his case more worthy of compassion. We will talk this matter over.

The authorities were apparently in no hurry to talk the matter over, and Robinson remained imprisoned. Nearly two more years were to pass before an event occurred that offered him an unexpected opportunity for promoting his cause. Ismenia Berry, now a young lady of eighteen, had married! In spite of Burrowes's dire predictions in court that she would be virtually unmarriagable because of her unfortunate experience with Robinson, Ismenia walked down the aisle with her soldier husband, Edward Archer Langley, on 8 April 1816.[52] The couple were wed in St George's church near Dublin's Mountjoy Square, described by a contemporary writer as 'not large, but of singular beauty'.[53]

Particularly happy to hear the news was the prisoner in Newgate. Within a few days of the wedding, he had acquired a copy of the marriage certificate from St George's parish and was sending a second letter to William Gregory. This time his mood was more confident.

> Sir,
> … I have been in confinement four years since 16 December last under a charge of bigamy at the suit of Mr Charles Berry of this city. The young lady who was the cause of my imprisonment was married last Sunday to Lieutenant Edward Archer Langley of the Staffordshire Regiment … from which circumstances I buoy myself up with the pleasing idea of obtaining my liberty through the clemency of His Excellency, the Lord Lieutenant, when he becomes acquainted with the fact – which, Sir, if you would be so condescending as to communicate to His Excellency, it would crown me with the highest obligation.

He signed the letter with a flourish: 'Robert de la Pere Robinson'.[54]

---

52 Copy of marriage certificate, NAI, PPC/1368, PPC/4065.
53 Jefferys, *Englishman's descriptive account of Dublin*, p. 91.
54 Robert de la Pere Robinson to William Gregory, April 1816, NAI, PPC/1390, PPC/4065.

This appeal had its effect. Robert Robinson was released from Newgate prison, having served nearly four-and-a-half years of his seven-year sentence.[55]

* * *

Even by the standards of the early nineteenth century, when trials for adultery, breach of promise and other marital entanglements were common, this trial for bigamy caused unusual interest and raised many questions about the characters of those who were involved. Why did Robinson think he could get away with marrying a girl of barely fourteen whose father knew so much about his affairs, including the existence of a wife and family in Tipperary? In the early nineteenth century, a good marriage held out the prospect of betterment, security and social status, if all went according to plan. An alliance, even an illegal one, might have seemed like a last opportunity for the desperate Robinson to extricate himself from his financial difficulties, provided that Mr Berry was amenable to compromise to save the family honour.

Robinson was used to getting his own way. As a boy of thirteen, he came into a large fortune, and was apparently free to spend it as he wished. The swift evaporation of his funds on horses, fine houses, liveried servants and high living suggests that by the time he appeared on Berry's doorstep, his extravagant and impulsive nature was well established. Perhaps the encounter with Ismenia Berry was just a continuation of this pattern of impetuous behaviour, spurred on by opportunism, and even a little love.

Marital misconduct was not unknown in the Robinson–Stoney families. In the previous generation, Andrew Robinson Stoney – an uncle of Ruth Stoney and cousin of Robert – had married two heiresses, the second, the extremely wealthy Countess of Strathmore. This was a stormy marriage, ending in divorce due to accusations of ill-treatment and extravagance. A vain, greedy man, Robinson Stoney had ultimately been forced to sell his gold snuff boxes and his jewellery to eke out a living.[56]

Why did Berry, who had allowed Robinson to live in his family home, not see the catastrophe coming? His lawyer, Peter Burrowes, described him as a busy legal man with a soft heart, and this may have simply been the case. And young Ismenia: why did she agree to an alliance with a man more than twice her age and in poor physical shape? The teenage girl lived with a

55 Ibid.
56 *Stoney annals*, p. 15.

neurotic mother, a weepy younger sister and a preoccupied father. Any diversion may have been a welcome change, and even Burrowes had to admit that Robinson had a certain polish, a taste for literature, and possessed 'that little artillery of accomplishments which makes a man agreeable, particularly to female society'.[57]

In the years after the trial, Charles Berry remained at his offices on Arran Quay, then moved to Richmond Street. By 1830, he is no longer listed as an attorney in the *Dublin Directory*. Peter Burrowes continued to practice at the bar. He was a judge of the insolvency court in his later years, and died in England in 1841.[58] Ismenia Berry and her husband are heard of no more. Robert Robinson, bigamist, went to live in London, at Burnett Street, in the parish of St James, Westminster, and had died by 1828. In a deed for the transfer of Robinson land drawn up in 1828, his demise is referred to, but not the date of, his death.[59]

And what of the woman he married in 1801, Ruth Stoney Robinson, she who had left her penniless husband and returned with her four small sons to her father's house? In the 1830s, she was resident at Ballinavin Castle, her husband's ancestral home. Living nearby at Park House, the property of William Trench, was her son, A.J. De La Pere Robinson.[60] In the 1840s, she is recorded as having land in fee in the townland of Ballinavin, parish of Modreeny, Tipperary, north riding.[61] For years, she was a regular Sunday visitor at gatherings of the extended Stoney family in north Tipperary.[62] In spite of her early tribulations, Ruth Stoney Robinson appears to have lived out her life in comfort, surviving all of her eleven brothers and sisters, her estranged husband and two of her four sons. She died in 1872 at the age of ninety-four.[63]

* * *

A hundred years after the trial of Berry versus Robinson, the academic and nationalist, Tom Kettle, compiled a collection of the speeches of historical characters such as Emmet, Tone and the Manchester Martyrs. An unlikely inclusion in *Irish orators and oratory* was an extract from the trial for bigamy

---

57 *Trial,* p. 10.
58 *Oxford dictionary of national biography,* viii, pp. 1018–19.
59 Robinson to Robinson, 9 August 1828, RD, 345 562 480.
60 *Lewis topographical dictionary,* 2 vols (London, 1837, reprinted 1995), ii, 375.
61 *Griffith valuation index 1845–1847,* p. 112.
62 *Stoney annals,* p. 72.
63 *Stoney annals,* p. 74.

of Berry versus Robinson. Apart from the eloquent opening address of Peter Burrowes in court, Kettle appears to have justified its selection simply because he was intrigued by the human story it told:

> This case may be classed among the documents which illustrate the social life of Ireland at the beginning of the last century, the simple facts constituting one of those astounding romances which sometimes vivify the arid pages of legal records. From the mystery of its illimitable folly one thing emerges luminous – the inexhaustible kindness of the Irish heart.[64]

---

64 Thomas Kettle [compiler], *Irish oratory and orators* (Dublin, n.d., *circa* 1915), pp. 263–4.

Sir John Bennett Piers, The Bold, Bad Baronet

Criminal conversation in county Kildare

KARINA HOLTON

> Oh! bold bad Baronet
> You need no coronet
> You sign your warrant with
> a bloody hand.[1]

The 'bold, bad baronet' refers to a gentleman called John Bennett Piers, a man from county Westmeath whose infamy spread far and wide during the early years of the nineteenth century. John Bennett Piers was descended from Captain William Piers who came to Ireland from Piers Hall, Yorkshire, in the 1530s. In 1562, Captain Piers was given a lease of lands at Tristernagh, near Ballynacargy in Westmeath and his descendants lived in an old Elizabethan manor house attached to the ruined Tristernagh Abbey.[2] Towards the late eighteenth century, Sir Pigot William, the son of Sir John Piers and Cornelia Gertrude Pigot, was head of the family.

On 17 April 1771 William married Elizabeth, daughter of John Smythe of Chancery Lane, Dublin and heiress to her father's fortune. Lady Elizabeth Piers was a regular member of the Dublin social circle, and was often seen attending such functions as the annual performances of Handel's *Messiah*.[3] They had four children, the eldest of whom was John Bennett Piers who

---

1 John Betjeman, 'Sir John Piers' in *Epsilon* (Mullingar, 1932). See also footnote 95.
2 Elizabeth Hickey, 'Some Notes on Kilbixy, Tristernagh and Templecross' in *Ríocht na Midhe*, vii (no. 1), 1980–1, p. 61.
3 *Belfast Newsletter*, April 1788, May 1789.

was born in 1772.[4] Pigot William Piers was an unpopular man in the local area. In 1783 he had the remains of Tristernagh Abbey torn down to obtain materials for enlarging his house. A neighbouring landowner offered to purchase the ruins to preserve them from destruction but his offer was refused by Piers.[5] Grose's *Antiquities* states that 'we may well wonder at that insensibility which could feel no compunction for the demolition of so noble and venerable a fabric.'[6] Local tradition claimed that the family never had any luck following the destruction of the abbey.[7]

John Bennett Piers was educated at Trinity College Dublin, which he entered on 5 July 1788, aged sixteen.[8] One of his fellow students was Valentine Lawless, the future Lord Cloncurry, who was destined to play an important role in Piers's life.[9] On 1 August 1796, Piers married Mary, daughter of Revd Joseph Pratt and Sarah Montmorres of Cabra Castle, Cavan. Mary died two years later. Following his father's death in April 1798, John Bennett Piers inherited the title and the estates.

The widowed Piers left Ireland and settled in Hampshire in England. He continued to visit Dublin, however. During 1801 he was seen at social events in the city.[10] The following year he became embroiled in a scandal when he 'carried off a dancer from Astleys'.[11] Astleys, a large amphitheatre fronting onto Bride Street, had been created by Philip Astley in 1784. It was known as 'the most fashionable place of entertainment in Dublin' for a number of years and hosted performances of musical pieces, dancing, tumbling and pantomimes.[12]

On the evening of the elopement, an announcement was made to that effect from the stage of the circus. The dancer's father threatened to lodge a claim against Piers, claiming that she had supported her family on the five guineas a week she earned in the show. A friend of Piers, who met with him that week, stated that 'he seemed to feel a conscious satisfaction in the degree of notoriety this has given him, as I never saw him in better looks or spirits.'[13] Yet, despite the outward show of bravado, Piers apparently feared

4   *Burke's Peerage*, 1911, p. 1485.
5   *Parliamentary Gazetteer of Ireland 1844* (Dublin, 1846), iii, p. 395.
6   Daniel Grose, *Grose's antiquities of Ireland* (Dublin, 1791), vol. ii, p. 51.
7   Paul Walsh, *The placenames of Westmeath* (Dublin, 1957), p. 37.
8   *Alumni Dublinenses*, (eds) George Dames Burtchaell and Ulick Sadlier (Bristol, 1935), ii, p. 669.
9   Ibid., p. 486.
10 Correspondence of Melesina Trench, 23M93/42/85, Hampshire Record Office.
11 Correspondence of Melesina Trench, 23M93/42/97, Hampshire Record Office.
12 Peter Pearson, *The heart of Dublin: resurgence of an historic city* (Dublin, 2000), p. 143.
13 Correspondence of Melesina Trench, 23M93/42/97, Hampshire Record Office.

12 Tristernagh Abbey, county Westmeath, as seen by Angelo Bigari in 1779. Pigot William Piers had the remains of the abbey torn down in 1783. Courtesy of *Ríocht na Midhe*

the repercussions of his actions. A memorial dated January 1802 in the Registry of Deeds shows that Piers transferred lands to his mother, Lady Elizabeth Marlay and her second husband, Thomas Marlay at that time in what was obviously an effort to protect the lands at Tristernagh from a charge being made against them in court.[14] The dancer was a lady called Elizabeth Denny, also known as Elizabeth King. They fled to Douglas in the Isle of Man where they lived together. Their first child was born in November 1803.[15]

Meanwhile, Valentine Lawless, Piers's fellow-student at Trinity, who had since become Lord Cloncurry, had embarked on the Grand Tour of Europe. In December 1802 he and his travelling companions arrived at Nice in the south of France. It was during this sojourn that he met Elizabeth Georgiana, daughter of Major-General Charles Morgan. General Morgan had had a distinguished career in the East Indies.[16] Elizabeth was a very beautiful girl by all accounts and had just turned sixteen at that time. She was described

14   594/52/401824, RD.
15   Baptismal Records, Manx National Heritage Library,
16   *A Full and Accurate Report of the Trial of Sir John Piers for Criminal Conversation with Lady Cloncurry taken in shorthand by an eminent barrister concerned in the cause* (Dublin, 1807), p. 7. Hereafter referred to as '*Trial*'.

as being 'lovely in person, highly accomplished, fascinating in her manners, innocent in her conduct [and] pure in her principles'.[17] Her mother had died while she was very young and her father had remarried in 1791.

On 1 February, Valentine and his party left Nice for Rome. Early the following month, the Morgan family arrived in Rome too. Soon Valentine had proposed marriage to Elizabeth. On 16 April 1803, Valentine and Elizabeth were married in the suite of the Duchess of Cumberland in Rome. The bride was sixteen years old and the groom almost thirty. The wedding was presided over by Revd Mr Burgess. Guests at the wedding included the Earl of Mountcashel and his brother, the Hon. William Moore, General and Mrs Morgan, and Valentine's two sisters, Mary and Charlotte Lawless.[18] That day, Valentine wrote to his agent Thomas Ryan at his estate in Kildare. The majority of the letter included details of estate business. Almost at the end he stated: 'In short, you must know I am married in case Mr Kelly wants to have any rejoicing … pray tell him to put them off until my return. I shall then best know whether I should rejoice at all.'[19] The statement is rather unusual for a man who has just been married. However, in a letter written in Naples in September by Valentine's sister Mary to Ryan, she stated that her brother Valentine was well and that his wife was a 'most amiable woman and promises him additional happiness in an increase to his family'.[20]

On 7 April 1804, Valentine and Elizabeth's first son was born. A second child, a daughter, was born the following year. Reports stated that the couple were 'united to one another' and that Lady Cloncurry was an exemplary mother 'nursing her own children, devoting to her domestic duties the most brilliant moments of her youth and beauty and absorbing every other feeling in her attachment to her lord, and her love for her offspring'.[21]

By June 1805 the family had begun to make preparations for their return to Ireland. The travelling party included General and Mrs Morgan, Lord and Lady Cloncurry and their two young children, and their servants. Signor Gaspare Gabrielli, an Italian fresco painter who had been commissioned by Lord Cloncurry to decorate his country estate, also joined them. On their arrival in London in November, Valentine settled a jointure of £1,000 per

17 *Trial*, p. 7.
18 William John Fitzpatrick, *The life, times and contemporaries of Lord Cloncurry* (Dublin, 1855), p. 270.
19 Cloncurry papers, Cloncurry to Thomas Ryan, Rome, 16 April, 1803, NLI, Ms 8492(3).
20 Cloncurry papers, Mary Whaley to Thomas Ryan, Naples, 1 September, 1803, NLI, Ms 8492.
21 *Trial*, p. 8.

annum on Elizabeth, while her father paid over £5,000 as part settlement of her dowry.[22]

They arrived at their estate at Lyons, in county Kildare, near Newcastle in November 1805 and by all accounts settled into the lifestyle of the aristocracy. They were well received at Dublin Castle.[23] They were visited by the nobility and gentry of the neighbourhood. Among those who became friendly with the young couple were their neighbours, Colonel Marlay and his wife, Elizabeth, the mother of Sir John Piers, Valentine's former fellow-student in Trinity, and widow of his father, Sir Pigot Piers. They lived nearby at Marlay Abbey in Celbridge.[24]

Sir John Piers visited his mother in February or March of 1806 and, while there, accepted an invitation to dine at Lyons. Valentine Lawless was delighted to renew his acquaintance with his old school friend and welcomed him warmly to his home. Piers had business to attend to in Westmeath and was absent until Friday 4 April, when he dined again at Lyons. It was noted that after dinner that evening, he left the society of the gentlemen earlier than usual, and instead, joined the ladies in the drawing room. On Easter Sunday, Piers and Lord and Lady Cloncurry were together at the house of Mr Browne of Castle-Browne near Clane.[25] Again, Piers left the gentlemen's company early. It was observed that on this occasion he seemed to pay particular attention to Lady Cloncurry. It appears that later that evening, while Eliza was seated at a harpsichord, Piers contrived to speak privately to her to disclose his passion for her. She appeared to be indignant at his boldness.

Following this incident, Piers began to write to Eliza 'declaring … that he could not live without her, that his heart was hers and that he must die if he were not gratified'.[26] In reply, Eliza stated that his passion was unrequited, that she loved her husband and her two children and that no one should attempt to destroy her family or her reputation. Less than a week later, Piers visited Lyons again. Valentine was out walking and Sir John was shown into the drawing room where Eliza sat. On learning that she was alone, he checked that the adjoining room was unoccupied. He then locked the door. What happened inside the locked room is not known. However,

---

22 Fitzpatrick, *life and times of Lord Cloncurry*, p. 281.

23 *The Drennan–McTier Letters, 1802–1819*, (ed.) Jean Agnew (Dublin, 1999), iii, p. 494.

24 Rolf Loeber and Magda Stouthamer-Loeber, 'Dublin and its vicinity 1797' in *Irish Geography*, vol. 35(2) (2002), pp. 133–55. This house is now known as Celbridge Abbey.

25 Now Clongowes Wood College.

26 *Trial*, p. 13.

unknown to Piers, the artist Gaspare Gabrielli was at work high above the adjoining room on scaffolding.

Piers did not visit Lyons again for several days. On 15 April, Lord and Lady Cloncurry went to Dublin. They lodged at Mr Warner's in 9 College Green. Lord Cloncurry returned to Lyons as he had business to attend to on the estate. He arrived back in Dublin on 17 April and continued to commute between Dublin and Lyons for the next month. While in Dublin, Valentine and Eliza attended social gatherings at Dublin Castle and parties at the Duchess of Bedford's.[27] During this time John Piers took lodgings at Nugent's at 11 College Green, and from there he paid regular visits to Lady Cloncurry during her husband's absences. He had a portrait done of himself which he presented to her together with a lock of his hair contained in a locket.

The Cloncurry family returned to Lyons on 15 May. Piers soon followed. He dined at Lyons on 23 and 24 May. Lord Cloncurry was not suspicious of his guest in any way. He regarded him as a friend. On the evening of 24 May a walking party set out to tour the grounds at Lyons. Lady Cloncurry refused to join the party, citing an indisposition as her reason for not accompanying her husband and guests. However, a few minutes later she was seen walking arm in arm with Piers in the gardens. Later that night in the privacy of their own bedroom, Cloncurry demanded an explanation. She immediately burst into tears and told him everything.

In the early morning of 25 May, Cloncurry, who was angry and emotional, rushed into Piers's bedroom, discovered he had gone outside and eventually found him shooting on the demesne. He managed to take the gun from Piers and then ordered him off the estate. On returning to the house, he declared that his wife should return to her father. Immediately he wrote to General Morgan, his father-in-law, informing him of recent events. Eliza was provided with a separate bedroom for herself and her maid. Within a few days, her uncle, Colonel Kyd, arrived from England to escort her back to her father's house.

Piers, in a letter addressed to Lord Cloncurry later on 25 May, stated that he was completely innocent of the charges made by the latter. He called on Cloncurry to 'state [his] reasons for such an unjust accusation … that [he] may have the opportunity of refuting the infamous and malicious falsehoods …'[28] When the letter received no reply from Cloncurry, Piers

27   Ibid., p. 43.
28   Ibid., p. 27.

13 Lady Elizabeth Cloncurry and Sir John Bennett Piers from *Saunder's Newsletter.*
Courtesy of National Library of Ireland

wrote again demanding an explanation. When he again received no reply, he copied both of the letters and sent them to Lady Cloncurry. He also wrote to her, beginning: 'My dear loved, ever adored Eliza'.[29] He continued to declare his love for her stating, 'should my angel Eliza trust her fate in my hands, she will ever find me the most attached of men ... my whole life shall be devoted to my Eliza, and were she this moment in my arms, never could I be perfectly happy till she was my wife ...'.[30] Lord Cloncurry intercepted this letter together with the copies of the letters originally addressed to himself. Piers now attempted to write to Lord Cloncurry a third time. In this letter he stated boldly that anyone who dared to attach infamy to Lady Cloncurry was a liar and challenged her husband to a duel. He wrote '... as to my conduct ... I never did, nor ever will be at the trouble of defending it but in the one way, in which you well know, my lord, I ever was and ever will, be ready to meet any man that supposes I have ill treated him.'[31]

This challenge was not unusual in early nineteenth-century Ireland. Duelling peaked in Ireland in the 1770s and 1780s when Piers and Cloncurry were in their youth. Duels were fought for many reasons including electoral rivalry, denominational animosity and 'the precarious financial and social circumstances of a large number of gentry'.[32] However,

29 Ibid., p. 29.   30 Ibid., p. 32.   31 Ibid., p. 83.
32 James Kelly, *That damn'd thing called honour: duelling in Ireland 1570–1860* (Cork, 1995), p. 150.

by the end of the eighteenth century, opposition to duelling was spreading and it was no longer dishonourable to refuse to rise to the challenge of duelling. Many gentlemen had grown disinclined to duel and to put their lives in danger. Instead, many quarrels which would once have been solved by duelling, were fought through the courts and those guilty of issuing challenges were being prosecuted. Another reason why Cloncurry may have refused to accept Piers's challenge may have been the widespread opposition to duelling in county Kildare in the late eighteenth century. The 'Kildare Knot of the Friendly Brothers of St Patrick' had operated in the north of the county for over thirty years until the early 1790s. Many of Cloncurry's friends and neighbours were members of this society which existed to 'stop the barbarous practice of duelling'.[33]

Cloncurry was advised instead to institute legal proceedings against Piers. Sir John Piers was accused of criminal conversation with Lady Cloncurry. In a classic case of criminal conversation, the husband sued the wife's lover for money damages to compensate him for the injury to his spousal rights caused by her adultery. The reference to the word 'conversation' denoted sexual intercourse.[34] Consequently, Piers was arrested and released on bail. On his release he fled the jurisdiction and returned to the Isle of Man. At that time persons having debts abroad or actions determined against them were safe on that island, although no asylum was afforded there for any one guilty of criminal conduct.[35]

The trial against Piers opened in Dublin on Thursday, 19 February 1807. The case was a sensation. The whole of Dublin was talking about 'Lady Cloncurry who [had] been found intriguing with Sir John Piers'.[36] The court room was crowded for the two-day hearing. Cases of criminal conversation had only recently begun to be heard before a jury when John Philpot Curran represented Revd Charles Massy against the Marquis of Headfort in the first Irish criminal conversation case to be tried by a jury in 1804, securing £10,000 in damages for the plaintiff.[37]

---

33 Patrick Guinness, 'The meeting book of the county of Kildare Knot of the Friendly Brothers of St Patrick 1758–1791' in *Journal of the co. Kildare Archaeological Society*, xix (part I) (2000–2001), pp. 116–160.

34 Laura Hanft Korobkin, *Criminal conversations: sentimentality and nineteenth-century legal stories of adultery* (New York, 1998), p. 20.

35 George Woods, *An account of the past and present state of the Isle of Man* (London, 1811), pp. 294–301.

36 *Drennan–McTier Letters*, p. 494.

37 *A report of the trial on an action for damages brought by the Reverend Charles Massy against the most noble the Marquis of Headfort, for criminal conversation with plaintiff's wife* (New York, 1804).

The case for the plaintiff in the Cloncurry trial was led by John Philpot Curran who claimed that at College Green on 21 April the previous year, Sir John Bennett Piers had assaulted, ravished, embraced, debauched and lain with Lady Cloncurry. Summing up his opening statement, Curran went on to claim that Lady Cloncurry had recently been delivered of a child, a boy. He stated that there was no doubt that this child was the result of the affair between Piers and Eliza. The *Dublin Evening Post* also reported the birth of a child stating that 'a spurious and illegitimate offspring is imposed on Lord Cloncurry [that] is well known to be the child of another.'[38]

Curran's opening statement was a classical example of sentimental narrative intended to win the jury's sympathy immediately for his client. After a lengthy recitation of the wrongs to which his client had been subjected by Piers, he concluded that [they] 'cannot compensate [his] broken-hearted client … by money, repair his injuries or heal his wounds … only impart to him that only consolation of which his excessive misery is capable – the sympathy of honest and good men.'[39]

The first witness to take the stand was the Earl of Mountcashel who had attended the wedding of Valentine and Eliza. He had seen the Cloncurrys regularly during their stay in Rome. In his evidence he stated that they had been devoted to each other during the early years of their marriage. Intriguingly, however, in a letter from Munich written the previous summer, Margaret, Countess Mountcashel, on hearing of the separation, had written that she was surprised that the people about Lady Cloncurry had not continued 'to direct her conduct as she [was] so very young and uncommonly silly and childish'.[40] Mountcashel's brother, William Moore, was next to take the stand. Under cross-examination he stated that Valentine and Eliza had married without a financial settlement having been reached. Colonel Burton, brother-in-law to Valentine, testified that on their return to Ireland the couple were still affectionate and loving towards each other. John Joseph Henry of Straffan, a neighbour of Cloncurry's, was next on the stand. He testified again to the closeness and intimacy that existed between the couple on their return from Rome to Lyons. This testimony as to the close, affectionate relationship that existed before the intrusion of a third party was a typical beginning to a case of criminal conversation. Comparable intro-

38 *Dublin Evening Post*, 24 February 1807.
39 *Trial*, p. 36.
40 Brian McDermott, ed., *The Catholic Question in Ireland and England 1798–1822; the papers of Denys Scully* (Dublin, 1998), p. 134.

ductions were made in several similar cases; for example in the case of *Mildmay* versus *Knapp*, which was heard a few years later in England, the opening statements set out to prove the affectionate state in which the couple had lived until the unfortunate incident had occurred.[41]

Signor Gaspare Gabrielli was then sworn in. Dr Pellegrini, a professor of Italian at Trinity College, acted as interpreter. Gabrielli stated that he had lived with the family for the previous seventeen months. During that time he had seen John Piers on many occasions. On a particular day in April 1806 he had been painting the billiard room which connected with the reception room. He stated that on his arrival that day, Piers had checked to see if the billiard room was occupied. Believing it to be empty, Piers shut the adjoining door, turned the key and covered the keyhole. He also locked the doors leading into the dining room and hall. Later, the door into the billiard room was unbolted by Lady Cloncurry as the artist came down off the scaffold to fetch some paint. Gabrielli testified that she was in a state of great surprise and her face was very flushed.

His wife, Frances, a maid at Lyons, then took the stand. Frances had been with Lady Cloncurry since before her marriage. She testified that Piers had visited Eliza regularly during her stay in Dublin while Cloncurry was absent. On the day of their proposed return to Lyons, Frances and the child's maid were waiting in the carriage for over half an hour with the hall door opened before Eliza appeared. She was accompanied to the carriage by Piers and 'was very much flushed, and so warm, that she was obliged to let down the windows'.[42] On previous occasions 'her hair was in great disorder … her habit shirt appeared as if it had been forcibly opened and was so much tumbled it was impossible to use it again.'[43]

A locket which Eliza kept under her pillow was produced. A miniature of Piers which he had given to her was also entered into evidence. Frances also testified that John Piers's groom had given her a letter on 26 May for her mistress. She had handed this letter directly to Lord Cloncurry.

John Comerford, the miniature portrait painter, and Thomas Manning, the locket maker, were then questioned. Manning stated that Piers had had a lock of his hair inserted in the locket. Jane McDowell, nurse maid to the Cloncurry's son, stated that Piers had been a frequent visitor to College Green in the absence of Cloncurry. While Cloncurry had been in town,

41 *Bell's Weekly Messenger*, 2 May 1830, *Mildmay* vs *Knapp*, Court of Common Pleas.
42 *Trial,* p. 55.
43 Ibid*.,* p. 56.

Piers was seen standing on the opposite side of the street or walking up and down looking towards the windows. When he visited Eliza, they were together for long periods in the drawing room. On one occasion Jane had entered the room to find her mistress in 'a very indelicate state' and Piers attempting to hide 'the discomposure of his dress.'[44] The couple spoke to each other in French so that the maid would not understand. Jane also testified that on the morning the family left Dublin, Piers had breakfasted with Lord and Lady Cloncurry. Lord Cloncurry had left town earlier in the day and when the maid went to the drawing room to check if her mistress was ready, she found her with Piers, crying bitterly and very upset. On other occasions when Eliza had been travelling in the carriage with her children and their maid, they had met Piers on the road. He had stopped the carriage and spoken to Eliza in a foreign language.

The testimony of the staff was typical of such a trial. House servants were privy to every activity in the place in which they worked and were intimately acquainted with the family's movements. Servants were 'witnesses to marital behaviour … ubiquitous and missed very little.'[45] In the *Mildmay* versus *Knapp* case, the servants were also called upon to testify that in the absence of their master, the defendant, Mr Knapp, called frequently upon the mistress of the house.

Laurence McDonagh, a footman, stated that he had carried letters to Lady Cloncurry from Piers. Nicholas Clarke, owner of a lodging house on Capel Street, who had known Piers for twelve years, was able to identify his handwriting on those letters. The full text of these letters was carried in the Dublin papers which disparagingly described Piers's declarations of love as 'perhaps the utmost range of this Baronet's education.'[46]

In cases of criminal conversation only two facts had to be proven: the plaintiff's marriage to the woman he accused of adultery, and the fact that sexual intercourse had subsequently taken place between the woman and the defendant.[47] Curran had done a good job in presenting these two facts to the jury. Witnesses to the wedding had clearly stated their evidence and proven their attendance there. The evidence of the servants had substantiated the claims of adultery.

44   Ibid., p. 70.
45   A. James Hammerton, *Cruelty and companionship in nineteenth century married life* (London, 1992), p. 116.
46   *Dublin Evening Post*, 21 February 1807.
47   Korobkin, *Criminal conversations*, p. 134.

On the second day of the trial, Peter Burrowes, representing Piers, declared that he had received instructions that morning from his client, not to give evidence in defence of his conduct, perhaps in order to spare Lady Cloncurry even more anguish. Burrowes, however, tried to sow the seeds of reasonable doubt in the minds of the jurors. He agreed that his client's behaviour had been reprehensible but did not agree that he was guilty of adultery. He claimed that Piers's behaviour towards Eliza was attentive but respectful in the drawing room at Lyons. He stated that Gabrielli's testimony was not deserving of credit and that while perched on the scaffold, he heard two doors close and then, nothing! He continued:

> Gentlemen of the jury, does this new importation from Italy expect to infect you and me with his own pruriency of imagination? Does he mean to persuade us that hearing NOTHING is a proof that SOMETHING BAD is going on? The closing of the doors of an apartment in very cold weather is necessarily a prelude to lewdness and adultery?[48]

Burrowes stated that nothing untoward could have happened on the day of the family's return to Lyons as the house was full of servants, the doors were seldom locked and the hall door stood open. The tumbled habit shirt and stained clothes were explained away as being the result of normal wear and tear. He went on to state that the evidence of Frances Gabrielli and Jane McDowell was so similar in nature that one was a servile imitation of the other. He dismissed the other witnesses as 'servants, dependants and syco-phants' and argued that no one of rank was asked to give evidence.[49] He further claimed that if adultery had been committed, it had happened the very first time Eliza had laid eyes on Piers, and that his client did not need to resort to violence or rape in order to destroy her character.

Throughout the trial, the reputation and character of Eliza had been continually cast in doubt. Her maids and servants attested to her strict upbringing and her education. Burrowes implied that her family were in a hurry to dispose of her through marriage. The discovery of any lapse of her character before her marriage that Cloncurry might have been aware of, would have led to mitigating circumstances and a considerably reduced amount of damages. The judge, in his instruction to the jury, stated that it was highly unlikely that rape had occurred and that it was possible that Cloncurry had 'lost a woman of no value' and that this fact could lead to

---

48 *Trial*, pp. 93–4.   49 Ibid., p. 97.

extenuated (reduced) damages for the plaintiff.[50] The jury then retired for half an hour and returned a verdict for Cloncurry, awarding him £20,000 in damages and 6*d.* costs. In his autobiography, written towards the end of his life, Cloncurry's only reference to the whole case mentions the dissolution of his 'hasty and imprudent marriage'.[51] Reports of the trial were printed by two rival publishers in pamphlet form and sales were immense.

Since she was neither a plaintiff nor defendant, Eliza's interests were not an issue in this trial. She was not called upon to testify. She was not legally represented. None of the couple's friends were called upon to give evidence in her favour. She had been returned to her own family the previous summer. Criminal conversation cases 'traditionally erase the wife's agency, reducing her to a species of "damaged goods". The husband's claim against his wife's lover seeks compensation for the injury to him caused by interference with his property interests in the exclusive use of his wife.'[52] The adultery, therefore, was viewed as a private commercial matter where the injury was seen as an injury to property and was therefore assessed in financial terms.[53] Cloncurry had claimed £100,000 in damages for the loss of comfort, society, love and affection of his wife.

Rumours had persisted from the earliest days of his marriage of Cloncurry's regret of his hastiness.[54] His biographer stated that these rumours were, of course, untrue and that never before had two people loved each other as much as Lord and Lady Cloncurry. Burrowes, in his defence of Piers, stated that the evidence given against his client was 'such as any husband who wishes to get rid of his wife could easily procure'.[55] While such cases were relatively common in those years, Cloncurry's pursuit of the charge of criminal conversation as opposed to a charge of rape almost guaranteed that the family unit would be destroyed and that Eliza's position as wife and mother would be severely compromised.[56] It was also widely rumoured at the time that John Piers may have entered into a wager or a bet, that in the event of the ruin of the Cloncurrys' happiness, a sum of

50 Ibid., p. 144.
51 Lord Cloncurry, *Personal recollections of the life and time of Valentine Lord Cloncurry* (Dublin, 1849), p. 254.
52 Korobkin, *Criminal conversations*, p. 93.
53 Ibid. p. 23.
54 Fitzpatrick, *Life and times of Lord Cloncurry*, p. 292.
55 *Trial*, p. 97.
56 Paul O'Higgins, *A bibliography of Irish trials and other legal proceedings* (Abingdon, 1986). O'Higgins cites four rape cases and fifteen criminal conversation cases that were published between 1790 and 1818.

money would be placed to his credit in a Dublin bank.[57] However, what did John Piers stand to gain from all of this? If indeed there was a bet and he had won that bet by breaking up the relationship of Cloncurry and his wife, the only recourse open to Cloncurry was to sue and cause Piers financial ruin. If the bet was not won, then Piers would not benefit from the action either. In fact, Piers had nothing to gain from his actions from a financial point of view. So what motivated him? Is it possible that in the heat of the moment Piers forgot himself and was overcome with a passion for Eliza? Yet, he was conducting a relationship with Eliza Denny on the Isle of Man throughout this time. They already had one child together and he was to return to her and spend the rest of his life with her.

Perhaps the focus of the investigation should be on the one person in the events whose story was not heard in the court – Eliza, Lady Cloncurry. She was little more than a child when she married Cloncurry, a man almost twice her age in 1803. He was already a man of the world at this time, having been well educated in Ireland and in London and having spent more than two years incarcerated in the Tower of London at the beginning of the nineteenth century on suspicion of treason. She had led a very sheltered life as was befitting of young girls of her class and had been left without a mother at a very young age.

There were some hints during the trial that the Morgan family had left England for reasons other than the bad state of Elizabeth's father's health at that time. Her maid testified that Elizabeth had attended boarding school in London and that she had been cared for by a guardian while her father served in India. The counsel for the plaintiff endeavoured to show that her father, General Morgan, had followed Cloncurry from Nice to Rome in great haste in order to arrange a match for his daughter. It was also implied that the match was hastily arranged and that even the financial settlements, common in such arrangements, could not be made until the parties could return to London.

Cloncurry's own observations on the very evening of his wedding that there may or may not be cause to celebrate his marriage, are of great interest. Worthy of note also are the comments of Lady Mountcashel on Lady Cloncurry's silliness and childishness. Is it possible that Elizabeth, bored with a husband with whom she had little in common, decided to play with fire and seduce Piers? Why did she not seek Cloncurry's help earlier if indeed Piers *had* been forcing his attentions upon her? Why did she not

---

57 Fitzpatrick, *Life and times of Lord Cloncurry*, p. 294.

refuse entry to her houses when Piers visited? Perhaps, in the heat of the moment, without undue consideration and reflection, Elizabeth flirted with Piers and his attentions, with little regard for the inevitable consequences. Those consequences would prove to be far reaching and terrible for her.

She had returned to her family in England in May 1806. Her marriage to Valentine, Lord Cloncurry, was officially dissolved on 7 April 1811 by an act of parliament. Parliamentary divorces were brought only on the grounds of the wife's adultery and were designed to safeguard property rights of a particular family, which would be undermined if illegitimate offspring were included among the legal heirs. Elizabeth never saw her two children in Ireland again. She reverted to her maiden name and in 1812, following the death of her uncle, Colonel Kyd, she inherited a considerable sum of money and property. In 1819 she married Revd John Sanford, rector of Nynehead, Somerset. They had one daughter, Anna Horatia Caroline who was born in 1823.[58] For many years, Thomas Ryan, Cloncurry's agent, corresponded with Eliza secretly, answering her regular enquiries after the welfare of her two children in Ireland.[59] Cloncurry remarried in 1811, his second wife being Emily Leeson, a widow and mother of the earl of Miltown.[60]

Following his release on bail, John Piers had fled to the Isle of Man. However, his troubles were far from over. On 24 December 1806, just a few months later, a difference of opinion arose over a bet between Piers and a Mr John Meredith. Piers, being an enthusiastic duellist, challenged Meredith. By 1806 there was considerable opposition to duelling in England and Ireland which 'not only attempted to show the dangers of duelling but suggested some methods to supersede or outlaw the practice'.[61] Others, like Piers, believed that it was a 'humane, sensible and equitable method of decision of right and wrong'.[62] Consequently, a duel was arranged for Friday 26 December.

Piers was attended by Major Warrington as his second, while Meredith had Mr Richards as his second. Seconds ensured the proper conduct of the

58 Ibid., p. 303. Eliza's daughter, Anna Horatia Caroline Sanford, married Frederick Henry Paul, Second Baron Methuen, an army officer and later militia ADC to Queen Victoria. Anna Horatia died on 3 March 1899 at Somerford Hall in Somerset, aged seventy-six years.
59 Fitzpatrick, *Life and times of Lord Cloncurry*, p. 302.
60 Ibid., p. 307.
61 Donna Andrew, 'The code of honour and its critics: the opposition to duelling in England, 1700–1850' in *Social History*, v (1980), pp. 587–8. For opposition in Ireland, see above note 32.
62 Bonamy Dobree, ed., *The letters of Philip Dormer Stanhope, fourth earl of Chesterfield* (6 vols, London, 1932), v, 206.

duel. Their duties included loading the pistols, handing them to the principals and the regulation of the firing. It was agreed by the seconds that three signals should be given before the principals should discharge their weapons and 'this arrangement was twice distinctly announced to the principals.'[63] However, in a most unusual occurrence, shortly after the first signal was given, Meredith took aim at Piers and discharged his weapon. Immediately, Piers advanced towards Meredith 'using many opprobrious epithets'.[64] Meredith fell to his knees begging for mercy. He claimed that his pistol had accidentally discharged. However, this was later refuted, as his pistol had no spring and only fired after Meredith had taken deliberate aim at Piers.

Meredith swore an affidavit on 29 December that the lock on the pistol was defective and that the gun could discharge at the least touch of the finger.[65] On 3 January 1807 the seconds, Richards and Warrington, stated that an inspection had been made of the pistol by several gentlemen, and that there was no defect found. By now, Meredith had been expelled from his gentlemen's club for his cowardice. The seconds also claimed that Piers had not advanced on Meredith and had actually placed himself between Warrington and Meredith calling out 'Warrington! Don't shoot the rascal.'[66] It was also discovered that while Piers had cleared his pockets before the duel, Meredith was found with a leather case of papers, a leather purse, two large handkerchiefs folded tightly and laid flat against the side shown to his opponent! It is assumed that all of these items were intended in some way to deflect the pistol shot from his person.

The controversy continued the following week. On 10 January Meredith stated again that the trigger of the pistol was indeed faulty and that his expulsion from the gentlemen's club was not as serious an incident as had been portrayed in the newspapers, the club having only ten members. Three of the members were Piers, Warrington and Richards. He also denied that he had attempted to flee the scene of the duel. He claimed that he was barely able to walk without the aid of a walking stick as he was severely afflicted with gout. The goods which were found upon his person following the duel were described and accounted for. He stated that the leather letter case was a mere four inches long by two-and-a-half wide and used to carry

---

63 *Walker's Hibernian Magazine*, January 1807, p. 60.
64 Ibid.
65 *A compilation of the different statements of a late duel in the Isle of Man between Sir John Piers, Bart., and John Meredith, esq.* (Douglas, 1807), p. 8.
66 Ibid.

half-crown tickets. The leather purse was two-and-a-half inches long by two-and-one-eighth wide and the handkerchiefs were carried because he was in the habit of taking snuff. Meredith also claimed that Piers carried a white handkerchief in his own pocket throughout the episode.

It is entirely possible that Piers's reputation was rehabilitated by this event. Like the Cloncurry divorce case, the Piers–Meredith duel was given extensive coverage in both the Manx and Irish newspapers. In his role as protector of Meredith's life, Piers could endeavour to recover his reputation as a gentleman in the eyes of the public. While Ireland's reputation as a 'hotbed of duelling' was beginning to change during the early years of the nineteenth century, men like Piers and other Irishmen abroad helped to keep the image alive and to 'perpetuate the stereotype of Irish gentlemen as incorrigible duellists'.[67]

There was still no respite for Piers from his troubles in Ireland, however. In early January of 1807 he began to attempt to raise money from his estate in Ireland by leasing the lands and its tithes to his brother, Edward, who lived at 12 Westmoreland Street, Dublin.[68] He leased the lands north of Tristernagh Abbey to Edward for the sum of £60 a year.[69] The following week he leased seventy acres south-east of the avenue leading to the Abbey.[70] In February he leased the demesne of Tristernagh for £300 annually and, in July, Edward leased the tithes of the local townlands.[71] The total income from all of these transactions would have amounted to about £1,000 annually.

Edward Piers, a solicitor in Dublin, had supported his brother throughout his difficulties. It had been claimed during the court case in Dublin that Valentine Lawless had loaned money to Piers and had instructed his law agent not to inconvenience the latter by demanding repayment. However, Edward Piers had written to the Dublin and Manx newspapers in early 1807, claiming that John had never borrowed money from Cloncurry and that the statement was 'infamously false'.[72] John Piers, himself, also refuted this allegation in his own letters to the newspaper in which he called on Cloncurry to declare that he had never been indebted to him.

67   Kelly, *Duelling in Ireland*, p. 240.
68   *Manx Advertiser*, 14 March 1807.
69   588/209/399438, RD.
70   588/210/399440, RD.
71   588/209/399439; 587/493/399733, RD.
72   *Dublin Evening Post*, 28 February 1807; *Manx Advertiser*, 14 March 1807.

Piers's troubles did not seem to depress him, however. A visitor to Douglas at that time wrote that 'the society of the English and Irish has given life and gaiety to the place, and there are frequent convivial meetings, assemblies, and card parties.'[73] In the spring of 1807 a dinner at the Globe Inn in Douglas to celebrate St Patrick's day was hosted by Piers. The meal was attended by other Irish exiles in Douglas and cost 10s. 6d. a head.[74] A commentator of the period stated that with Piers's past escapades in Dublin, and the duel involving Meredith, the patron of the Globe Inn 'must have felt a distinct sense of relief when the last of the diners passed through the door on their homeward way'.[75]

By this time, the Manx administration was becoming concerned about the number of persons who were seeking refuge in their jurisdiction from charges in other jurisdictions. On 10 July 1807 a warrant was issued in the Isle of Man for the arrest of Piers who stood 'indicted in Ireland for sending a challenge to Lord Cloncurry'.[76] Instructions were sought from Whitehall as to the best course of action to take. In his reply, Lord Hawkesbury stated that the case did not warrant any 'extraordinary interference of His Majesty's Secretary of State'.[77]

However, other events overtook the administration. Newspaper reports in August 1807 stated that Piers had been arrested by 'six bailiffs and committed to Castle Rushen' on the Isle of Man.[78] Cloncurry, fearing that Piers would skip bail while measures were being put in place for his arrest, had taken matters into his own hands. He had his own agent watching Piers's movements on the island. The agent had Piers arrested and held in custody for eight days. However, the agent himself was forced to flee the island soon afterwards as a warrant was issued for his arrest for the false imprisonment of Piers![79]

Woods, in his history of Man, states that Cloncurry did not pursue Piers further for the damages awarded by the Dublin court as, although Piers was a man of property, he had taken care that none of it was liable to seizure. He

---

73 Nathaniel Jefferys, *A Descriptive and historical account of the Isle of Man with a view of its society, manners and customs* (Newcastle-upon-Tyne, 1808).

74 Neil Mathieson, 'Old inns and coffee houses of the Isle of Man', in *Isle of Man Historical and Archaeological Society,* v (no. 4), pp. 411–433.

75 Ibid.

76 Letter from Lieut. Governor Smelt to Lord Hawkesbury on the subject of persons taking refuge in the Isle of Man, Manx Library, MS 1053C, p. 36.

77 Letter from Lord Hawkesbury to Lieut. Governor Smelt, Manx Library, AP 126 (2nd) 1.

78 *Manx Advertiser*, 29 August 1807.

79 *Saunder's Newsletter and Daily Advertiser*, 15 August 1807.

also stated that Piers's credit was good in Douglas and that the Chief Deemster had declared in open court that he 'should consider his security for the payment of a debt equal to a bank note'.[80] Later in August 1807 a letter appeared in the *Manx Advertiser* signed by 'A. Bystander'. This letter, which was obviously written by Piers himself, stated that the description of his arrest which had appeared in the Irish newspapers, had been erroneously and grossly exaggerated. The author went on to say in defence of Sir John Piers, 'having done with due submission to the laws of the land which protect him from the dire effects of an intemperate and vindictive verdict, obeyed without hesitation the summons'.[81] Following his release he was now free to resume his business without fear of further interference from 'Lord Cloncurry's *respectable* agent'.[82] He continued in a defiant tone that Cloncurry ought to visit Man to enlarge his sphere of knowledge and to learn of its laws, privileges and immunities.

In October 1809 Piers was again in trouble with the law. A case was heard in the courts of the Isle of Man of a disturbance at the theatre in Douglas, caused by Major-General Stapleton who, in jest, pushed a Mr Johnson forward onto the stage. The General, Sir John Piers and Piers's friend, Captain Edwards, were summoned to appear at Castle Rushen to answer charges.[83]

Life began to settle down for John Piers after these incidents. He had been living with Eliza Denny since before 1803 and they had seven children. The eldest son, Henry Piers, was born on 7 November 1803. John Edwards Piers was born on 16 December 1807, William Stapleton Piers was born on 20 November 1808 and George in December 1810. Piers married Eliza Denny in the Isle of Man on 27 May 1815.[84] He had attempted to have his brother, Revd Octavius Piers, perform the ceremony two years earlier, but Octavius was unable to travel due to domestic matters. Therefore, the celebrant was an Irish clergyman, Revd T. Orpen Stewart, curate of the parish of St George in Douglas.[85] Piers's friend, John Edwards, a captain in the regiment of Ancient Britons, was the main witness. Two daughters were born after the marriage – Florence Anna Maria Stapleton and Louisa

---

80 George Woods, *An account of the past and present state of the Isle of Man 1811*, book 2 (London, 1811), vii.
81 *Manx Advertiser*, 29 August 1807.   82 Ibid.
83 *Manx Society*, vol. xxiv, pp. 97–121.   84 *The Times*, 20 March 1849.
85 Revd Thomas Orpen Stewart, the son of Revd Walter Stewart and Agnes Orpen was married to Mary Scott. Ironically, in February 1816, Richard Oliver Smith Esq., who accused Revd Stewart of seducing his wife, brought a case of criminal conversation against him. Smith sued for damages of £4,000. The jury awarded damages of £1,000 after a trial which lasted for five days. (*Manx Advertiser*, 15 February 1816).

Adelaide. There was no question, of course, of children born before 1815 being legitimised by the marriage. The family settled for a time at Leece Lodge which lay within two-and-a-half miles of Douglas. The house, which was cosy, containing two parlours, two kitchens, four bedrooms and attics with outbuildings and ten acres of land.[86]

Piers and Eliza returned to live in Ireland in 1821 and celebrated their marriage for a second time in St Catherine's church in Dublin. In August 1836, he executed a deed which appointed a jointure of £600 per annum on his wife and created a charge of £4,000 for his two daughters. This financial agreement had been made by his late father, Sir Pigot Piers. John made his will on 30 May 1842 in which both of the arrangements against the estate were further ratified.[87] In July 1842 his daughter, Florence Anna Maria, married Count Louis le Coat de Kervéguen. On her marriage, her father covenanted to her, her portion of the £4,000. Louisa Adelaide became a chanoinesse of the royal order of St Anne of Bavaria.[88] It is said that Piers returned to Tristernagh and lived his last days in a small house behind a high brick wall, 'venturing beyond the gates only on a Sunday when the waiting bailiffs could not execute their warrants'.[89] The house was in a ruinous condition by now and in 1837 John O'Donovan wrote that the house of Tristernagh was in a most deplorable state of dilapidation and was said to have suggested to Maria Edgeworth the first idea of Castle-Wreck (*Castle Rackrent.*)

John Piers died on 28 July 1845 and, as he was without lawful male heirs, he was succeeded by his nephew, Sir Henry Samuel Piers, son of John's brother, Frederick Piers. Soon after John's death a disagreement arose between his heir, Sir Henry, and his two daughters. Sir Henry claimed that his uncle had not been legally married until his marriage in Dublin in 1821 and that as a consequence, his two daughters were illegitimate and therefore not entitled to their share from the estate in Tristernagh. Louisa and Florence Piers took their uncle to the court of chancery in Dublin in 1847 in order to compel him to raise the money due to them against the estate. They claimed that a *de facto* marriage had taken place between their parents in 1815. Lady Piers (née Denny) claimed that the marriage had been kept secret as John Piers's mother was still alive at that time and, as she controlled

---

86 *Manx Sun*, 9 November 1838.
87 *The Times*, 20 March 1849.
88 *Burke's Peerage*, pp. 1485ff.
89 Elizabeth Hickey, 'Some notes on Kilbixy, Tristernagh and Templecross', p. 60.

the greater part of the family estates, her son feared offending her by a marriage which she might not consider advantageous.[90]

Sir Henry's defence claimed that while the 1815 ceremony may have taken place in Sir John's private residence at Leece Lodge, that no licence was issued by the bishop for such a marriage and that there was no entry in the marriage register. The Bishop of Rochester, who in 1815 was Bishop of Sodor and Man, swore that he had no recollection of having given a licence for the marriage.[91] It was proven that a marriage had taken place in St Catherine's church in Dublin on 19 March 1821 and it was claimed that this was the first and only legal marriage. The plaintiffs claimed that as the celebrant of the 1815 marriage was the curate of the bishop and had been celebrating marriages and other solemnities on the island for at least five years, he was aware of the legal and other necessities required. They also proved that it was possible that a special licence had been granted by the bishop. A recent case in the same courts had proven that the same bishop had forgotten that he had issued a marriage licence and that it was not unusual for marriages to remain unregistered on the island at that time. It was confirmed that it was customary during those years for Irish people who had been married in a foreign country, to be married again upon their return to Ireland and that this explained the 1821 ceremony. It was further stated that:

> It is a constant course for persons in a certain station in life, who make what is commonly called a runaway or irregular marriage, afterwards to marry in *facie ecclesiae*, for the purpose of quieting the scruples of persons of nice conscience, but also for the purpose of putting down any public clamour that may have arisen.[92]

The lord chancellor declared that he would consider whether a solemnised marriage had taken place in 1815 if the bishop would travel to Ireland to allow himself to be examined by the court. The bishop refused to travel to Dublin and the case was dismissed without costs on 10 May 1847. Piers's daughters lodged an appeal in March 1849 in London. The judge quoted a previous case which stated that 'the presumption in favour of marriage is not at liberty to be repelled on a mere balance of probabilities. The

---

90 *Piers* versus *Piers* 1849, p. 1120, HLC.
91 *Freeman's Journal*, 24 March 1849.
92 *Piers* versus *Piers* 1849, p. 1133, HLC, 331.

circumstances to repel it must be strong, distinct, satisfactory and conclusive.'[93] He found, therefore, that the decree of the Lord Chancellor of Ireland should be overturned and that the 1815 marriage ought to be recognised with a subsequent charge to be made upon the estate in favour of the two appellants.

Sir John Piers's wife, Lady Elizabeth, died at Lucca in Italy on 17 February 1862. Their youngest son, William Stapleton Piers, who had married at the British Embassy in Brussels in February 1842, died after a painful illness at Dinan in Brittany in 1863.[94]

Sir John Bennett Piers had led a colourful life. He was at times impetuous and high spirited. His involvement in the Cloncurry case left him financially ruined. His impulsiveness got him into trouble many times throughout his life. Yet, he seems to have been a man of some honour and character. His attempts to save Meredith's life in the failed duel and his challenges to Cloncurry to fight a duel to protect Lady Cloncurry's reputation may be further signs of his impulsive nature or of his honourable character. He refused to have Eliza, Lady Cloncurry's good name sullied in the court case and instructed his legal team not to pursue that course of action. On his enforced exile from Ireland, he returned to his mistress, Elizabeth Denny, eventually marrying her in 1815 and again in 1821. He attempted to make adequate financial provision for his wife and children through the terms of his father's will.

In the 1930s the poet, Sir John Betjeman, came across the story of Piers and Lady Cloncurry in the *Annals of Westmeath*. He was so taken by the tale that he composed the poem *Epsilon* which gives a rather fictionalised account of the seduction of Lady Cloncurry. The poem concludes with a description of the now ruined Tristernagh.

> In the ivy dusty is the old lock rusty
> That opens rasping on the place of graves,
> 'Tis no home for mortals behind those portals
> Where the shining dock grows and the nettle waves.
> Of the walls so ferny, near Tristernagh churchyard,
> Often the learned historians write,
> And the Abbey splendificent, most magnificent,
> Ribbed and springing in ancient night.[95]

93 *The Times*, 23 March 1849. The ruling of the validity of a marriage ceremony in the Piers case was used in a court case in 1998 heard by the High Court of the Solomon Islands.
94 *The Times*, 2 September 1842, 2 December 1863.
95 'Epsilon by John Betjeman, copyright estate of John Betjeman. Reproduced by permission of John Murray (Publishers) Ltd.

Felon or Fenian Martyr?

Peter O'Neill Crowley: accidental hero from east Cork

DENIS A. CRONIN

O n the night of 5 March 1867, the long-predicted and long-awaited Fenian rebellion in Ireland burst briefly into life. Localised, badly co-ordinated and deeply compromised by betrayals, the rebellion was easily snuffed out by the combined forces of the police and military. But the Fenian movement had by then put down deep roots in Irish society and the failure of the rebellion did not diminish the strong impression it made on Irish nationalism. Local memories of incidents during the Fenian 'rising' helped to fill and maintain a deep reservoir of support for armed rebellion which was drawn upon during the struggle for Irish independence after 1916. One of these incidents and the consequences of rebellion for some of its participants is related below. The particular circumstances of that incident helped to turn one of the rebels into a patriotic icon for those in his locality who regarded armed rebellion as neither criminal nor treasonous.

In 1867, the district of east Cork around Midleton and Castlemartyr was a stronghold of Fenianism. According to the local unionist press, it abounded in disaffection – 'drillings at night' and 'meetings on Sundays' – and local police believed that, if a rebellion was to break out, this district would become a centre of disturbance.[1] In the early days of March 1867, police intelligence and reports of 'certain indications in the demeanour of the working men' led the authorities to believe that something was afoot. They arrested, among several local Fenian suspects, 'Captain' P.J. Condon, the American officer in charge of the Midleton district, and James Sullivan,

---

1 *Constitution or Cork Advertiser*, 7 March 1867; *Cork Examiner*, 7 March 1867.

the local leader or 'Centre'.[2] Despite this setback, a number of local groups went out as arranged on the evening of Shrove Tuesday, 5 March, to raid the police stations at Midleton and Castlemartyr and the coastguard station at Knockadoon in order to capture badly-needed guns and ammunition. It was intended that these groups would then make contact with each other and join the expected wider uprising. The Midleton and Castlemartyr arms raids failed ignominiously, however, which effectively ended the rebellion from these quarters. The raid on the coastguard station was more successful.

At about 9.00 p.m. on the evening of 5 March, a group of perhaps sixty men raided Knockadoon coastguard station, situated a few miles south-west of Youghal, county Cork.[3] They were led by an American Fenian, later identified as 'Captain' John McClure, and by a local tenant farmer named Peter O'Neill Crowley.[4] McClure had been staying in Crowley's house at Ballydaniel near Ballymacoda for about a fortnight before the rising, and was being passed off as Crowley's future brother-in-law. He moved about the locality quite openly under the name of Cronin, although his true identity did become known to some locals a few days before the rising.[5]

In carrying out the attack on Knockadoon coastguard station, McClure, Crowley and their followers crossed the line from disaffection to subversion. They were now engaged in an act of rebellion and were thus guilty of the crime of high treason against the crown. This was an act described at the time as 'the highest crime known to the law ... not merely the greatest of political offences but the greatest of moral offences', and one which was still punishable by hanging and quartering.[6] Any Fenian who went out in the rising of 1867 had to be aware that the consequences of failure could include being condemned to death as a traitor. Who were these men who gambled their lives by taking part in this abortive rebellion and what drove them to do so?

---

2   *Cork Examiner*, 7 March 1867; John Devoy, *Recollections of an Irish rebel* (reprint, Shannon, 1969 of original edition, New York, 1929), p. 213; Íde Ní Choindealbháin, 'Fenians of Kilclooney Wood' in *Journal of the Cork Historical and Archaeological Society (JCHAS)*, vol. 49 (1944), p. 128.
3   Capt. Thomas Miller, HMS Royal George, Kingstown, to Maj. Gen. Thomas A. Larcom, 7 March 1867, NAI, CSORP 1867/3635; *Cork Examiner*, 7 March 1867. John Devoy in his *Recollections* stated that Crowley's entire command of a hundred men went out with him but the official estimate of sixty seems nearer the mark.
4   Ní Choindealbháin, 'Kilclooney Wood', p. 128.
5   Statement of Philip O'Neill, Ballydaniel, in High Treason Brief for Cork Special Commission (hereafter cited as Cork HTB), p. 195. Available in NLI.
6   *Speech of the Solicitor-General at the County of Limerick Special Commission, 19 June 1867* (Dublin, 1867), p. 4.

Peter O'Neill Crowley, aged thirty-four years in 1867, was a respectable farmer, who held about one hundred acres of land 'at a nominal rent' at Ballymacoda, between Youghal and Knockadoon Head.[7] As a member of the strong farmer class, he was unusual in becoming actively involved in the Fenian movement, a fact particularly noted by Fenian leader John O'Leary in his memoirs.[8] Crowley's main motivation seems to have come from his family's history of republicanism. His mother was a niece of a Fr Peter O'Neill, parish priest of Ballymacoda, who was arrested and flogged by soldiers for alleged complicity in the 1798 rebellion. He was afterwards transported to Botany Bay, and served five years of a life sentence before being allowed home. According to one unsympathetic later observer, 'the rancour engendered by this seems to have been cherished in the family and to have made treason an heirloom with its descendants.'[9]

Crowley was named after this grand-uncle and, although only a small child when Fr O'Neill died in 1835, he is said to have inherited under his will 'all that the priest was worth in the world, including his residence'.[10] Crowley's impeccable republican pedigree combined with his social standing as a strong farmer made him the natural leader of the Fenian movement in his locality.

John McClure was born in America in July 1846, in Dobbs Ferry, near New York city, the son of a Tipperary mother and a Limerick father. At the age of only seventeen, he joined the Union army in December 1863, fought in a New York cavalry regiment during the last two years of the civil war, and was promoted to lieutenant in 1865.[11] Like many other young men of Irish birth or descent in the American armies, he became active in the Fenian movement after the war. From the dock during his trial, he explained his motivation as follows:

> Although not born upon the soil of Ireland, my parents were, and from history, and tradition, and fireside relations, I became conversant with the country's history from my earliest childhood … A desire to aid

---

7 *Irish Times*, 3 April 1867.
8 John O'Leary, *Recollections of Fenians and Fenianism* (London, 1896), pp. 238–9.
9 *Constitution or Cork Advertiser*, 4 April 1867, quoting a report in the *Freeman's Journal*.
10 Fr Patrick Lavelle's letter in *Irish People*, New York, 4 May 1867, quoting the *Cork Herald*; Risteárd Ó Foghludha, 'Note on "Fenians of Kilclooney Wood"' in *JCHAS*, vol. 50 (1950), pp. 63–4.
11 Letter from William J. McClure published in *Irish People*, 13 July 1867; Devoy, *Recollections*, p. 218; William F.K. Marmion, 'American soldiers in Ireland, 1865–67' in *Irish Sword*, xxiii, no. 91 (Summer 2002), p. 126.

poor Ireland rise from her moral degradation took possession of me
… I am no fillibuster or free-booter *but* a man willing to suffer in
defence of that divine, that American principle – the right of self-
government.[12]

Most of the rest of the Knockadoon party was composed of local labourers
and tradesmen, several of whom were known by name to the coastguards.
The insurgents were badly armed: McClure had a Colt revolver, Crowley
had a rifle and some others had old shotguns or pikes, but many had to
make do with makeshift weapons such as 'sharpened rasps, fastened to rake
handles with waxed hemp'.[13] A shortage of arms did not prove to be a
handicap on this operation, because overwhelming numbers and the element
of surprise easily carried the day. The chief boatman, Robert Hoyle, was
overpowered in his quarters with another man, James Taylor, and the other
four coastguards were in turn surprised in their cottages. All later reported
that they had 'surrendered in the face of overwhelming odds', helped by
repeated threats, from Peter Crowley in particular, that their houses would
be burned down with hand-grenades.[14] The entire operation, including the
search for arms, took about two hours.

The insurgents took the coastguards' supply of arms – 'about 20 stands of
arms, pistols and cutlasses' – and marched off in military formation towards
Ballymacoda, bringing Hoyle and four of his men with them.[15] McClure
allowed the sixth coastguard, Peter Nicholls, to remain behind to nurse his
seriously ill wife on condition that he remained in his house.[16] When the
party reached Ballymacoda, Hoyle complained of being tired, so the rebels
'procured a cart, with some straw' and let him sit into it. Later on, while on
their way to Killeagh, they allowed the other coastguards to join him.[17]
When the group reached Mogeely, near Castlemartyr, at about 6.30 a.m.,
they were persuaded by Hoyle to release their prisoners.[18]

12 *Cork Examiner*, 25 May 1867.
13 Devoy, *Recollections*, p. 213.
14 Capt. Miller, HMS Royal George, Kingstown to Maj. Gen. T.A. Larcom, 8 March 1867,
    NAI, CSORP 1867/3835; Statements of Robert Hoyle and others in Cork HTB,
    pp. 181–94; *Cork Examiner*, 7 March 1867.
15 NAI, CSORP 1867/3635. John Devoy in his *Recollections* inflated the number of
    coastguards to ten.
16 Statement of Peter Nicholls in Cork HTB, p. 190.
17 Statement of Robert Hoyle in Cork HTB, p. 182.
18 Ibid.

14 Pursuit of the Fenians in 1867, as seen by the *Illustrated London News*

The statements given by the coastguards in the days following the Knockadoon raid contain fascinating insights into the state of mind of the rebels. A small leadership group of committed revolutionaries like McClure, Crowley and another strong farmer, Thomas Walsh from Ardnahinch, Shanagarry, were determined to attempt an armed insurrection. Coastguard Peter Nicholls recalled meeting Thomas Walsh on the night of the raid and expressing surprise at his involvement in 'the like of this'. Walsh's answer was, 'It is so, and cannot be otherwise. We intend to overthrow the Government.'[19] Most of the raiding party on the other hand seem to have been reluctant rebels. Several men who spoke to the coastguards on the march to Mogeely claimed that they were forced into joining the Knockadoon action. Typical of this number was Thomas Bowler Cullinane, a farm labourer from Ballymacoda, who was reported to have said: 'I could not help it; I was forced; I am in it now, I cannot help it.'[20] Another man, David Joyce, claimed later that Thomas Walsh and others had threatened to burn down his house if he did not join them.[21]

19   Statement of Peter Nicholls in Cork HTB, p. 189.
20   Statement of Timothy McCarthy in Cork HTB, p. 186.
21   Statement of David Joyce in Cork HTB, p. 226.

Some accounts of the incident state that, on their way from Knockadoon to Mogeely, McClure's party linked up with members of other Fenian groups from Ladysbridge, Midleton and Castlemartyr.[22] This was no doubt their intention but in fact it seems that they were joined by only one small group, led by another American Fenian, John Edward Kelly. This man had been a compositor with the *Cork Herald* in Cork city, but left his job on 1 March, met up with McClure at Ballymacoda a couple of days later and was sent to Youghal, perhaps to drum up support.[23] When Kelly saw no prospect of action in Youghal on the night of the rising, he left with a small group just after 11.00 p.m. and met up with McClure near Killeagh, where, in accordance with the arranged plan, they cut the telegraph wires to disrupt military communications. The rest of the plan involved the converging groups of Fenians waiting at Killeagh in order to stop the first train on the line from Youghal or Cork.[24]

However, as already mentioned, the failures in other parts of east Cork caused this plan to go badly awry. During that early morning, McClure sent Thomas Cullinane on several scouting missions 'to see if he could get tidings of any parties', but he returned on each occasion without making contact with any other rebels.[25] The coastguards who travelled with them gave evidence that not only did the Knockadoon party fail to link up with any other rebel force but that their own numbers dwindled away as the night went on and as prospects of a wider rising faded. Hoyle claimed that by the time he and his men were released after daybreak, the numbers in the Knockadoon party had reduced from about sixty to twenty.[26]

In spite of their communications being disrupted, the authorities reacted swiftly to the outbreak of violence. The police in Youghal roused the local magistrates and military, and by mid-morning a force of some fifty military and police reached Mogeely by train and began searching the area for rebels. They were later reinforced by a party of troops who came by train from Cork.[27] Despite reports that the rebels had mustered about 2,000 strong on a hill near Castlemartyr, the military search revealed no trace of insurgents

22 *Cork Examiner*, 7 March 1867.
23 *Cork Examiner*, 6 April 1867; Devoy, *Recollections*, p. 214; Ní Choindealbháin, 'Kilclooney Wood', p. 130.
24 *Cork Examiner*, 7 March 1867; Devoy, *Recollections*, p. 214.
25 Statement of Patrick Fitzgerald in Cork HTB, p. 192.
26 Statement of Robert Hoyle in Cork HTB, p. 182.
27 Constable Peter Guildea, Youghal, 6 March 1867, NAI, Fenian papers, F2707.

apart from some lost or discarded rifle cartridges and a coastguard's pouch.[28] Only the most committed and well-armed remained in the field by then, including a group of about twelve men led by McClure and Crowley. This group eventually continued north in the hope of linking up with active rebels in the Galtee mountains in county Tipperary.[29]

The authorities immediately began the task of rounding up suspected insurgents. One of the first prisoners taken was McClure's scout, Thomas Bowler Cullinane, who was stopped on horseback at Castlemartyr at about seven o'clock on the morning of 6 March.[30] Provisions for a military campaign were found on him, including 'some coffee, a bag of salt, some biscuits, and 39 bullets'.[31] Other men involved in the Knockadoon raid who were subsequently apprehended included David Joyce, who was caught hiding in a farmer's house (the farmer was also arrested for harbouring him), David Cummins, a plasterer, and Bartholomew Buckley, a discharged sailor in the Royal Navy.[32] Most of the men identified as taking part in the raid were farm labourers or craftsmen such as plasterers or shoemakers.

The incident at Knockadoon had been one of the few notable successes, 'the neatest job done by the Fenians in the Rising' on the night of 5 March.[33] The coastguard station was captured without firing a shot or spilling blood, and the acts of allowing one prisoner to tend his sick wife and the early release of the others added a chivalrous lustre to the incident. Nevertheless, Knockadoon would be worthy of little more than a footnote in the history of the Fenian rising if subsequent tragic events had not propelled Peter Crowley to iconic status in the history of Cork republicanism.

* * *

The small group of rebels who moved into the hills above Killeagh in the early morning of 6 March disappeared from the view of the authorities for over three weeks. It was later reported that McClure and some others had

28 NAI, F2707.
29 Devoy, *Recollections*, p. 214.
30 According to the statements of Philip O'Neill of Ballydaniel and Robert Pumphret of Ballymacoda, the horse ridden by Cullinane was 'borrowed' by him under false pretences early on the evening of the Knockadoon action. See Cork HTB, pp. 195–6.
31 *Cork Examiner,* 7 March 1867 and 14 March 1867.
32 Sub-Inspector Fanning, Castlemartyr to Inspector General, 16 and 20 March 1867, NAI, Fenian papers, F3288; *Cork Examiner,* 14 March 1867.
33 Devoy, *Recollections*, p. 213.

initially tried to escape in a small sloop called the *Ariel* but were driven back to Queenstown by bad weather.[34] They then moved north in the hope of joining with other Fenian bands in the border areas between Cork, Limerick and Tipperary. They may have tried to reach Mallow in north Cork at first but, finding no active Fenians there, turned east towards the Galtee mountains before halting in the area of Ballinacourty, across the border in county Limerick, a few miles from Mitchelstown.[35] The group appears to have been aided by some sympathetic families in this area. John Devoy, who spent some time in prison with McClure, reported many years later that they 'were very comfortable in a dilapidated old house, and were living off the fat of the land'.[36]

It was almost inevitable that the authorities would hear rumours that a number of 'American' Fenians were hiding out in the area. On 21 March, a party of twenty-two policemen raided the house of a man named Lee but failed to find any wanted men. It appears that the men they sought had been given advance warning of their approach and had moved to an abandoned house near a small wood at Kilclooney, on the Cork side of the border.[37] About a week later, isolated and unsure of the state of the country, Peter Crowley set off in disguise for Cork city to make contact with the surviving Fenian organisation.[38]

Stories about the presence of rebels near Kilclooney Wood persisted and so, on Saturday, 30 March, a party of police again began to search the area where they were thought to be hiding. They surprised the sentry, Thomas Walsh, who ran to a stable where the others were sleeping and alerted them. When the rebels emerged to make a fight of it, they found to their relief that the police had moved away to surround the wood, and so they managed to slip through the police lines before they were properly formed.[39] By a remarkable coincidence, while these men were hiding in a field near the wood, they met Peter Crowley returning from his visit to Cork and were able to warn him in time 'that he was going into the lion's jaw'.[40] Accounts of subsequent events on that night are confusing but it seems that McClure

34   *Irish Times*, 3 April 1867.
35   Ní Choindealbháin, 'Kilclooney Wood', p. 129.
36   Devoy, *Recollections*, p. 215.
37   *Cork Examiner*, 2 and 3 April 1867. Devoy's account makes no mention of an earlier escape by the Fenians (see Devoy, *Recollections*, pp. 214–5).
38   *Cork Examiner*, 6 April 1867; Devoy, *Recollections*, pp. 214–5.
39   Quoted in Ní Choindealbháin, 'Kilclooney Wood', pp. 130–1.
40   Ibid., p. 131.

and Kelly linked up with Crowley and spent the night with him at a safe house in the area while the remainder of the group made their escape.[41]

The noose was now tightening on the three leaders. At about 4.00 a.m. on Sunday morning, 31 March, a large party of about 120 soldiers attached to the Waterford Flying Column (a military rapid response unit) along with twenty local police, entered the area under the command of Major Bell of Fermoy barracks, accompanied by H.E. Redmond, RM of Dungarvan.[42] One group under Redmond began to search houses on the hill above the wood and the second group under Major Bell began to surround and search the wood itself.[43] At about the same time, Crowley, McClure and Kelly started to move southwards in an effort to escape the area before the net closed in on them. They soon encountered the Flying Column and were forced across country. Losing Kelly on the way, the other two crossed a river into Kilclooney Wood, hoping to escape from it under cover. They were challenged by another party of soldiers hiding behind a hedge on the other side of the wood and so they retreated back towards the river, exchanging fire with the military until they were forced back into the water.[44] Confronted on the far bank by Redmond and some of his men, McClure was arrested after a brief struggle, while a fatally-wounded Crowley was pulled out of the water onto the bank. Kelly was found elsewhere hiding behind a hedge and gave himself up without a struggle.

Accounts of this incident by those involved differ little in the main details. The only major point of disagreement was over who first began shooting. This was of course a key point which had the potential in the first place to influence the inevitable coroner's jury on Crowley's death and might subsequently influence the battle for public opinion over the incident. In his initial account to government, Redmond was clearly aware of the importance of emphasising that the Fenians had opened fire:

> When I came up in the rear of the troops in the wood I at once asked them 'have we been fired at', they answered 'yes, they fired at us first, and are firing at us now', at this place the wood was so thick that I could not see the party opposed to us, but I heard firing within the

41 Letters of Thomas Walsh and John McClure quoted in Ní Choindealbháin, 'Kilclooney Wood', pp. 130–1.
42 *Cork Examiner*, 2 April 1867.
43 H.E. Redmond, R.M., Mitchelstown to Military Secretary, 31 March 1867, NAI, CSORP 1867/5647.
44 Letter from John McClure to Catherine Crowley, transcribed in Bill Power, *Images of Mitchelstown* (Mitchelstown, 2002), pp. 52–3.

wood, therefore directed the troops to defend themselves – I proceeded rapidly to the front of the skirmishers and saw then two armed
men dodging from tree to tree firing at us as they went and making
for the river. I presently saw them stand and aim at us. The troops fired
at them. The two men gained the river bank (at this time I had
ordered the troops to cease firing and they had done so).[45]

Redmond's account was backed up by his men in their subsequent statements.
Each one repeated his contention that the troops had fired only when fired
upon and had ceased firing when the men jumped into the river.[46] One
man, Private James Pye, 6th Regiment of Foot, stated that he was fired on
by Crowley and added 'I returned the fire and 3 or 4 of us pursued after
them …'[47] On the other hand, in a letter to Crowley's sister, John McClure
alleged that it was the soldiers who had first opened fire, even before
Crowley and he had first crossed the river to reach the wood. When the
two men encountered a line of skirmishers at the other side of the wood:

> We turned again and moved back towards the river, under cover of the
> trees – the soldiers having opened on us a deadly fire. Finding that we
> were completely surrounded and being subject to a heavy fire from all
> sides of us, I told Peter to take a tree – that is to get behind one – and
> we returned their fire until their skirmish line came so close that we
> were compelled to get to the river.[48]

Edward Kelly, who had become separated from the other two early in the
skirmish, also contended that the flying column had opened fire:

> … his party did not fire a shot till they had been fired upon repeatedly
> by the military – that, in fact, when assailed, they were unarmed, and
> had to rush for their weapons to a part of the wood, where they were
> concealed, before they could reply to the first fire of the military; and
> that they did so then in self defence.[49]

45 NAI, CSORP 1867/5647.
46 Copy of various statements re engagement in Kilclooney Wood, NAI, CSORP 1867/5710.
47 NAI, CSORP 1867/5710.
48 John McClure to Catherine Crowley, quoted in Ní Choindealbháin, 'Kilclooney Wood',
    p. 132 and Power, *Mitchelstown*, p. 53.
49 *Cork Examiner*, 6 April 1867.

Other contemporary documents are ambiguous on this question. Redmond told the coroner's inquest that, as he lay dying, Crowley told him he had fired only when fired on. Yet, Constable James McEnroe of Kildorrery gave evidence to the inquest that he too had spoken to the dying man and that Crowley had told him, 'I did not fire at all; my rifle was loaded and I would have fired but it missed'.[50] The version of events given by Fr Patrick Lavelle in his letter to American Fenians a week later projected a heroic stance by Crowley in which thirty policemen had 'fired a volley at him without effect. He returned the fire, it is rumoured, with a vengeance.'[51]

As it turned out, the contradictory accounts of who opened fire did not cause too many problems for the authorities. Despite expressing 'some difficulty as to the right of 60 men to fire on four' the inquest jury accepted the military evidence that the men had been determined to resist arrest and found simply that Crowley had died from injuries caused by the firing of the military party 'in the execution of their duty'.[52] John Devoy's account of the incident in his memoirs seems to have accepted Redmond's original contention that the rebels opened fire by stating:

> Crowley and McClure reached Kilclooney Wood, but were soon confronted by a soldier, who shouted at them to halt and give the countersign. Crowley levelled his rifle and fired at him, saying: 'there's the countersign for you.' The bullet did not hit the soldier and they were fired on from several points at once.[53]

What seemed to matter most to Fenian sympathisers and the wider nationalist population was that Crowley had fought heroically against impossible odds and died for the cause of Irish freedom. Within twenty-four hours of his death he was being treated as a new member of the pantheon of republican martyrs.

After their capture, John McClure and Edward (Ned) Kelly were brought before Neale Brown, RM at Mitchelstown and committed for trial to the Special Commission on a charge of high treason.[54] There was never any doubt of their guilt. Found with them at Kilclooney Wood were weapons

50 *Cork Examiner*, 2 April 1867. 'Missed' here presumably means 'misfired'.
51 'Fr. Patrick Lavelle's letter, Mount Partry, 9 April 1867' in *Irish People*, New York, 4 May 1867.
52 *Irish Times*, 3 April 1867; *Cork Examiner*, 2 April 1867.
53 Devoy, *Recollections*, p. 215. Devoy's account of these episodes tends to be inaccurate, and exaggerates the Fenian role in events.
54 *Cork Examiner*, 2 April 1867.

and ammunition, military plans and a diary, copies of Hardy's *Military Tactics* and a small green flag.[55] At the Special Commission held in Cork, four of Crowley's associates were put on trial: McClure, Kelly, Thomas Cullinane and David Joyce. Three of the men pleaded not guilty but McClure pleaded guilty, 'at the instance it is said of his father', who had travelled to Ireland for the trial and had brokered a deal in which the U.S. government would intercede for his release.[56] Neither McClure nor Kelly expressed regret for their actions. McClure stated he was 'made to believe by traitors that I came to assist an oppressed people' but did acknowledge that he was glad no blood was spilt on 5 March.[57] Kelly expressed his views in strongly Protestant evangelical terms. Neither Cullinane nor Joyce spoke in their defence, the latter because he could speak no English.

Defence counsel for the men did not contest the evidence in the case but attacked the suitability of the evidence of informers and argued that high treason was not an appropriate charge for the men, in that their acts did not amount to the 'levying of war'.[58] Nevertheless, all four were found guilty and were sentenced to be hanged, beheaded and quartered on 19 June.[59] In line with the government's general policy of not inflaming the situation any further by creating new martyrs, these sentences were soon commuted to life imprisonment.

John McClure initially served time in Millbank prison, moving to Chatham prison in the spring of 1869 where he became acquainted with Jeremiah O'Donovan Rossa.[60] When royal commissioners enquiring into prison conditions arrived at Chatham in July 1870, McClure declined to take part in the inquiry in protest at the 'torturous living death' he had been forced to endure since his death sentence was commuted.[61] On 5 January 1871, McClure, O'Donovan Rossa, John Devoy and several other prominent Fenians were released from prison and went to America.[62] He joined his brother's law practice in New York and lived into the twentieth century.[63]

---

55 Ibid.
56 Neale Browne, RM, Imperial Hotel, Cork, 22 May 1867 to Sir Thomas Larcom, NAI, CSORP 1867/9162; William J. McClure in *Irish People*, 13 July 1867.
57 *Cork Examiner*, 24 May 1867.
58 Ibid.
59 Ibid.
60 Jeremiah O'Donovan Rossa, *Irish rebels in English prisons*, Thomas J. Cox (ed.), (new edition, Dingle 1991), p. 213.
61 O'Donovan Rossa, *Irish rebels*, p. 254.
62 Ibid., p. 274.
63 Devoy, *Recollections*, p. 218; Joseph Denieffe, *A personal narrative of the Irish Revolutionary Brotherhood* (reprint Shannon, 1969 of original, New York, 1906), p. 143.

Edward Kelly was informed at Millbank prison on 24 September 1867 that he was to be transported for life to Australia. He travelled out on board the *Hougoumont*, the last ever convict ship to Australia, which carried 280 convicts to Freemantle in Western Australia. Sixty-two of them were Fenians, several of whom were involved in incidents in Cork, including Kelly, David Joyce and Thomas Bowler Cullinane. The Fenians were kept separate from the other prisoners and, to pass the time during the voyage, produced several issues of a handwritten newspaper, named 'The Wild Goose' by Kelly.[64] Some of Kelly's poetry, suffused with religious and patriotic images, was included.

One of the men who evaded the flying column at Kilclooney Wood was Thomas Walsh, who had farmed seventy-five acres at Ardnahinch, Shanagarry. He made his way to Boston in the aftermath of the rising. In April 1868, his wife petitioned the government to allow his return, citing her difficulty in keeping the farm going to feed her three young children and promising to guarantee his future conduct. The petition was turned down with the comment that a pardon might give encouragement 'to many of Walsh's class to continue in their disloyalty'.[65]

* * *

While accounts of what happened at Knockadoon coastguard station and at Kilclooney Wood may vary somewhat in their detail, the broad brushstrokes are the same. Knockadoon represented a rare but minor Fenian success, Kilclooney Wood a brave battle against overwhelming odds. Neither incident would have gained much notoriety if Peter Crowley had survived. His death raised the Kilclooney incident out of the ordinary and gave him cult status in Cork and well beyond.

An important element in the raising of Crowley to the status of a martyr lay in the extraordinary confluence of religious and specifically Catholic imagery that accompanied accounts of his death and which obviously aroused strong conscious and unconscious emotions among the local population and among Fenian sympathisers in general.

Crowley was widely known to have had a deep attachment to his Catholic faith: he was said to be a member of four Catholic lay orders and

64 Walter McGrath, 'Convict ship newspaper, The Wild Goose, re-discovered' in *JCHAS*, lxxiv (1969), pp. 20–26.
65 County Inspector's Office, Cork, 20 April 1868, NAI, Fenian papers, 2372R. Walsh did return to Ireland eventually and gave an oration at the unveiling of the O'Neill Crowley monument at Ballymacoda in 1879.

to have taken a vow of celibacy.[66] At the inquest into his death more details emerged of his religious devotion. As he lay dying on the road, he requested Dr Segrave, the doctor accompanying the flying column, to read to him from a prayer book. He survived long enough for a priest, Fr Tim O'Connell, curate of Kildorrery (who was intercepted on his way to Sunday Mass in the nearby chapel at Knockanevin), to arrive and anoint him.[67] Fr O'Connell spoke of Crowley's death as being 'very happy and most edifying'.[68] He later wrote:

> On my arrival at Kilclooney Wood I found Dr. Segrave, surgeon to the flying column, busily engaged staunching the fatal wound with one hand, whilst from a prayer book in the other he read aloud at the young man's request, the litany of the Holy Name of Jesus. I was deeply touched by the scene, and especially by the exclamation 'Thank God, all is right now', and turning to the doctor, he said, 'Thank you very much, the priest is come; leave me to him.'[69]

Another indication of Crowley's religious devotion that was soon widely reported was that, while on the run, the party of rebels recited the Rosary every evening, and that Kelly, although a Protestant, joined in the prayers.[70]

Reports of Crowley's attachment to prayer were one thing. A number of other extraordinary occurrences were reported that added further sheen to his status as a martyr. One of the bullets fired at him was reportedly stopped by a small silver religious medal of the Immaculate Conception that he was wearing, 'which it indented so as to give it the shape of the bowl of a spoon'.[71] He was reported to be also wearing a large bronze crucifix, and this was said to have stopped another bullet.[72] The bullet which killed him was said to have been fired when his back was turned.

Reports also highlighted other elements which seemed to carry echoes of the death of Jesus. Crowley was placed on a door carried out of the wood by the soldiers and 'it is stated that while he lay on the roadside, some women of the neighbourhood, with whom he seemed to be acquainted, visited him, cried over and embraced him'.[73] There was even an incident of

---

66 *Cork Examiner*, 8 April 1867; Devoy, *Recollections*, p. 217.
67 *Cork Examiner*, 2 April 1867.
68 *Cork Examiner*, 8 April 1867.
69 Quoted in Devoy, *Recollections*, p. 216.
70 *Cork Examiner*, 8 April, 1867.   71 Ibid.
72 *Irish People*, 4 May 1867.
73 *Cork Examiner*, 3 April 1867.

rejection or betrayal by one who could have helped him: when the police sought a comfortable house in the vicinity in which to lay the dying Crowley, a man named Hennessy and his wife refused to allow him in, forcing them to continue on towards Mitchelstown, en route to which Crowley died.

These powerfully emotive stories must have circulated almost as soon as the flying column reached Mitchelstown and they inflamed local opinion. By the following day, Major Bell was forced to request that he remain on in the town with his troops because of the hostility – which included verbal abuse and stone-throwing – shown by some of the townspeople to them.[74] When the inquest on Crowley's death was held that afternoon in the boardroom of Mitchelstown workhouse, the authorities found it difficult to persuade 'respectable persons' to attend as jurors. Although the jury did vindicate the authorities' handling of the affair at the end of the inquest, the powerful emotions aroused by Crowley's death were to have an outlet on the following day. There was an enthusiastic public demonstration of support for the dead man when his body was being handed over to his sister Catherine for burial. A large crowd of men, women, and children gathered outside the workhouse, forced open the large gate of the yard and took the coffin in procession through the town, accompanied by Catherine Crowley and by three priests.[75] Many of the women carried green boughs and the town's Catholic shopkeepers closed their shutters while the funeral passed through the town towards Fermoy.[76]

At Fermoy there was an equally fervent display of emotion as the cortège passed through. 'Green boughs were displayed, and the coffin was almost covered with laurels. Children crowded in the street and bore little green banners before the hearse. The demonstration, however, was characterised by decorum.'[77] The procession was watched from the terrace of St Colman's College above the town by a young student named Patrick Sheehan, who would become famous as the novelist Canon Sheehan. He later recalled the impression made on him by Crowley's funeral:

74 Major Bell to Chief Secretary, 1 April 1867, NAI, CSORP 1867/9163.
75 It was reported to the government some time afterwards that Crowley had a first cousin, 'Mr Ahearne' who was a Catholic curate in Mitchelstown. See Neale Browne, RM to Sir Thomas Larcom, 21 April 1867, NLI, Larcom papers, Ms 7594.
76 *Cork Examiner*, 8 April 1867.
77 Ibid.

I remember well the evening on which that remarkable funeral took place. It was computed that at least five thousand men took part in the procession and shouldered the coffin of the dead patriot over mountain and valley and river, until they placed the sacred burden down there near the sea and under the shadow of the church at Ballymacoda.

I remember how a group of us, young lads, shivered in the cold March [sic] wind there on the College Terrace at Fermoy, and watched the dark masses of men swaying over the bridge, the yellow coffin conspicuous in their midst. We caught another glimpse of the funeral cortege as it passed the Sergeant's Lodge; then we turned away with tears of sorrow and anger in our eyes.[78]

Crowley was buried in Ballymacoda churchyard on Wednesday, 3 April and it was reported in the press that 'a large and respectable concourse of people' followed his remains to his burial place.[79]

Fr O'Connell, the priest who had administered the last rites to Crowley, preached from the altar at Knockanevin chapel, near Kilclooney Wood, on the following Sunday, and asked for prayers for the dead man. He also chided his congregation for shunning Hennessy, the man who had refused to let the dying Crowley into his house, and also for assuming that he was responsible for informing the authorities of the rebels' whereabouts.[80]

Almost immediately, too, strong rumours began to circulate that several military or police had been wounded or killed in the affray at the wood. Stories were told of soldiers seen falling, of bodies covered with greatcoats being carried to Fermoy, of secret burials, of the body of a policeman being found. A newspaper reporter who returned to the area to investigate these rumours found them hard to substantiate. But, needless to say, they added to the legend of the 'affray' at Kilclooney Wood.[81]

The strong emotions aroused locally by the Kilclooney incident took some time to settle. The local resident magistrate reported on 4 May that Crowley's death had acted as a kind of catalyst for nationalist feeling in the locality, stating that even the shopkeeper class 'have cast off concealment'.[82] He grumbled that:

78 P. A. Canon Sheehan, 'The moonlight of memory' in *The literary life and other essays* (Dublin, 1921), pp. 178–9.

79 *Cork Examiner*, 4 April 1867.

80 *Cork Examiner*, 8 April 1867. Hennessy's reason for refusing to take Crowley in was that 'he feared it might cause him annoyance afterwards and cause his house to be visited by other troops'.

81 *Cork Examiner*, 8 April 1867.

82 Neale Browne, RM to Sir Thomas Larcom, 4 May 1867, NLI, Ms 7594.

Every girl has green ribbons & my servant girls who have red ribbons in their bonnets have been told as they left church on Sunday by young girls on the street that 'the red is damned'. The young girls have cast aside all respect for ranks and are saucy and insolent – it will take some time and trouble to tame them down again.[83]

Almost two months after Crowley's death, a correspondent from Mitchelstown to the *Cork Examiner* reported a row between some local men and four off-duty soldiers on the evening of the local fair, and reminded his readers, 'You are all aware, at least we people of Mitchelstown are, that the poor, indeed those of the middle class, for ten miles around Kilclooney, are not very kindly disposed towards either the soldiers or the police ...'[84]

The process of creating a martyr out of Crowley began from the moment of his death and continued for many years. It suited the purposes of both republicans and sympathetic members of the Catholic clergy to have a very Catholic Fenian martyr, in order to counter episcopal allegations that Fenians were godless and had put themselves outside of the Church. Fr O'Connell wrote twenty years after Crowley's death that his dying words were: 'Father, I have two loves in my heart – one for my religion, the other one for my country. I am dying today for my Fatherland. I could die as cheerfully for the Faith.'[85]

This link between Fenianism and faith was initially made within ten days of his death by Fr Patrick Lavelle, the radical Mayo priest, who told his American readers that Crowley had died 'true to his country, true to his God' and asserted that his 'edifying death' was a clear refutation of the view held by some bishops that members of the Fenians had lost their faith or, worse, deserved 'a longer eternity and a hotter hell than exists'.[86] Lavelle argued also that the scale of public sympathy at his funeral was proof that, contrary to the 'West British' view that Ireland was largely content under the British *imperium*, there existed a massive level of discontent which needed only the prospect of success to ignite into rebellion.[87] Ironically, Cork's unionist newspaper, the *Constitution*, took a line similar to Fr Lavelle by insisting that disloyalty was 'insinuated so constantly' in nationalist society that the involvement of a strong farmer like Crowley in rebellion was evidence of widespread support for Fenianism.[88]

---

83   Ibid.
84   Quoted in *Irish People*, 22 June 1867.
85   Quoted in Devoy, *Recollections*, p. 216.
86   'Fr Patrick Lavelle's letter', *Irish People*, 4 May 1867.   87 Ibid.
88   *Constitution or Cork Advertiser*, 5 April 1867.

Lavelle and other supporters of extreme nationalism, stung by the ignominious collapse of the rebellion, wanted also to demonstrate the nobility and seriousness of the Fenians in order to counter the scorn that rained down upon the rebels from the unionist establishment. The rebellion had been attacked by the unionist press from the outset as 'an extraordinary piece of human folly and wickedness' undertaken by 'ignorant and infatuated fools', who were easily routed by a few policemen.[89] After its rapid collapse, some of the conservative press were quick to contend that the rebellion was an aberration and that all was well in Ireland.

Commenting on the Kilclooney incident, the *Irish Times* emphasised that it was an isolated case, that 'the peasantry are taking advantage of the happy change of weather and are working in the fields', and that 'the recollection of the Fenian rising is forgotten almost as quickly as the rising itself was put down.'[90] The magistrates of east Cork, perhaps more attuned to local sentiment, took a less sanguine view of the Fenian movement. At a meeting held early in April, chaired by Lord Fermoy, Fenianism was denounced as a cover for Socialism, led by a 'set of rowdies from America and a mob of communists in this country', whose real aim was to turn out the farmers and shopkeepers and grab their property.[91] In this atmosphere of abuse, the Kilclooney incident became important for the morale of republican supporters and sympathisers.

Images of martyrdom multiplied as the story of Crowley's death was retold. A.M. Sullivan, editor of the *Nation*, wrote an account of the Kilclooney incident as early as the autumn of 1867, asserting that Crowley was 'greatly loved in the neighbourhood' and that even before his death 'the peasantry revered him almost as a saint'.[92] He also restated the story that Crowley and his comrades nightly 'knelt around the embers of their watchfire, and recited aloud the Rosary' but, squeezing out an extra touch of pathos, added that 'at the moment of their surprise by the soldiery they were at their morning prayers'.[93] He also repeated the reports that Crowley's miraculous medal and bronze crucifix had stopped bullets.

Kilclooney Wood rapidly became a place of pilgrimage for Fenian supporters and sympathisers, who began visiting the locality on Sunday

89   *Southern Reporter*, 7 and 11 March 1867.
90   *Irish Times*, 2 April 1867.
91   *Cork Examiner*, 8 April 1867.
92   A.M. Sullivan, 'The history of Ireland from the rebellion of Robert Emmet to the Fenian insurrection' in Sylvester O'Halloran, A.M. Sullivan, and others, *The pictorial history of Ireland: from the landing of the Milesians to the present time* (Boston, 1884), p. 35.
93   Sullivan, 'The history of Ireland', p. 35.

afternoon outings. On the anniversary of Crowley's death in 1868 a few hundred people visited the wood, and the same happened on Sunday, 4 April 1869 and on several subsequent Sundays.[94] Most of the reports, however, emphasised the peaceful and 'insignificant' nature of the outings.[95]

On 15 August 1869, several hundred people from the neighbouring parishes were reported to have attended the wood, where they were addressed by a man named O'Neill from Cork, described as 'a well known Fenian' and by Fr Fitzgerald, the Catholic curate from Kilfinane. This meeting fell short of the number expected because of opposition from some of the local clergy and from the local prisoner amnesty committee, which reportedly accounted for the 'total absence of the *respectable* and *independent* farming classes'.[96] Here the fault line between mainstream nationalists and the republicans was already apparent. Constitutional nationalists acknowledged the courage and sacrifice of the Fenians and had united behind a campaign to secure an amnesty for Fenian prisoners but they disapproved of armed rebellion and shows of support for separatism.

This fault line can be clearly seen in the late autumn of 1869, when two public meetings were held in north Cork to promote the nationalist cause. The first meeting was part of a series of demonstrations in support of the Fenian prisoners and was held in Mitchelstown on 31 October. The meeting was a large one, dominated by the Catholic clergy and chaired by the parish priest of Mitchelstown. Respectability was the order of the day, with large numbers of groups from parishes in Cork, Limerick and Tipperary marching behind banners and pipers. Cards with the words 'Order and Sobriety' were handed out and rosettes were distributed to participants after 'last Mass'. The procession was led by children from the local Christian Brothers schools 'each carrying a small cross-crowned banner, having the word "Amnesty" inscribed upon it in letters of gold'.[97] They were followed by five local priests leading a thousand men from Mitchelstown. Speeches emphasised that this meeting was seeking fair play and justice for Ireland. The anxiety of the Fenians to serve their country was acknowledged but, while one or two banners supported the 'Manchester

94 NAI, Fenian papers (R series), 3934R, 3992R, 3954R.
95 For example, Thomas O'Brien J.P., Mounteagle House to Sub-Inspector Rudge, Mitchelstown, 16 April 1869, NAI, Fenian Papers, 4010R.
96 Richard Eaton, 16 August 1869, NAI, Fenian Papers, 4507R.
97 *Cork Examiner*, 2 November 1869.

martyrs', Allen, Larkin and O'Brien, there was no report of public support for Crowley or his associates at the meeting.

In contrast, the second meeting, held at Kilclooney Wood on 7 November, saw the sanctification of Crowley as a Catholic nationalist martyr reach its zenith. Local clergy in county Cork strongly disapproved of this meeting taking place and had reportedly dissuaded many of their parishioners from attending.[98] Nevertheless, a large crowd of several thousand people attended, the majority from county Limerick. The main demand from the platform was a core Fenian one: 'the inauguration of a new national policy, which parting once and for all with parliamentary agitation, pledged its participants to at least a legislative severance between this country and England'.[99] Any notion that those attending the meeting were 'the opponents of religion and social order' was strongly rejected by the platform, whose main speaker was Fr Fitzgerald, the curate of Kilmallock.

The most striking feature of the report is the description of demonstrations of hero worship of Crowley. A banner was displayed which showed a painting of the struggle in the wood on the fateful morning. The tree beside which he was believed to have been shot was treated with great veneration: the top part had already been shipped off to America, while hundreds gathered round the rest of the tree, 'some kissed it reverently, others securing the smallest chip of the sacred wood; and all muttering strange manly prayers for the poor fellow whose blood had sanctified it.' A bullet claimed to be one of those which pierced Crowley was handed around reverently among the crowd.[100]

Crowley's death continued to be honoured by nationalists in subsequent decades. For instance, during the struggle for the land in the 1880s the local tenant right branch was called the Peter O'Neill Crowley National League.[101] During the 1798 centenary commemorations, the Midleton committee expected large groups of Irish-Americans to visit Fenian-related sites like Crowley's grave in Ballymacoda.[102] During that year also the *Cork Examiner* noted the death of Mrs J. Murphy of Roxbury near Boston, 'the last surviving sister of Peter O'Neill Crowley, the heroic soldier-martyr of Kilclooney Wood' and made the connection between her family and the events of 1798. By commenting on her 'ardent devotion to Faith and

98 Richard Eaton, Mitchelstown, 8 November 1869, NAI, Fenian Papers, 4887R.
99 *Cork Daily Herald*, 9 November 1869.
100 Ibid.
101 *Cork Examiner*, 6 April 1898.
102 *Cork Examiner*, 5 March 1898.

Fatherland', it also echoed that constant *motif* of Catholic nationalism that accompanied Crowley's death.[103]

Thus is illustrated the schism in Irish nationalism that was obvious in 1914, where the moderate majority obeyed their leaders in the Irish Parliamentary Party and supported the British Empire in the European war, and the revolutionary minority refused and sought another opportunity to strike at their ancient enemy. Canon Sheehan of Doneraile, the young student who watched the funeral procession of Peter O'Neill Crowley from a distance, wrote a fictional account of the Kilclooney incident in his novel, *The graves of Kilmorna*, published posthumously in 1916, and he linked it approvingly to the then fashionable concept of the role of blood sacrifice in regenerating the manhood of a nation. And so, almost fifty years after his death, Peter O'Neill Crowley, a traitor in the eyes of the law in 1867, continued to personify for many extreme nationalists in Cork and its neighbouring counties the ideal of breaking the law in pursuit of a political cause.

103 *Cork Examiner,* 2 April 1898.

From Dublin to Botany Bay

Experiences of Fr James Harold, a convict priest

MAEVE MULRYAN-MOLONEY

Readers of the *Belfast News Letter*, 11 January 1799, noted that 'on Sunday 6 January 1799, the celebrated Holt' – leader of the United Irishmen – 'was conveyed from the Castle on board a transport vessel now lying in the River [Liffey] for the purpose of being carried to Botany Bay'. Among his companions on board ship was Father James Harold, parish priest of the west county Dublin town of Rathcoole. In conversation on the ship, Holt asked Father Harold why he was being sent to Australia. Was he a rebel? 'No'. Did he sustain great losses by oppression? 'No'. Was he taken in battle? 'No'. Did he rob anyone? 'No'. So why was he on board? Holt was straightforward in telling Father Harold that in his opinion he deserved 'to be transported, if it was only for your stupidity. You had nothing to complain of. You have not, like myself earned what you have got; you should have done something to entitle you to have your passage paid by the Crown.'

It is to the memoirs of the celebrated Joseph Holt that we are chiefly indebted for an account of Father Harold's journey to and sojourn in Australia.[1] Due to celebrate his silver jubilee as priest, James Harold, who as a 30-year-old man had been ordained by the Archbishop of Dublin, John Carpenter, on 12 March 1774, was in January 1799 facing a life sentence in the Australian penal colony.

In 1794 Father Harold was transferred to Saggart and lived at the priest's house in Rathcoole in the foothills of the Dublin mountains.[2] The town

---

1   Joseph Holt, *Memoirs of Joseph Holt in 1798,* 2 vols (London, 1838).
2   Maeve Mulryan-Moloney, *A history of Saggart and Rathcoole parishes* (Rathcoole, 1998).

centre had no Catholic church. Father Harold's keen administrative skills found plenty to do in caring for the parish churches at Saggart and Newcastle, each about a mile from his home. Rathcoole was a military town from the mid-seventeenth century. The priest's house was halfway between Clinch's big house on the Dublin side, and the road junction with Woolpack road where carts of wool from the west Wicklow area came around the corner at the west end of town.

The priest was in the centre of all local activity. His comings and goings were clearly visible from the military barracks. Loud chatter of the men from Ransford's public house and coach-yard came clearly. Men and women at the newly-refurbished Saggart paper mills were fully employed making paper for bank notes for the Bank of Ireland, founded in 1783. The bleaching green for linen woven from locally grown flax was an oasis for the women and girls. The carriages of the Protestant gentry lined the street during divine service in the ninety-year-old Protestant church. Schoolboys and girls from the more affluent local families walked to and from Daniel Brady's school just off the main road. Girls from the charter school attended twenty acres of schoolhouse land to milk cows and tend vegetable plots. Neighbours gathered for fresh spring water from the well fifty yards from Harold's home.

Outwardly all was calm but the legacy of injustices to previous generations simmered in the background. In the early seventeenth century, Saggart lands were confiscated from long-established Irish owners. Tensions were high when in January 1642, English troops under Sir Thomas Armstrong attacked the town of Rathcoole and after much fighting the locals were defeated. Months later, families, fearing another attack on their town, fled to a nearby furze-covered hill. The hill was surrounded by troops, set ablaze and a fearsome death toll of the inhabitants ensued. The place still bears the name Tootenhill – from the Gaelic meaning blazing hill.

Peace was gradually restored to the Rathcoole area. A monument in Saggart cemetery commemorates an event in the history of the parish around the time of Father Harold's arrival. Edward Byrne, chairman of the General Committee of the Catholics of Ireland, a member of the local strong farming class, was in London to meet with King George III. A petition was drafted at the convention of Irish Catholics at Tailors' Hall in Back Lane in Dublin under the chairmanship of John Thomas Troy, Archbishop of Dublin, in December 1792. Byrne was one of five delegates from the Back Lane parliament to go to London to present the petition on behalf of the Catholics of Ireland. The outcome was further alleviation of Catholic grievances, but excluding the right to be members of parliament.

15 Late eighteenth-century cross and chalice found in Rathcoole, where Fr James Harold ministered before his transportation to Australia. Photograph by the author

Father Harold settled into his prominent parish. The tombstone of his predecessor, Father Simon Barlow, in Saggart graveyard is inscribed thus:

> To a primitive simplicity of manners he joined the most solid strength and penetration of mind. Charitable without ostentation, and always feeling for the distresses of his people, he carried with him to the grave no other riches than of their tears and affections.[3]

Father Harold was of the same mould. On the feast of the Ascension, 20 May 1798, when he kissed the cross on his linen amice, wrapped it across his white alb, muttered in Latin 'Gird me, O Lord, with the girdle of purity' and tied his cincture around his waist, he could not in his wildest nightmares

---

3   Mulryan-Moloney, *Saggart and Rathcoole*, p. 79.

foresee how his life would change by Pentecost Sunday, ten days later. He exhorted his parishioners to forbearance and peace. He urged them to shun all discord and disorder. He went on to rebuke the yeomanry and military for the reckless barbarity they displayed.[4] Then he left home, probably on the Cork mail coach that trundled past his front door. He took a well-earned change of scene at the home of his friend, Father John Leonard, in county Cork. Fifteen years would pass before they could enjoy each other's company again.

Father Harold was aware, possibly through the long hours he spent in his confessional over the Easter period, that the United Irishmen were recruiting in his parish. The military were also aware that Captain James Ormsby's Rathcoole yeomanry corps was a vital backup in tracing the movements of those who pledged their allegiance to the rebels. Some, such as the priest's 18-year-old neighbour, John Clinch of Rathcoole House, had membership of both groups. Ormsby commissioned Clinch as lieutenant and 17-year-old John Walsh as sergeant. Walsh was taken in for questioning by the military and disclosed that Clinch was in the United Irishmen.

Clinch was arrested in the last days of May 1798. His family was a well-known and long-established farming family. The *Freeman's Journal*, 2 June 1798 wrote 'a young man named Clinch, the son of a respectable farmer who lived at Rathcoole, has been apprehended and yesterday was in the guard house in the [Dublin] Castle. He stands charged with being an officer in the rebel army. He is a young man and was a member of the Rathcoole yeomanry.'

His arrest caused alarm in the neighbourhood. He was court-martialled on Friday 1 June 1798. Offered pardon if he betrayed others, he mentioned Father Harold. The journalist from the *Freeman's Journal* wrote 'Clinch was sworn by a priest some time ago against his king, his country and that God who has commanded subjection to the lawful and constituted authorities of the land.'[5] The death sentence was imposed. The news of John Clinch's arrest and sentence sent shock waves through the parish. Young Clinch wrote bravely to his father:

> I expected to have seen or heard from you before this … it would be a great satisfaction to see you before I die … and if you could bring or send a priest to me I think I could then die happy … as I hope for salvation, I declared the truth at the court-martial.[6]

4   Cardinal Moran, 'The Irish convict priests of '98', in *Irish Rosary* (1898), p. 189.
5   *Freeman's Journal*, 5 June 1798.   6   Mulryan-Moloney, *Saggart and Rathcoole*, p. 82.

Father Harold, in Cork, was probably unaware of the drama in his parish. A friend to his parishioners, he had a particular affinity with young people. He was a first-rate preacher and led his congregation in choral singing. The British deemed him a man who knew the state of affairs within his parish. His absolute refusal to divulge information gained through confession brought him under suspicion. He identified with his people and refused to violate confessions. A sociable man, he made friends on both sides of the religious divide, from the Clinch family in their mansion just up the street from the presbytery, to the Rourke family who kept the tollgate three miles to the west, to Protestant confidants four miles away at Hazelhatch.[7] The authorities wished to speak with him and issued an order for his arrest. He returned to Rathcoole and was taken in for questioning.

The *Freeman's Journal*, 2 June 1798, stated that a Roman Catholic clergyman 'was on Thursday brought up to town from the neighbourhood of Rathcoole, a prisoner, who is accused of being an abettor of the rebels in that part of the country'. Father Harold was possibly questioned and released. Then he obtained a protection order from the military at Drogheda. Eleven weeks later, *The Times* reported:

> On Saturday 18 August 1798, Harold, the Romish priest of Rathcoole, who was accused by the unfortunate Clinch in his dying moment as his seducer from his allegiance, was apprehended on the bridge of Hazelhatch by one of the Rathcoole cavalry. He made some objections to his arrest and shewed a protection, which he had received from the general commanding at Drogheda, but was, notwithstanding, brought under an escort to this city [Dublin], and was on Monday lodged in the Castle.[8]

The protection order proved valueless. The government would seek to get Father Harold away from Ireland.

Father Harold was placed on board the sloop, the *Lively* in Dublin. Archbishop Troy had cautioned his priests in his Lenten pastoral six months earlier to avoid any collusion or part in the anti-government cause. Now, it seemed he was dismissive of Father Harold's plight. He allowed four months to elapse before contacting him. His petition dated 10 December 1798 requested the authorities to allow his representative, Revd Barnaby Murphy

---

7   *Irish Rosary*, 1898, p. 189.
8   *The Times*, 20 August 1798.

of Townsend Street chapel, to meet with Father Harold aboard the *Lively*.[9] The *Freeman's Journal* referred to Clinch's incriminatory evidence during which he allegedly said 'how horrible is a civil war, but how tenfold horrible when directed by the spirit of religious bigotry.'[10] A spirit of religious bigotry could not be laid against Father Harold.

On 13 February 1799, Judge Robert Day sentenced Father Harold to transportation for life. A formal writ to detain him was sent to the commander of the *Lively* with the following instructions:

> We command you that you have the body of James Harold detained in your custody, as it is said, under safe and secure conduct, or by whatsoever other Name, addition of Name, or Sirname, the said James Harold is called in the same before the Honble. Robert Day, fourth justice of our Court of Chief Place in Ireland, or in his absence, before any of his Brethern Justices of said Court, in Dublin … Immediately on sight or receipt hereof, together with the day and cause of his being the said James Harold so taken and detained, to do and receive what shall then and there be considered concerning him, and have you then there this Writ.[11]

Joseph Holt recalled that the journey from Dublin to the south of Ireland Cove of Cork took two days. It must have been a harrowing journey in the spring of 1799, from Dublin, south by Wicklow Head, and westwards around Carnsore Point to the magnificent harbour called the Cove of Cork. Personal comforts for convicts were considered an unnecessary expense due to the shortness of the journey, so neither clothing nor bedding was provided – instead each was given a plank of wood as a seat by day and a bed by night. They rested their weary heads on a bundle of hay. Father Harold spent about five months – February to August 1799 – on the *Lively*. Timothy Mahony of Blackpool in Cork got a priest's kit of chalice, vestment and altar linen to him.[12] Some returned convicts informed the Inspector General of Prisons, Mr Archer, that they underwent more suffering and sickness on the *Lively* than in sailing from Cork to Botany Bay. Archer attributed the appalling conditions endured by the convicts to the length of time they were held on the *Lively*, since few convicts were allowed to breathe in the air on deck at any one time.[13]

9 NAI, MS SPP 161.   10 *Freeman's Journal*, 5 January 1799.
11 Writ of George III to Commander of the *Lively*, cited in *Irish Rosary*, 1898, p. 187.
12 *Irish Rosary*, 1898, p. 188.   13 NAI, CSOOP/1815/439/5.

In mid-summer, the 558-ton *Minerva* sailed slowly into Cork harbour. A fine sea-worthy ship, fitted for her voyage, and in every respect calculated for the long uncertain sea journey to the other side of the world.[14] Everything appeared clean, orderly and proper on board; decency, decorum, and discipline appeared in every department. The passengers were well kitted out with two jackets, two pairs of trousers, two shirts, two pairs of stockings, and two pairs of shoes, a small flock bed, a blanket, and a rug to each of the 165 men prisoners. The twenty-six females were equally well kitted out. Holt, according to his memoirs, was much impressed.

Petitioning the lord lieutenant was the only real hope of obtaining a commutation of sentence. It was a slow cumbersome process. Petitions, also known as memorials, were prepared by the convict, or by a representative, and presented directly in the first instance to the lord lieutenant. He then referred them through the chief secretary's office to the trial judge, and to the local constabulary. The system was tortuous. On 22 February 1799, Father Harold, 'aged 55, a pastor in the parish of Rathcoole, Co. Dublin prays to be removed from the *Minerva*, which is due to sail for Botany Bay.'[15] All petitions were investigated thoroughly. Father Harold awaited a positive response to his plea for *habeas corpus*. None came. The year was 1799, August, the shadows were beginning to lengthen, as Father Harold left Cove on board the *Minerva*. The well-wooded arena of hills around Cove gradually faded in the distance. Father Harold was determined that his mission henceforth would be one of consolation and pastoral ministry to his companions.[16]

The first few days were an easy sail at an average speed of somewhat less than 100 miles a day through the Bay of Biscay – a 400-mile passage in open sea with no landmarks, and no possibility of shelter from its storms. Then they sailed across to the Canary Islands. Guided by the shape of the swells, they were blown steadily in the warm trade winds across the equator and on to Rio de Janeiro. The convicts, unaccustomed to the intense heat and humidity, suffered extreme thirst, and the salted meat added to their discomfort. The daily water allowance was a little over half a litre per person. They made landfall at Rio de Janeiro on 22 October 1799.[17]

While at Rio, Father Harold wrote to his nephew, William Vincent Harold, who was a Dominican seminarian in Lisbon. The nephew was

14 Anne-Marie Whitaker, *Unfinished revolution, Ireland 1798* (Sydney, 1994), p. 43.
15 NAI, SPP 628; *Irish Rosary*, 1898, p. 191.
16 Ibid.   17 Ibid.

much impressed with his uncle's acceptance of his fate and considered joining the Catholic mission to Australia.[18] At Rio the ship got provisions, including maize, pineapples, and sweet potato, and was adjudged capable of the almost 7,000-mile trans-Pacific trip to Sydney. On 8 November 1799, it travelled from Rio down the east coast of South America, round by Cape Horn, and on to the South Pacific. Christmas 1799 was spent on the high seas. It was a relatively idyllic voyage with no great storms encountered. Humane treatment was meted out to the passengers. Father Harold was on good terms with the captain and crew. The peace and harmony of the *Minerva* may have been due in part to his priestly ministry, and his accomplishments as an entertainer and group leader.[19] The death toll for such a long voyage was less than usual, with only three passengers breathing their last between Cove and Sydney.[20]

The New South Wales penal colony was barely a decade in existence. The first shipload of convicts bound for Australia had left Ireland in the spring of 1791. Only three years before that, in 1788, the first convicts travelled from England to Port Jackson. More advanced seafaring methods had prompted authorities to send what they deemed their more trouble-some citizens to the new colonies, first America from the seventeenth century, and then following the American War of Independence, to Australia. The first Irish statute, which mentioned transportation to America, or else-where out of Europe, was in the early years of the eighteenth century. Transportation sentences were for periods of seven years, ten years, fourteen years or life. On 11 January 1800 the *Minerva* sailed through Port Jackson to Parramatta. The prisoners and crew were on board for a total of five months.

The Scottish-born, classically-educated second governor of New South Wales, John Hunter,[21] greeted the passengers. He looked through the charge sheets and was none too pleased when he met them. He needed good strong workers to turn a remote wilderness into a place of trade, commerce, farming – in short a self-contained, highly functioning community. Generally, health was good, the country was level, and ideal for healthy living. In a letter to the authorities in London, Hunter wrote:

> Many of the prisoners have been either bred up in genteel life, or to professions unaccustomed to hard labour. Those are a dead weight on

18 Ibid., p. 192.
19 Harold Perkins, *The convict priests* (Victoria, 1984), p. 11.
20 Whitaker, *Unfinished revolution*, pp. 44, 48.
21 *Australian dictionary of biography*, 1788–1850, 2 vols (Melbourne, 1866), A–H.

the public store ... we can scarcely divest ourselves of the common feelings of humanity so far as to send a Roman Catholic priest to the grubbing hoe or timber carriage.[22]

In 1800, Sydney, with its population of 2,500 (43 per cent were convicts), needed people who could contribute to the common good. Everyone was expected to have a role in community life. The Unitarian minister, the convict Thomas Fyshe Palmer, welcomed Father Harold. Would he dine with him the following evening? Father Harold's conviviality and good company were welcome. After dinner he regaled Palmer and the company with his rendition of *Exile from Erin*.

> There came to the beach a poor exile of Erin
> The dew on his thin robe was heavy and chill
> For his country he sighed, when at twilight repining
> To wander alone by the wind-beaten hill.

He was encouraged by the enthusiastic crowd on a nearby beach to provide an encore. Irishmen and women gathered around to hear the latest news from home.[23] Some felt the need to meet with Father Harold in his priestly ministry. Holt remembered that Father Harold was housed in a private house. The authorities kept close watch and he was forbidden to exercise his ministry openly. On the 23 April 1800, he reminded Governor Hunter that he was accustomed to higher society, but that those he regarded as his equals in the colony found it their duty to keep him at a distance. He was, therefore, obliged to associate with less respectable persons.[24]

Shortly afterwards, at the beginning of May 1800, Governor Hunter's officers opined that the convicts from Ireland resented the English. They allegedly held unlawful meetings, with passwords and hand signals devised and freely exchanged in a bid to gain recruits. A general secret search of all convicts did not yield the slightest evidence of disloyalty. Their examination of Father Harold yielded no information 'for nothing appeared to criminate him, though the fact was universally acknowledged'.[25] What was the governor to do in the circumstances? Generally, there was no smoke without fire!

---

22 *Historical records of Australia*, ii, p. 450.
23 Whitaker, *Unfinished revolution*, pp. 47–50.
24 Perkins, *The convict priests*, p. 11.
25 *Irish Rosary*, 1898, p. 235.

The governor judged it necessary, in consequence of these rumours, to issue warnings. He examined government papers against seditious corre-spondence or unlawful assemblies of the people. He altered them so as to suit the position he found himself in; then published them as a proclamation so that none might plead ignorance of the existence of such laws.[26] The proclamation was displayed prominently in the colony, and on Sunday 24 May was proclaimed after divine service. All was outwardly calm for a period.[27]

Nearly four months later, some very serious whisperings circulated early in September. Would the Irish convicts try to gain control of the colony? They had many pikes! The governor nominated a committee of inquiry under judge advocate, Richard Dore. Father Harold was the first witness called before Dore. He refused to give any information.[28] He may be regarded as respecting the confidences of confession. From his language and behaviour, Father Harold, suspected of being concerned in the intended attack on the government, was imprisoned.[29] Then he undertook to discover the several hundred concealed weapons. He implicated several of his countrymen, and they, on being questioned, accused others. Pikes were buried in the ground of a settler, according to him; but on searching every part of it, none was found. He then mentioned the harbour, but again none was found.

Had Father Harold definite information, or was he in Holt's words 'aiming at making himself of consequence'?[30] In any event, Father Harold was shortly afterwards transferred to Norfolk Island in the Pacific. Governor Hunter was recalled to London and left for England on 28 September 1800. Of his sojourn in Australia he said that he 'could not have had less comfort, although he would certainly have had greater peace of mind, had he spent the time in a penitentiary'. Life in an emerging colony was fraught with difficulties. Conditions for the prisoners were possibly as good as the conditions of most other people there.

Norfolk Island had been discovered by James Cook in 1774, a rugged volcanic island, a landscape of steep hills, with a very pleasant climate. At about the time of Father Harold's arrival on the island, the authorities in London wanted the penal colony to cease.[31] The lieutenant governor

26 Holt, *Memoirs,* ii, pp. 109–10.
27 Ibid., p. 32.
28 Whitaker, *Unfinished revolution,* p. 50.
29 *Irish Rosary,* 1898, p. 235.
30 Holt, *Memoirs,* ii, p. 111.
31 *Irish Rosary,* 1898, p. 239.

allowed Father Harold to open a school there for his own accommodation. He was about sixty years of age, and with the hardships of several severe bouts of dysentery he was hospitalised for a month, and his school closed. He then went to live 'with a poor, honest, industrious, moral man'. He missed his life on the mainland and the regime on Norfolk Island was a very severe one. He felt too old and unwell to climb up those hills.[32] All convicts, including Catholics, had to attend prayers led by the commandant, since the Protestant chaplain never visited the penal settlement. Any person absent from church during divine service would be imprisoned. It was compulsory to attend at least once each Sunday, and the penalty for non-attendance was deduction of three pounds of flour from the ration of each overseer or two pounds from the flour ration of each labouring convict.

Father Harold wrote several times to family members, but did the letters ever leave the colony? He never received a reply, or had any family contact in the four years since his departure from Ireland. He was in a melancholy mood during his illness, saying 'my existence here can be but short and miserable.'[33]

> Erin, my country, though sad and forsaken
> In dreams I revisit your sea-beaten shore
> But, alas, in a far foreign country I awaken
> And sigh for the friends who can meet me no more.

For a time, he had the companionship of another Irish priest, Father Peter O'Neill from county Cork, who had been unjustly accused of being involved in killing a government soldier. He was sentenced to transportation. The two priests empathised with each other. On further investigation, Father O'Neill was pardoned and on 8 January 1803, he was granted his freedom to return to Ireland. This news further increased Father Harold's depressed state. Father O'Neill was in a better financial state than Father Harold, whose home at Rathcoole had been burned to the ground, so presumably his entire worldly goods were destroyed. He depended on Father O'Neill's generosity for any little extras he needed.

On 8 January 1803, Father Harold wrote to his nephew that Father O'Neill 'brought with him a property sufficient to afford us the necessaries of life, and had just as much left as paid his passage etc when his release

32 Ibid.
33 Ibid.

arrived. Every shilling he could spare he left me, but any consideration of this nature is but a miserable compensation for his absence.'[34] Father O'Neill would take a letter to the Harold family, to begin a renewed process towards his liberty. The letter read:

> It may be said 'why should I not continue in Port Jackson?' Were I guilty of any misdemeanour I should remain silent on that head, but I solemnly declare that I was not. I endeavoured at all times to prevent any disturbance and to preserve the peace of the colony.
>
> As there is now a general peace, I am inclined to suppose that a proper application to Government might procure me liberty to retire to some of the Portuguese or Spanish settlements, without the privilege of returning to his majesty's domain.
>
> I should have written to Colonel Wolfe and to Most Reverend Dr Troy on that subject, but certainly I am not able in the short space, for, only this day, Friday, Mr O'Neill, agreed with the captain of the ship, and on Sunday morning early he must be on board. However, with the advice of your friends, you may apply to these gentlemen in my name. This miserably written letter will serve for your introduction. I have a thousand questions to ask and many persons to inquire about, but I apprehend I should not be answered.
>
> I am particularly anxious about my nephew William, and often think of little James. You know those to whom I am sincerely attached; make them my affectionate remembrance, and write to me accordingly. As soon as you receive this letter, write to Mr O'Neill, and enclose a letter to me, which he will take care to send me. In the meantime write by post. The manner of conveyance, and whether the letter is to be paid to London, some gentleman will let you know, or you will be informed at the post office in Dublin.[35]

Father Harold suggested an appeal to Colonel Wolfe whom he was possibly acquainted with. Lord Chief Justice Arthur Wolfe, created Lord Kilwarden in 1798, was a trustee of the toll road that ran by the parish house. He would have felt confident placing his case before him. Father Harold had no idea of events in his home parish. It was in turmoil. On Saturday 22 July 1803, a group of men at Thomas Street Dublin attacked Wolfe's coach, on his journey from his home at Newlands, Clondalkin to Dublin Castle. His

34 Ibid., p. 238.
35 Ibid., p. 239.

companion and nephew, Revd Mr Wolfe, was killed and Wolfe himself was injured. Felix Rourke of Rathcoole, an acquaintance of Father Harold, was arrested, tried on 24 August, and on 10 September he was executed at the burnt-out ruins of the priest's house in Rathcoole.[36] Father Harold would not see the Dublin foothills for another decade.

The Cornish man, Philip Gidley King,[37] former governor of Norfolk Island, replaced Governor Hunter. He was the person to move the colony to a more settled state. His main ambition was to break the power of the officers, so he forbade importation and trading of spirits. King, like Hunter, was in constant conflict with officers. King proceeded with the settlement of Tasmania near the present-day Hobart, and Father Harold was removed there from Norfolk Island. Allowed to celebrate mass,[38] he felt confident that under King's more enlightened attitude that some day he would be free. He was refused permission to go to Spain, Portugal or Ireland.

> Buried and cold, when my heart still her motion
> Green be your fields, sweetest isle of the ocean
> And your harp-striking bards sing aloud with devotion
> Erin, mavourneen, Erin-go-bragh.

In 1806, William Bligh, a keen disciplinarian,[39] was appointed governor in the hope that he would be able to end the domination of the officer clique under its leader John Macarthur. The last of the convicts was removed to Tasmania in 1807. In 1808 Bligh was ousted.

Bligh's successor, the Scot, Lachlan Macquarie,[40] sailed from England with the seventy-third regiment on 22 May 1809. New Year's Eve, 31 December 1809, marked his official landing in Australia. His account of conditions there show the grimness of the lives of officials, settlers and convicts. The country was 'threatened with famine, distracted by faction, the public buildings in a state of dilapidation; the few roads and bridges almost impassable, the population in general depressed by poverty ... the morals of the great mass of the people in the lowest state of debasement, and religious worship almost neglected'. Macquarie assumed office without delay. He replaced all office holders with his own men. A waterfront produce, livestock

---

36 *Freeman's Journal*, 13 September 1803.
37 *Australian dictionary of biography*, vol. A–H.
38 John Kingston, *Parish of Fairview* (Dundalk, 1953), p. 81.
39 *Australian dictionary of biography*, vol. A–H.
40 *Australian dictionary of biography*, vol. I–Z.

and poultry market had grown around the King's Wharf, which was the main landing place for ships from England. It was unsightly, so was moved inland to a site where on 20 October 1810, a large market place, which became the hub of the new city of Sydney, was proclaimed. Father Harold entered the wharf in 1810.

Macquarie considered the plight of the convicts, and keen on their rehabilitation, he brought some of them on his side as magistrates. He successfully reorganised a police force. He reckoned that a positive approach to formal education was essential so free schools were funded at Sydney and Parramatta. The first post office opened on 23 June. Just as some ordered life came to Sydney, Father Harold succeeded in his efforts to be granted his liberty.[41]

On 14 July 1810, a notice appeared in the *Sydney Gazette and New South Wales Advertiser* stating that: 'All claims and demands on the Rev. James Harold are requested to be presented for payment, he designing to leave the country per *Concord*.' Father Harold's homeward departure meant that Australia was without a Catholic priest until 1819, when two Roman Catholic priests were officially authorised by the British government to minister to the day-to-day spiritual needs of Catholic colonists.

The *Concord* sailed northwards up the east coast of South America. Father Harold spent some time in Rio de Janeiro, then sailed across the equator and up the east coast of North America to Philadelphia. He made contact with his nephew, Father William Vincent Harold,[42] who by now was vicar-general for the diocese of Philadelphia. Father James was assigned to St Mary's cathedral, under Limerick-born, newly-appointed bishop Michael Egan, a Franciscan. Father Harold returned to priestly dress as laid out by Pope Benedict XIII in 1725. He wore his best black biretta and donned his black full-length cassock and Roman collar and went freely among his parishioners. When the Harolds became party to a dispute with trustees of the parish, Father Vincent resigned his post, and uncle and nephew sailed for Ireland and arrived in April 1813.

Father Harold was back in his homeland. The memoranda book for 1816 of Archbishop Troy of Dublin records him as parish priest of Kilcullen, the parish he left over twenty years earlier. His next appointment was as administrator at the church of the Visitation at Fairview, just north of Dublin city-centre. His Australian years left Father James with failing health. He

41 *Irish Rosary*, 1898, p. 240.
42 *New Catholic encyclopedia*, 2nd ed., vii (America, 2003), p. 237.

went to live with his cousin Michael Ryan at 21 Lower Dominick Street Dublin. His eventful life came to an end on 15 August 1830, in his eighty-fifth year. He lies in Goldenbridge cemetery beside the Grand Canal at Inchicore.[43]

* * *

The Rathcoole happenings that led to Father Harold's exile were commemorated in a ballad:

> My curse attend you … and …
> My curse attend you night and day
> You hung John Clinch and sent the priest away.

Many years later, a late eighteenth-century cross and chalice were found hidden in Rathcoole town. The cross was found in the priest's hiding place in the older part of Rathcoole House. The chalice was found in the rafters of a thatched house, formerly a schoolhouse. Rathcoole public library was built on the site of the house where Father Harold lived during his time as parish priest from 1794 to 1798. On the bicentenary of his leaving the parish, on Sunday, 5 July 1998, the Main Street of Rathcoole was thronged as church and state came together to remember a man who was possibly wrongly accused by a young man from the big house, which still stands forlorn and empty up the street. Bishop Eamonn Walsh and Revd Olive Boothman led a commemorative ecumenical prayer service and Ms Mary Harney, TD unveiled a monument. It reads:

> This stone was erected to commemorate
> Father James Harold
> John Clinch, Richard Fyans
> J. Molloy, Felix Rourke
> And the people
> Of the area associated
> With the 1798 rising.[44]

---

43   *Irish Rosary*, 1898, pp. 240–1; Kingston, *Parish of Fairview*, pp. 81–2.
44   Mulryan-Moloney, *Saggart and Rathcoole*, p. 79.

Westmeath versus Westmeath

Adultery, cruelty, greed and perjury

PAUL CONNELL

On 3 January 1825, George Thomas John Nugent, eighth Earl and first Marquis of Westmeath, began a private prosecution against six individuals in a Dublin court. It was one of the most unusual and sensational trials of the period. The six defendants were indicted for 'a conspiracy, by corrupt means and by false oaths, to establish a charge of adultery against his Lordship'.[1] The trial was only one of a series of legal actions involving the marquis and his wife, Emily, resulting from the breakdown of their marriage. Their legal battles, between 1818 and 1834, impoverished both of them to the tune of some £30,000, an enormous sum at the time.[2] It was one of the most acrimonious marital splits of the age, one that eventually had important implications for custody and divorce law in England. To the end of their days, both parties remained embittered, as detailed in their separate and conflicting accounts of the whole affair that were published in 1857.[3]

Their relationship had not always been so acrimonious. When in 1812 George Nugent, Lord Delvin, the 29-year-old son and heir of the seventh

---

1   *A full and complete report of the trial, the King, at the prosecution of the Marquis of Westmeath, against Anne Connell, John Monaghan, Bernard Maguire, Patrick Farley and William McKenzie, at Green Street, Dublin, at the Commission of Oyer and Terminer* (Dublin, 1825), p. 2 (hereafter *Trial*).

2   For a full account of their legal battles see 'Westmeath v. Westmeath, The wars between the Westmeaths, 1812–1857, in Lawrence Stone, *Broken lives, separation and divorce in England 1660–1857* (Oxford, 1993), pp. 284–346. I am greatly indebted to this work for the legal background to this saga.

3   E.A.B.E. [Emily Anne Bennet Elizabeth] Westmeath, *A narrative of the case of the Marchioness of Westmeath* (London, 1857); Westmeath, *A reply to the narrative of the case of the Marchioness of Westmeath* (London, 1857).

Earl of Westmeath, was paying court to the 23-year-old Lady Emily Cecil, second daughter of the first Marquis of Salisbury, an Anglo-Irish acquaintance noted in her diary:

> Lady Emily Cecil is going to be married to Lord Delvin, Lord Westmeath's son. He is very poor, and I think it is a wretched match for her, but they have long been in love.[4]

Apart from his relative poverty, George had other drawbacks. His mother had been divorced for adultery, so he was regarded as coming from a scandalous family. In addition, he had fathered a child by an Irish mistress, something that Emily knew, having been told by her brother, Lord Cranborne.[5] It must be assumed, therefore, that such a marriage between a Cecil and the heir to an impoverished Irish peerage was a love match. The marriage in financial and political terms was certainly a step-up for the Nugents. This connection with the Cecils would certainly have helped George attain the rank of marquis from the Tory government in 1822.

The couple lived for a year after their marriage in Dublin and at Hatfield House in Hertfordshire, home of the Cecils. In 1813 they moved to Clonyn Castle, the marquis's ancestral home, near Delvin in county Westmeath, where they lived until 1815. It was here that their daughter Rosa was born in 1814. By then the couple were already quarrelling bitterly. Clonyn was a real backwater for Emily. She had been brought up at the court in London where her father had been Lord Chamberlain until 1804. A run-down Irish castle was a far cry from the luxury that she was used to at Hatfield. By 1815 their situation had deteriorated to the extent that a family friend had to intervene to bring about reconciliation. Part of the difficulty lay with George continuing to see and support his Irish mistress.[6] The agreement that emerged included an undertaking by George that he would never see her again. The couple set off for a nine-month stay in France, mostly in Paris, where relations deteriorated once again. At one point George hit his wife in a fit of temper. In the summer of 1817 Emily left George and decided to sue him for legal separation on the grounds of cruelty.[7]

In the following month, George wrote Emily a series of letters expressing his sincere repentance for his previous behaviour towards her.

---

4 Stone, *Broken lives*, p. 284.
5 Court of Arches Mss D 2240: 107–9, 491, 1021, Lambeth Palace.
6 Ibid., 127, 357–9.
7 Ibid., H 365/10.

> Pardon me for so much brutality. I was a hell to you ... Tell me you do not hate me, Emily ... I really do think that in the state I have been for a month past, I shall not hold out. I only wish and pray to die.[8]

Once again, a reconciliation was achieved, thanks to George's contrition and to the absolute hostility of the Cecils to even a private separation, much less to the public scandal of a suit in the ecclesiastical court. The Marchioness of Salisbury, Emily's mother, went down on her knees to beg them 'not to make themselves the talk of the town'.[9]

Emily drove a hard bargain, however. In return for her withdrawal of the threat to sue George for legal separation on the grounds of cruelty, and her agreement to renew cohabitation and sexual relations, George agreed to settle on their daughter, Rosa, the reversion of much of his own Nugent estates, if he and Emily did not produce a male heir. This was a very unusual arrangement since it separated the descent of the property from that of the title and cut George's brother out of the inheritance. He also agreed that if a separation occurred in the future, he would give custody of Rosa to Emily and grant her an allowance. The reconciliation held for three months and by March 1818 Emily was pregnant again. Fresh quarrelling broke out soon after, and in May 1818 George and Emily again parted beds, this time forever. Emily left the Nugent town house in London and rented a smaller one, where in November 1818 she gave birth to a son.

Meanwhile, under further pressure from her parents, Emily had agreed not to sue through the ecclesiastical court but to accept instead a private deed of separation. As a result, George settled a generous allowance of £1,300 a year on her, let her have full custody of the children and promised not to sue her in the ecclesiastical court for 'restitution of conjugal rights'. He did request, however, permission to occupy a bedroom in what was now Emily's home so as to conceal from the world their situation. Emily agreed but was always careful to sleep behind locked doors and ensured that her maid slept in the antechamber as a further protection.[10]

At Easter 1819, George began to press Emily to surrender the separation agreements. Emily refused and began to remove some of her possessions from the house. George appealed to her childhood friend, the Duke of Wellington, but his efforts were to no avail. Emily would not budge. George

---

8   Ibid., D.2240: 171–85.
9   Westmeath, *Reply to the narrative*, p. 75.
10 Court of Arches Mss D 2240:141–3, 457, 1047, 1127, 1153, 1157, 1207–211, Lambeth Palace.

went so far as to quarrel with the duke and even challenged him to a duel. The duke apologised and the matter was dropped but it did not prevent George from attempting to ban the duke from visiting his wife's house again. A further row developed when George attempted to dismiss the housekeeper and broke into the household accounts cabinet. Emily, following the advice of her solicitor, left the house, bringing the children with her. There is reason to believe that George suspected the duke of having an affair with his wife and contemplated taking an action against him for criminal conversation. If this had gone ahead it would have been the trial of the decade, possibly denting severely the reputation of the great hero of Waterloo. George did have the duke watched on his visits to Emily, but he took the precaution of always visiting her in the company of others.[11]

George then sued for custody of the children and won, despite the existence of their previous separation agreement, which, because it was private, was held to have no validity in law. He now made offers of a new separation agreement but insisted on the cancellation of the previous ones. Emily refused because they protected her daughter Rosa's claims to inherit George's estates, guaranteed her allowance and provided proof of George's ill-treatment. Before either side could begin litigation, their baby son became very ill and Emily rushed to Clonyn Castle to be with him, arriving just after he died.

Through negotiations conducted by her brother, Lord Cranborne, George allowed Emily to return to London with Rosa. In March 1820, however, George resumed custody and sent Rosa to live with Lord Buckingham, a friend and close relative. Emily went to court to try and regain custody but failed. Years later, she recalled how in 1825 she managed to see her daughter while she was attending dancing lessons. The child, then aged eleven, refused to kiss her mother or shake her hand, and said to her: 'Papa and the Duke of Buckingham have pointed out to me what sort of woman you was.'[sic][12]

The bitter struggle over custody of their daughter was merely the opening engagement in a long drawn-out legal battle between Emily and George. Emily attempted to validate in law the private separation agreements. George opposed this and sued in the ecclesiastical court for 'restoration of conjugal rights', a device that would have left him no longer

---

11 Westmeath, *Narrative of the case,* pp. 84–5; Westmeath, *Reply to the narrative,* pp. 24–33; Stone, *Broken lives,* pp. 307–10.
12 Ibid., pp. 313–14.

responsible for her debts or maintenance.[13] Their respective suits gave rise to a series of appeals to higher courts and also spawned subsidiary suits in other courts. The net result was a total of seventeen lawsuits before eleven or more different tribunals, embracing all three legal systems in England.[14] It was one of the most complex and expensive legal battles of the age.[15]

Emily was advised that the best method of defence in the ecclesiastical suit was attack. She, therefore, launched in 1821 her own counter-suit in the same court for separation from bed and board on the grounds of thirty-three charges of cruelty. She had good witnesses to George's cruelty to her, in particular her maid, Sarah McKenzie, who could testify to verbal abuse and occasional physical blows. However, George could produce counter-witnesses who were able to testify to his affectionate and proper manner towards his wife. Worse still, by continuing to live with George until 1819 she might be regarded in law as having condoned his previous acts of cruelty.

Fearing defeat in this arena, she further charged George a year later with twenty-five new counts of adultery.[16] She accused him of consorting with five different low women, two of whom he was alleged to have slept with in London. The evidence was weak, however. One of these women was described by the Countess of Glengall, her former employer, as a 'respectable elderly servant'.[17] The other three were Irish women whom George was alleged to have slept with in Clonyn or Dublin. Emily requested her Irish lawyer, Bernard Maguire, to find evidence to support the charges of adultery. He succeeded in doing so, but the witnesses he produced gave contradicting and unconvincing evidence before the ecclesiastical court.

George decided to sue these witnesses for conspiracy. Based on the evidence of their collective perjury in return for money and promises in the ecclesiastical court in London, he sued them in Dublin in 1825. He was hoping that if they were convicted of perjury this would discredit Emily's witnesses in the cruelty case and would lead to the collapse of her suit for separation.[18]

13 In the Church of England, the ecclesiastical courts are a system of courts, held by authority of the Crown, whose holder is the Supreme Governor of the Church of England. The courts have jurisdiction over matters dealing with the rights and obligations of church members, now limited to controversies in areas of church property and ecclesiastical disciplinary proceedings. Up to the late 1860s they had jurisdiction over marital cases.
14 The civil courts, the ecclesiastical courts and finally the House of Lords.
15 Stone, *Broken lives*, p. 315.
16 Westmeath, *Reply to the narrative*, p. 57.
17 Stone, *Broken lives*, p. 321.
18 Ibid., pp. 324–5.

A FULL AND COMPLETE

REPORT OF THE TRIAL,

THE KING,

AT THE PROSECUTION

OF

THE MARQUIS OF WESTMEATH,

AGAINST

ANNE CONNELL, JOHN MONAGHAN, BERNARD MAGUIRE,
PATRICK FARLEY, AND WILLIAM M'KENZIE,

AT GREEN-STREET, DUBLIN,

AT THE COMMISSION OF OYER AND TERMINER,

JANUARY, 3RD, AND TWO SUCCEEDING DAYS.

———

ALSO,

AN APPENDIX,

CONTAINING

A MOTION FOR NEW TRIAL, &c.

AND ALSO

THE DOCUMENTS AS PROVED BEFORE THE COURT ON THE
PART OF THE PROSECUTION, &c. &c.

═══════

DUBLIN:

FOR JOHN CUMMING. No. 16, LOWER ORMOND-QUAY:
AND JOHN RIDGEWAY, PICCADILLY, LONDON,

1825.

16 Title page from trial pamphlet showing the names of those accused
of conspiracy against the Marquis of Westmeath in 1825.

When the trial opened in Dublin, six defendants stood in the dock. Emily's lawyer, Bernard Maguire, was charged with conspiracy along with John Monaghan, Edward Bennett, William McKenzie, Patrick Farley and Anne Connell. They were all charged with conspiring to procure false evidence of adultery against the marquis, evidence that had been deposed by them in the suit taken in the ecclesiastical court in London by the marchioness against her husband.

The case was heard before Justice Moore and Justice Vandeleur and a jury of twelve. Nine lawyers represented the defendants, and Daniel O'Connell was one of the five prosecuting lawyers. Obviously, O'Connell had no qualms about representing the marquis, who was well known for his anti-Catholic views and was an implacable opponent of Catholic Emancipation.[19]

Interestingly, Mr Crampton, who opened the case for the prosecution, went out of his way at the very beginning to clear the marchioness of any wrongdoing.

> Let me not, my Lords and Gentlemen, be here understood to state, that the noble Lady Westmeath is chargeable with the base and odious practices which I impute to the prisoners at the bar … No, I acquit her Ladyship of all the guilty part of this combination. She has been the dupe and the instrument, not the accomplice, of the Traversers.[20]

While it is not certain, George may have astutely concluded that to include his wife in the prosecution or to imply guilt on her part might have had the effect of putting at risk a successful prosecution by a jury who would be reluctant to convict someone of her standing. Crampton had no hesitation, however, in vilifying the six defendants. He described Bernard Maguire as a very active and zealous solicitor, the sub-sheriff of the county of Westmeath and the 'avowed enemy of the noble prosecutor'. John Monaghan was described in the indictment as a farmer but in reality the active agent of Maguire and 'the soul and centre of the conspiracy'. He described Bennett, Farley and McKenzie as mere mercenaries, dismissed servants of Lord Westmeath who had been bought.

Crampton reserved his most vitriolic comments for the only female defendant, Anne Connell.

19 Stone, *Broken lives*, p. 296.
20 *Trial*, p. 3.

> The last and lowest of the tribe is Anne Connell, spinster, as she is described in the indictment. No words of mine can paint the infamy of this woman's character. She will be proved before you to be a prostitute of the most degraded class, and of the most abandoned character, and to have been, to the knowledge of the other Traversers, utterly unworthy of belief.[21]

Having identified the defendants, Crampton went on to give the background to the case, outlining the breakdown of the marriage and the reasons for it. His description was somewhat one-sided. Alluding to the fact that Emily had found Clonyn Castle a bit of a backwater when compared to her previous residence at the Court of St James, he further blamed her background by sarcastically remarking that:

> Gentlemen, Lord Westmeath is a man of easy and forgiving temper; but he had a foolish notion that he should be master in his own house. The Marchioness however, Gentlemen, had her own notion on this interesting subject; she is a genuine descendant of the great Cecil, the minister and favourite of the glorious virgin Queen, and inherited from her progenitor a natural propensity to petticoat government.[22]

The other problem with the marriage he identified as Emily's jealousy, aroused in particular by false stories about her husband's 'ante-nuptial gallantries'. He noted that Emily's family were not supportive of her position and in fact were taking the side of her husband. He suggested that she had fallen into the hands of poor advisers who encouraged her to take the various legal actions regarding custody of her daughter and now that of a cruelty and adultery suit in the ecclesiastical courts. Because her advisers were fearful of losing the cruelty suit they had decided to pursue a different course. 'Who was the protecting genius that intervened?,' Crampton asked the court.

> You must anticipate that I mean Mr Bernard Maguire. Mr Maguire is accordingly invoked; his genius soon suggested a case. Her Ladyship's weak side he knew was jealousy. The Marquis had had two children by a woman of the name of —. This, her ladyship had been acquainted with before her marriage. It was easy to persuade her *now* that the Marquis's gallantries had continued after she had become his wife.[23]

---

21 Ibid., p. 4.   22 Ibid., p. 6.   23 Ibid., p. 8.

Crampton charged that a plan was devised, money was distributed among the defendants and a case was concocted. The case of adultery would be produced by Emily's Irish agent and supported by Irish witnesses and then sworn before a credulous English judge. The bones of the case were as follows. Anne Connell, one of the defendants, a common prostitute, was prevailed upon to claim that she often had sexual relations with the marquis. These events had occurred supposedly in his house, under the trees at Clonyn, and in the Leinster Hotel in Dublin. In 1815 the marquis was purported to have purchased her favours by giving her a deed promising her £15 a year for life, and £10 for every child she produced for him. She had borne him two children, a boy and a girl. This story was corroborated in some parts by oaths sworn by Monaghan, Farley and Bennett.

Having outlined the case, Crampton proceeded to pour scorn on it, claiming it was a complete fabrication. Anne Connell, he claimed, had made her deposition before the ecclesiastical court in London but had failed to corroborate her own evidence. She had said that she was in the habit of letting herself into the house at Clonyn in the evening, where she generally took tea with the marquis and slept with him. She was, however, utterly unable to describe the room in which she slept or to describe any part of the house. To explain this peculiarity she claimed that the marquis gave her drink and:

> so happily adjusted the dose, that she was just sober enough to find her way home, but too drunk to have remarked or known the way.[24]

When questioned in the ecclesiastical court about the hotel in Dublin she had been equally unclear. She found herself in the marquis's bedroom there, but how she got in or where it was situated, she did not know. Crampton described the story about the children as 'a romance, a monstrous and incredible lie'. He promised that the marquis himself would take the stand to deny ever meeting Anne Connell. Other witnesses would be produced to support the charge of conspiracy. Crampton was at pains to point out that the fact that Maguire was Emily's solicitor did not exonerate him from conspiracy. He had been informed that the charges were false yet had failed to abandon them, so he also was guilty of conspiracy. Crampton concluded by giving the legal definition of conspiracy, as established by the lord chief justice of Ireland in the case of *The King* versus *Forbes*:

24 Ibid., p. 9.

> His Lordship there describes a conspiracy to be where two or more
> persons confederate together for the effecting of an illegal purpose, or
> to effect a legal purpose by the use of unlawful means, although such
> purpose should not be effected. The confederacy alone, though the
> object be not effected, constitutes the crime.[25]

An hour-and-a-half was then spent on legal argument before the first
witness for the prosecution was called. The prosecution, it was claimed by
the defence, should have produced the evidence from the ecclesiastical court
in London but had failed to do so. The judges agreed to take this into
account and the trial then resumed.

Michael Corcoran was the first defendant to take the stand. He began by
stating that he knew all the other defendants with the exception of Bennett.
He had known Anne Connell from infancy. On 22 August 1822 he
described how he had been approached by John Monaghan, one of the
defendants, who enquired of him where Connell lived. Monaghan told him
that he was looking for a document given to her by the Marquis of
Westmeath, settling £15 for life on her. He wanted it for the marchioness
who needed the document in order for her to get a divorce.

Corcoran went to see Connell and asked her had she such a document?
She replied that she had but went on to lead him a merry dance as to its
whereabouts for over a week, giving him a different answer each time.
When she stated that she had given it to Smith, the Quaker, in Queen Street
for £7. 10s. 0d., Bernard Maguire, the solicitor, produced £8 to cover the
cost of reclaiming it. But this story didn't hold up. Connell then said her
brother had the document. All this time, Corcoran claimed, Monaghan was
supporting Connell with money.

By early October, Corcoran said that Monaghan was despairing of ever
finding the document and instead set out to find the two children. Anne
Connell claimed that they were staying at the house of a Mrs Mulvany, but
when Corcoran had accompanied her there, Connell had refused to go into
the house. A further attempt to get Connell to say where the children were
had also ended in failure. She told them to go to the devil despite being fed
with broth, meat, spirits and porter. He reported back to Monaghan and said
to him that in his opinion there were no children. Monaghan replied:

25 Ibid., p. 12.

> Let her go to the devil, I can prove everything myself … I saw Lord
> Westmeath with her in Clonyn Wood, committing adultery with her
> … I was going home one morning before day, and Lord Westmeath
> was out duck shooting, and Connell was with him in the wood.[26]

Under cross-examination by the defence, Corcoran admitted that he had
lived in Lord Westmeath's dairy the previous November and that when he
went to London the marquis paid him 17s. 6d. per week for his support. He
had only agreed to help Monaghan when he was promised £50. He did not
realise how important the document was until late August. He admitted to
being a conspirator in the beginning but he had turned against the others in
October, only waiting first to be paid by Monaghan.

The next witness for the prosecution was Margaret Shields. Anne
Connell had told her that she had two children by the marquis and assured
her that if she was prepared to swear that she had seen the children in the
lying-in-hospital she would never see a poor day again. Maguire, the
solicitor, later sent for her and asked if she would go to London and make
that declaration for the marchioness. When she declined to do so, he told
her that she had to go and he gave her a sovereign and a pound note to buy
clothes. Shields told the court that she was taken to London and had
stayed there for about eight days. While there, Anne Connell asked her to
corroborate her story:

> She wanted me to say that I had lived as a servant at the Leinster Hotel,
> and admitted her (Connell) into the house at unseasonable hours of the
> night; and that on one occasion when I handed a glass of wine to Lord
> Westmeath in his bedchamber, I saw Anne Connell with him.[27]

Margaret Shields went on to tell the court that Monaghan, who had
accompanied her to London, had told her she was to go to St James's Palace
to tell this story to the marchioness.[28] Shields said she would say it but
would not swear to it and did not take an oath, despite being promised that
if she remained in London she would be given a guinea a week. She was
very emphatic about not being willing to swear such an oath, declaring that
she could not go into court before the Lord and swear to what she knew to
be false.[29]

---

26 Ibid.   27 Ibid., p. 18.
28 Stone, *Broken lives*, pp. 333–4.   29 *Trial*, p. 19.

Under cross-examination by the defence, Margaret Shields said that Monaghan had taken her to St James's Palace where she met the marchioness, who shook hands with her and told her that she had a great many friends coming from Ireland whom she did not know. She had told Lady Westmeath and Monaghan that she knew nothing and wanted to go home. They thought she was afraid of Lord Westmeath and tried to reassure her but the reason she was afraid was that she knew that what they wanted her to say was wrong. She returned to Ireland and since then had lived in Roscommon at Lord Westmeath's lodge. After Shields finished giving evidence her sister, Sarah Taylor, was called to the stand and confirmed all that she had said.[30]

The next witness for the prosecution was Henry William Spinks. A dyer by trade, his association with the case came about in an unusual manner. His evidence to the court and his relationship with one of the defendants, Patrick Farley, is recorded in the trial transcript:

> Knows Patrick Farley. Became acquainted with him at Holyhead. Slept with him there. Farley came *promiscuously* to lodge in witness's room. He came there on the 1st August. Witness had been there since the 12th of June. He slept with witness from the 1st August 1824 to the 18th. Conversed with him about Lord and Lady Westmeath. After they became acquainted, in consequence of sleeping together.[31]

Spinks went on to tell the court that Farley had filled him in on the details of the case and that the object was to help Lady Westmeath by proving adultery against her husband. He told him that to support the case Monaghan had brought over to London a 'dreadful prostitute' named Nance Connell. Farley had given Spinks three reasons why he had agreed to give evidence against Lord Westmeath. Firstly, Lord Westmeath had sacked him after twelve years in his service. Secondly, he was being well paid for what he was doing. The final reason caused great hilarity in the court. Farley, Spinks alleged, claimed he was also doing it because 'his Lordship's forefathers destroyed the monastery at Fowre at the time of the Reformation.'[32]

Spinks said that he had asked Farley how much he was getting, and Farley had replied that he was owed seventy pounds. When questioned as to why Farley would volunteer all this information, Spinks's reply caused much

30 Ibid., pp. 17–24.   31 Ibid., p. 24.   32 Ibid., p. 25.

laughter when he said that he believed it was because they had slept together. When asked to identify some letters to Lady Westmeath, Spinks confirmed that they were in Farley's handwriting; he had seen him write several letters in their lodgings.

Spinks was then cross-examined by Mr Doherty, acting for the defendants, Farley and Bennett. His approach was rather sarcastic.

> Mr Spinks, you are an experimental *liar*, I believe? [Loud laughter]. Oh, I beg your pardon, I meant dyer; you are an experimental dyer? *A.* I am. *Q.* And you went to Holyhead to practise dying? *A.* I went on the invitation of Mr. Moran. *Q.* You made but little proficiency; Holyhead is not a good place for dying then? *A.* No; it is too small. *Q.* Then you did not dye much before you became acquainted with Farley; but since you became acquainted you have dyed to some purpose? *A.* I don't follow dying now. *Q.* No; you follow Farley, I believe? [Laughter].[33]

Spinks told Doherty that he had found a copy of one of Farley's letters in their lodgings and kept it. Later in Delvin, he had met Corcoran and told him he had slept with Farley and that Farley had written a great deal. He had seen some of these letters and he did not think them proper. The defence lawyer continued to try and undermine Spinks's evidence about the letters and finally recommended him to return to dying, as his new trade as a handwriting expert 'will never do for you!'[34]

A number of other witnesses for the prosecution were then called, including George Elvidge, proprietor of the Leinster Hotel, who declared that he had never seen Anne Connell there. It would simply not have been possible that any woman would have gained access to Lord Westmeath there without his knowledge.[35]

At this point in the trial, the marquis took the stand and was questioned by Daniel O'Connell for the prosecution. Apologising for having to put the question, he asked the marquis had he ever had sexual relations with Anne Connell? He replied that he had never seen her before and, therefore, could not possibly have done so. He had never given her a document promising her £15. He had never admitted her to his bedchamber, in the Leinster Hotel or anywhere else. He had never seen her in his bedroom and no one else had either. He had never made her drunk and let her out of his house secretly.

---

33 Ibid., p. 26.   34 Ibid., pp. 24–7.   35 Ibid., pp. 28–32.

Cross-examined by Mr Wallace for the defence, the marquis said he had heard only lately that Connell had lived in a miserable cabin on part of his Roscommon estates. Wallace then began a series of searching questions about various women. Had he known a Jane Smith? The marquis replied that he knew a girl by that name; she was his daughter's maid in London. Wallace then asked the marquis if he knew a woman by the name of Irwin living in Leeson Street? The marquis stated that he had never known a woman of that name living there or any lane off it. He had known a woman named Irwin before his marriage and she had borne him two children, and added: 'I do not choose to remain under insinuations: since you ask me a question, you shall have an answer.'[36]

At this point Judge Moore intervened and objected to the type of questioning. Wallace continued his cross-examination by asking about his relationship with the witnesses, Corcoran and Shields. He then asked the marquis if it were true that he harboured ill-will towards Bernard Maguire as he had been the cause of a judgment for £6,000 in favour of Lady Westmeath? The marquis agreed that he did not like Maguire as he felt he had been trying to ruin him financially. In addition, he had been heavily involved in the conspiracy against him now before the court. Wallace concluded by asking how had Maguire's letters to Corcoran and Monaghan's to Maguire, all now produced in court, come into his possession? The marquis replied that they had been sent to him anonymously.[37]

When the case resumed the following day, a great deal of time was taken up by the reading of the depositions made by Connell, Farley and Monaghan in the ecclesiastical court in London. In doing so, the prosecution was trying to highlight contradictions in Connell's evidence. When the prosecution case closed, Mr Wallace made an application for dismissal on behalf of his client, Bernard Maguire, as there was little or no evidence against him. With the agreement of the judge, the jurors and the prosecution, Maguire was dismissed.

The case was then opened for the defence by Mr Gould, who stated that the charge against his client, Monaghan, was a 'concatenation of horrid perjury and wickedness'. He was at pains to emphasise that in law there was no conspiracy if the parties to it do not realise that the evidence is fabricated. He made much of the fact that while one of the marquis's forefathers had allegedly destroyed the abbey at Fowre, he had still hired Daniel O'Connell as one of his counsel, therefore implying that the

36 Ibid., p. 35.   37 Ibid., pp. 33–8.

marquis, who was well known for his anti-Catholic views, could put them aside when it was in his own interests.

The marchioness, he said, had left her husband and taken an action in the ecclesiastical court. Upon hearing rumours of her husband's infidelity she had, quite rightly, approached Monaghan to look into the matter. Monaghan, in turn, had approached Corcoran to assist him. Corcoran's evidence was simply untrustworthy; he had broken off because he got no money. Monaghan then had approached the marquis, whose hatred of Maguire had spawned the prosecution. Monaghan was merely guilty of putting too much faith in the evidence of such ruffians as Connell, Shields and Corcoran. It was they who were the true conspirators, not Monaghan.[38]

Another defence lawyer, Mr North, then spoke on behalf of his client, William McKenzie. He explained that the defendant had acted as steward and gardener for the marquis. He had married Lady Westmeath's maid and since his promotion to a situation in the ordnance, his duties required him to reside at Feversham in Kent. He was not in Ireland, therefore, when all the events had allegedly taken place. The witnesses from Ireland were brought to his house, where it was his duty to keep them from being tampered with. He was being made out to be an odious person simply for doing a duty for Lady Westmeath, who trusted him.

Mr Doherty, speaking for Farley and Bennett, said they were humble human beings not capable of the charges against them. The case was not the King versus the Traversers but rather the Marquis of Westmeath versus the Marchioness of Westmeath.[39] Defence lawyer, Mr Jackson, told the court on behalf of his client, Connell, that she had not been charged with perjury, merely conspiracy. If the other defendants were found not guilty then his client could not be found guilty either. None of the witnesses had proved anything against her. He suggested that the marquis had given evidence that could not be trusted as he was in such an agitated state and might easily have mistaken the identity of Anne Connell.

After a number of witnesses had been called for the defence, the Marchioness of Westmeath took the stand and was questioned by Gould for the defence. She stated that she had lived for some time at Clonyn Castle and that she knew Monaghan, although not well. She was present at the meeting in London between her solicitor, Mr Iggolden, and the witness, Margaret Shields. She did not assist Shields with her answers except when

38 Ibid., pp. 38–44.   39 Ibid., p. 46.

she varied on dates. She said she knew Farley very well. He had been a ploughman but had been promoted to steward since she left Lord Westmeath. She had received a letter from him seeking his expenses and she had sent £10 to Bernard Maguire, her Irish solicitor, for him. She also knew Bennett, who was a person of good character. In reply to questioning from Mr North, she stated that she knew McKenzie well and that the witnesses who attended the ecclesiastical court had been sent to his house in Kent under an arrangement made by her solicitors. In conclusion, the marchioness confirmed that she had met Anne Connell in London and had mentioned her name to Maguire when he began seeking evidence to support her case.[40]

Daniel O'Connell was chosen to sum up the case on behalf of all the prosecution team. It was a performance combining humour with a devastating dissection of the defence case, a real tour de force. He began by alluding to the fact that the court luckily would not have to listen to all the prosecution team. On the downside, however, they would have to listen to him. He was not joking. When he eventually finished, the trial transcript records that he had spoken for two-and-a-half hours and 'at one time became so exhausted as to be obliged to retire for a few moments'.[41] In hiring him, the marquis certainly got his money's worth.

Having taken humorous pot-shots at the defence team, he then commended the jury for acquitting Maguire, but went on to assure them that he would prove beyond doubt the guilt of the other defendants. He intended to show them that the whole story of an affair between the marquis and Connell, and the existence of children, was not only false but an impossibility. If the whole business was concocted by Connell alone, then there was no conspiracy. If, however, she was aided by others who knew the matter to be false that certainly was conspiracy.

He was scathing about Anne Connell. She had children by three or four men and swore that her marriage to a man called Keogh was not legal. He further went on:

> She is of that class of creatures, Gentlemen, who are degraded in the scale of humanity; who, while they excite our pity, at the same time arouse our abhorrence; who are outcasts from society; who make crime their sport, and perjury their pastime; and are, therefore, the more proper to be made the instrument of nefarious artifices.[42]

40 Ibid., pp. 50–1.   41 Ibid., p. 65.   42 Ibid., p.54.

O'Connell noted that in her deposition to the ecclesiastical court in London, Anne Connell had stated that, seven years before, she had been before Lord Westmeath, in his capacity as a magistrate, to swear that a certain man was the father of one of her children. Yet, in her cross-examination in the ecclesiastical court she had sworn that this event had occurred twelve years before. 'But then perhaps the jury would be so accommodating as to believe she carried the child for five years!' Turning to the supposed affair with the marquis he outlined the evidence she had given.

The whole story was simply not to be believed, O'Connell contended. The same was true of the document promising her £15 a year for her life and £8 for every child she bore the marquis. 'The child bounty accounted for Mr Jackson's zeal on behalf of his client. He, I suppose, was to have this amiable progeny as pupils![43] Connell had claimed that she had a child, now four-and-a-half years old. Where was the child? Could there be any stronger evidence', he argued, 'than the production of the child if it ever existed?'

He went on to refer to Connell's sworn evidence that she had slept with the marquis on the night his little son, Lord Delvin, had died. 'This foul accusation, which had even penetrated the court in London, could not have come from her alone.' O'Connell stressed that he was not departing from his instructions from the marquis that he not malign the marchioness. 'She was not capable of such conduct, she was merely the victim of a foul conspiracy.'

Referring to Jackson's claim on behalf of Connell that the marquis was agitated in his testimony and that it therefore could not be depended upon, he had this to say:

> … [was he] so broken down, that he does not know whether he is swearing truly or falsely; in short, that he might have had these two children by Anne Connell while he was asleep? [Laughter] That is what you are required to believe, Gentlemen.[44]

He argued that Connell had sworn so stupidly in her deposition in London that she could not possibly have done so without the collaboration of others. Monaghan had claimed in his deposition that he had seen the marquis with her in Clonyn wood, and Connell had confirmed that she was that woman. Monaghan may at first have been convinced by Connell, but in his letter of 22 September he referred to her as a 'notorious liar' who had

---

43 Jackson, defence lawyer, was also secretary to the Kildare Place Society.
44 *Trial*, p. 56.

led him on a merry dance to find the children. Even though he called her a liar, he still did not abandon the search, and was prepared to go to London to confirm statements under oath that he knew to be false.

Turning to the defendant, William McKenzie, and to his role in the sheltering of the witnesses, O'Connell satirised the military nature of the position he held at the ordnance in Feversham.

> We have had a letter of McKenzie's, Gentlemen, stating that the persons in his care are *comfortable and happy*, and that they never go out but when he is with them. Here is honest McKenzie, faithful as we are told to his patroness, converting the Ordnance store-house at Feversham in Kent, into a lock-up shop for this vile harlot and the crew of infamy in her train; drilling them for the approaching campaign in London.[45]

Why, he argued, did they need the surveillance of McKenzie if they were genuine witnesses?

Lest the jury find fault with the marquis for producing as evidence private letters which were the property of others, O'Connell stated that given the nature of the charges levelled against him he was entitled to do so. The letters particularly identified Farley as a conspirator. By his own hand, he had convicted himself of working for hire and promising money to others if they joined the cause. Bennett, on the other hand, should be acquitted as the evidence against him was not compelling. O'Connell concluded his address by urging the jury to convict the 'prostitute Connell' and the other participants. His client, the noble marquis, looked to them to vindicate his reputation. As he sat down he was lauded by all present with an immense burst of applause.[46]

It was left to Judge Moore to sum up the case for the jury. The charge was that the defendants had conspired to accuse the marquis of adultery and of having children with Anne Connell. A conspiracy was normally only proved by implication and inference arising from the evidence. Against Bennett there was really no evidence. It was up to the jury to find whether McKenzie was a conspirator. The fact of sheltering witnesses was not necessarily a crime, he pointed out.

The whole inquiry had begun with Monaghan. If he had persisted despite being aware that the evidence was false, then he was worthy of

45 Ibid., p. 60.
46 Ibid., pp. 51–65.

conviction. Turning to Farley, he said the jury could only find him guilty if they thought he had involved himself in the conspiracy. He reminded the jury that the nub of the whole case was whether the defendants had assembled false evidence of adultery deliberately or whether they were merely pursuing fair testimony for the ecclesiastical suit. If it was the former, they should convict them, if the latter they should be acquitted.[47]

The case had taken two-and-a-half days to try and was widely reported in the newspapers.[48] After only one hour's deliberation the jury delivered their verdict. Monaghan, Connell and Farley were convicted, McKenzie and Bennett were acquitted.[49] A subsequent appeal was rejected.[50] John Monaghan was fined £20 and imprisoned in Newgate for eighteen months. Anne Connell and Patrick Farley were fined one mark each and also imprisoned for eighteen months.[51]

* * *

George, no doubt, was well pleased with the verdict although he must have hoped for a better result against his wife's solicitor, Bernard Maguire. He arranged for the transcript of the trial to be published in full. However, apart from the Dublin trial, there were many more trials and appeals to follow in other courts. Because of its complexity, the suit in the ecclesiastical court dragged on for years. In 1826 the court found for George, dismissing the evidence relating to the alleged adultery, no doubt drawing on the result of the Dublin case. George had been guilty of acts of cruelty but not after the reconciliation in 1817 and so Emily was ordered to return home.[52] Emily appealed to the court of arches and the case was heard there in 1827. Here, the judge reached a different conclusion. He agreed that the adultery charges should be dismissed. The renewal of cohabitation and sexual relations after 1817 were also a bar to separation, but leaning on the cohabitation after 1818, he found that Emily had a reasonable case to fear personal violence and granted her a sentence of separation. It was a spectacular victory for Emily. George appealed to the court of delegates, but in 1829 it upheld the decision by a majority of four to three and awarded her £700 a year alimony and costs of £1,600.[53] George did not give up,

47 Ibid., pp. 65–77.   48 *The Times, Freeman's Journal*, 4, 5, 6 January 1825.
49 *Trial*, p. 77.   50 Ibid., pp. 78–80.   51 Ibid., pp. 81–5.
52 Stone, *Broken lives*, pp. 327–8.
53 The court of arches was the court of appeal for cases appealed out of the ecclesiastical court. The court of delegates was the final court of appeal in ecclesiastical matters.

17 Portrait of Lady Emily Cecil, Marchioness of Westmeath, *circa* 1850.
Courtesy Marquis of Salisbury

however, and won a victory in 1831 when the court of chancery set aside
the separation agreements of 1817 and 1818, thus depriving Emily of her
maintenance of £1,300 for life.[54]

After the trial in Dublin, Emily did not forget her Irish witnesses, and
using her connections with the Duke of Wellington, she saw to it that they
were looked after. At the end of his prison term in Dublin, John Monaghan
persuaded the duke to give him two places in the ordnance office. A year
later, William McKenzie got similar treatment, he already having held such
a position at Feversham at an annual salary of £80 a year. Bernard Maguire
was also rewarded by the duke, being appointed a government solicitor.
Patrick Farley, according to George, was given the means to set up a shop in
Dublin. There is no indication of what became of Anne Connell.[55]

54 Stone, *Broken lives*, pp. 328–32; Westmeath, *Reply to the narrative,* pp. 57–86.
55 Westmeath, *Reply to the narrative,* p. 70; Westmeath, *A sketch of Lord Westmeath's case*
    (Dublin, 1828), p. 21; Stone, *Broken lives*, pp. 326–7.

Emily was very short of money throughout the 1820s. She was successful in exploiting her connections with her childhood friend and brother-in-law, the Duke of Wellington and also the royal family.[56] She was granted a rent-free apartment by King William IV in St James's Palace and was appointed extra Lady of the Bedchamber to the Queen in 1830, a position that carried a salary of £275 a year. Despite a lot of opposition from the lord lieutenant, Wellington arranged in 1829 that she be granted a pension of £385 on the Irish list. The benefit of this was reduced somewhat when George success-fully sued to have the £700 alimony reduced to £315 a year on the strength of her new pension. Still, by the 1840s her income came to some £1,500 a year and she acquired her own house in Piccadilly. But she was a deeply embittered woman and ill-health forced her to spend a lot of time abroad. She was excluded from all contact with her daughter Rosa until she came of age and, even after this, their relationship remained estranged and difficult.[57]

Many years later, when parliament debated a new divorce bill in the 1850s, she took her revenge on all her enemies by publishing, at her own expense, a pamphlet outlining her case.[58] George was no shirker himself when it came to defending his position. He had already published the court transcript back in 1825, and in 1828 published a pamphlet giving his side of the story, one that was not very flattering to the Duke of Wellington.[59] Now, in 1857, he replied in kind to Emily with his own pamphlet finishing it, however, with the remark:

> Considering the very few years which are left to either of us, it is time that malice and ill will should be at an end, and that unhappy differences and discords should not be revived and aggravated by such a proceeding as the composition and publication of the Narrative exhibits.[60]

George had some better fortune in affairs other than those of the heart. He was created first Marquis of Westmeath in 1822. In 1830 he was also elected a representative peer of Ireland in the House of Lords, where he was noted for his anti-Catholic views. He kept a French mistress whom he called Lady Delvin and he settled £10,000 on their three children. All of them pre-deceased him, however. Right up to Emily's death, which occurred in early 1858, he tried to free himself from her. He supported several measures

56 Emily's sister, Georgiana, was married to the Duke's brother, Henry Wellesley, Lord Cowley.
57 Stone, *Broken lives,* pp. 333–42.
58 Westmeath, *A narrative of the case.*
59 Westmeath, *Sketch of Lord Westmeath's case.*
60 Westmeath, *Reply to the narrative,* p. 97.

introduced into the House of Lords to make divorce easier, including one allowing remarriage after twenty years' separation. All of them failed. Within four weeks of Emily's death he remarried but divorced his new wife four years later in the newly-established matrimonial causes court. Undeterred, he married yet again in 1864, a marriage which lasted until he died in 1871 at the age of eighty-six. Having no male heir, the title of marquis lapsed and the earldom of Westmeath went to a cousin. His daughter Rosa inherited all his estates, made possible, ironically, considering their estrangement, by Emily's insistence so many years before.[61]

61 Stone, *Broken lives,* pp. 342–3.

The Paul Singer Affair

Drama in Shanahan's Stamp Auctions, Dún Laoghaire

AUSTIN STEWART

Paul Singer was born on the 31 July 1911 in Bratislava, the capital of present-day Slovakia, and in 1925 his family moved to Austria. Singer attended school in Vienna and later the University of Lausanne in Switzerland, where he obtained a doctorate in political and social science. In 1930 the family, being Jewish and fearful of anti-semitic feeling, moved to London while Singer himself studied international law in Paris. Singer's father set up a finance company in London and shortly afterwards Singer joined the firm.[1] Three years later in 1953 the firm dramatically collapsed and went into liquidation with assets of £12,326, and owing a sum of £58,150 – the equivalent of approximately €1.5 million by the twenty-first century – to 345 creditors.[2]

Singer couldn't wait to escape London. In January 1954 he flew into Dublin to explore the possibility of re-establishing himself in business. He had an idea that he might turn a life-long amateur interest in philately into a business concern. He succeeded, at least in the short term. In an extraordinary turn-around of financial fortune he made millions of pounds in the auctioning of stamps, out of a small father-and-son auctioneering firm, called Shanahan's, in Dún Laoghaire, county Dublin. Five years later, the auction business was in ruins amid accusations of fraud and fraudulent conversion. The matter went to court over a three-year period, made Irish legal history, and raised questions about the integrity of the Irish

1 Brian Lawlor (ed.), *Encyclopaedia of Ireland* (Dublin, 2003), p. 992.
2 House of Commons research paper 02/44, 11 July 2002, 'Inflation: the value of the pound 1750–2001' (www.parliament.uk). The arrival of the Irish punt in 1979 broke the link with sterling.

government of the day. When finally resolved, thousands of Irish people who had invested in the stamp auctions had lost millions of pounds of hard-earned cash and life-savings, and the affair became the *cause célèbre* of the decade.

On a February morning in 1954, Singer arrived out of the blue at Shanahan's auction rooms at 38 Corrig Avenue, Dún Laoghaire, for the first time. Jerome Shanahan, an established auctioneer, was a man in his sixties. He ran the auction rooms with the help of his son, Desmond, a noted athlete and sportsman. The premises are long gone and a modern garda station and district court occupy the area. As Shanahan's Stamp Auctions went from strength to strength, the company in 1958 moved to the main street in Dún Laoghaire to a building at 29 George's Street Upper.[3]

Before Singer arrived Shanahan's auction business was a modest affair. On Singer's first visit there he bought an antique item in the auction rooms and returned the following day to pay. It was then he suggested to Jerome Shanahan that together they set up a stamp auction business.[4] Singer argued that it would be the first such auction initiative in Ireland and that the venture had enormous potential. The Kerryman, Jerome Shanahan, with the property business in the doldrums, saw the possibilities of new income, and a deal was struck between the Shanahans and Paul Singer. They formed a company with a capital sum of £200. Singer put up £100, the Shanahans matched it and Shanahan's Stamp Auctions Ltd came into existence. During the next five years the business became a £5 million enterprise. By 1959 it enjoyed the reputation of being the largest stamp auction in the world.

Years later, Desmond Shanahan recalled how plausible and persuasive Singer was on that first contact. He appeared a master of rhetoric, was a larger-than-life person and had a terrific personality. He was a huge man, almost twenty stone in weight, and his dominant physical characteristic was a nervous tic in his face. When Diana Shanahan, Desmond's wife, met him for the first time she thought he was winking at her.[5] As the stamp auctions prospered, Singer kept all the cogs of the business in the palm of his hand. He made all the decisions and it was really a one-man show. He had a huge ego and loved being referred to as 'the brains' behind the company. In business he was ruthlessly single-minded. His great aim in life was to create a world-wide market for stamps in Dublin.

3   *Thoms Directory*, 1958.
4   *Irish Independent*, 25 August 1959.
5   *Paul Singer, the stamp of scandal*, 3 October 1996, RTÉ library and archive.

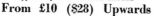

PROFIT FROM STAMPS

Without Risk

Stamps mean different things to different people. What can they mean to you ? If your problem is a small Capital which you want to invest with absolute security, but with an unusually large return, then Stamps are the solution to your problem.

We give you the opportunity to invest small amounts

From £10 ($28) Upwards

and participate (without overhead expenses) in the large profits attended to Stamp trading and that with our absolute guarantee for the safety of your Capital.

Your money will be outstanding for a period of four months. During this period we shall buy, in your name in Britain and on the Continent, Stamps which *we know* will fetch higher prices in our own Auctions here. The Stamps would be invoiced to you direct and treated by us as your property.

These Stamps will then be entered in our next available Auction. You will be advised of your lot numbers and after the Sale we publish the results in our next Catalogue.

Four months after receipt of your Investment we will post you our cheque for your Capital and Profits.

And remember your Capital is *absolutely guaranteed* by us and will be returned to you intact, whatever else happens.

This proposition has been tried out many times and our friends have *always* made a profit. This varied between 25% and 250% per annum of the Capital invested. Please turn over for further details.

The only charge to you is our Standard rate of selling commission (minimum 10%). We don't make any charge at all for buying the Stamps for you.

If you are interested, fill in the coupon below and enclose your cheque.

Yours sincerely,

SHANAHAN'S STAMP AUCTIONS, LTD.

39 Upr. Gt. George's Street, Dun Laoghaire.
Telephone 86933.   (Please turn over)

To SHANAHAN'S STAMP AUCTIONS, LTD.   Date..

    39 Upr. Gt. George's Street,

      Dun Laoghaire, Dublin.

Please find enclosed herewith my remittance for .... This amount to be used to purchase Stamps for me. These Stamps to be suitably lotted and entered into your next available Sale. The total proceeds of the Sale of these lots (less your standard commission [minimum 10%]) to be remitted to me not later than 4 months from to-day. But should the net proceeds be less than my investment then you will make good any shortage.

Kindly confirm acceptance by return.

Yours faithfully,

Nọ 279469

NAME (in block letters)...

ADDRESS..... ....

18 Advertising leaflet, Shanahan's Stamp Auctions, Dún Laoghaire.
Source: Shanahan's promotional bulletin

The stamp auctions grew bigger and better, and to attract buyers and collectors to Dublin, Singer organised lavish parties at his home, Cairn Hill, in Foxrock. These parties were an attempt to generate publicity and to provide generous copy to the society columns of newspapers and magazines, both at home and abroad.[6] The fifth and final party,[7] to celebrate the fifth anniversary of Shanahan's Stamp Auctions, came the night after the firm was burgled. It was a wild night of champagne and caviar. Singer wanted to believe that, despite the audacious burglary the previous evening, the company was as strong as ever. By all accounts, he lost the run of himself on the night and he 'drank champagne from a slipper which he wrenched from some woman's foot. He got up on the band stage and made a fighting speech, filled with bombast and liquor, in which his general theme was that despite the robbery "we'll carry on". The staff dutifully cheered him.'[8]

Within days, Shanahan's auction rooms were the centre of a police investigation and word spread through the city and afar, that Shanahan's was at the hub of a financial scandal the like of which the country had never seen. It was to prove a nightmare for thousands of ordinary Irish people who invested in Shanahan's Stamp Auctions Ltd. They literally lost millions of pounds. In late May 1959, Paul Singer, his wife Irma, Jerome Shanahan and his son Desmond, all directors of the firm, were brought before the Irish courts accused of fraud and corruption.

In ways, Ireland in the late 1950s was experiencing the end of an era of innocence in matters of culture and economics.[9] The first decade after Independence in 1922 was a period of turmoil and disquiet. After the economic war in the 1930s and wartime rationing, many believed that there had to be better times ahead. It was not to be. Legions continued to emigrate as there were too few jobs for those who remained at home.[10] The 1950s saw a mass exodus from Ireland. The government of the day lurched from one economic dilemma to another in a series of balance-of-payments crises. The conventional economic response was to impose higher taxes and cut expenditure to reduce demand. It was late in the decade before T.K. Whitaker's five-year Programme for Economic Expansion enabled Ireland to emerge 'phoenix-like from the economic morass'.[11] In the words

---

6 *Irish Independent*, 28 August 1959.
7 *Irish Independent*, 9 May 1959.
8 Séamus Brady, *Doctor of millions* (Tralee, 1965), p. 32.
9 Brian Fallon, *An age of innocence: Irish culture 1930–60* (Dublin, 1998), p. 257.
10 Dermot Keogh, Finbar O'Shea, Carmel Quinlan (eds), *Ireland in the 1950s: the lost decade* (Cork, 2004), p.11.
11 Ibid., p. 80.

of Dr Whitaker, the Irish people had 'plumbed the depths of hopelessness'[12] and the difficulties experienced in those years 'left semi-permanent scars on the lives of individuals and on society itself'.[13] Plans were afoot in the country's Department of Finance to 'extricate the Republic from its current dire economic plight'.[14] It was the eve of an exciting 'New Departure'.[15] Shanahan's Stamp Auctions arrived on the cusp of this momentous change.

In retrospect, it is extraordinary that in times that were reportedly frugal, and the economy struggling, huge amounts of money were invested in Shanahan's Stamp Auctions in the late 1950s. Despite all the hardship in mid-century, Ireland in the late 1950s was still in a pre-PAYE era and had the lowest rate of personal taxation in Europe. Real product per capita grew at an unprecented 2.2 per cent per year and industrial output expanded at 2.8 per cent per annum. Farming output grew at 3.4 per cent per year.[16] If you were lucky enough to have a job there was money out there and a scheme like Shanahan's Stamp Auctions was a mecca for surplus funds.

Tax inspectors in the 1950s often reported how difficult it was to collect due taxes. In desperation it was not unknown for tax collectors to visit small employers on pay-days to collect something on account from employees.[17] In the late 1940s there was much talk of the revision of income tax law but it was not until February 1957 that a commission on income tax agreed the radical change to Pay As You Earn (PAYE), and on 6 October 1960, PAYE came into operation 'almost unheralded'. As a result, the number of taxpayers rose dramatically and tax cases to be processed trebled.[18] On the cusp of this tax reform, Shanahan's Stamp Auctions surely offered to investors, mainly from the self-employed ranks, a window of opportunity that might not be open to them should there be any further revision of income tax law.

To advertise and propagate their new stamp venture, Paul Singer and Jerome Shanahan published a simple magazine cumbersomely titled *Green Ireland's Stamp Lovers Edition Philately*. The first edition contained a letter from the then Lord Mayor of Dublin, Alfie Byrne, to Jerome Shanahan.[19] He warmly welcomed the new venture declaring a personal interest in

---

12 Ibid., p. 114.
13 Ibid., p. 106.
14 J.R. Hill, *A new history of Ireland* (Oxford, 2003), vol. 7, p. 693.
15 Tom Garvan, *Preventing the future* (Dublin, 2004), p. 92.
16 J.W. O'Hagan (ed.), *The economy of Ireland: policy and performance of a small European country* (Dublin, 1995), p. 34.
17 Publications/corppubs/1950 (www.revenue.ie), 7 November 2004.
18 Ibid.
19 *ISLE Philately and Shanahan's Auctions* (hereafter *ISLE*), NLI, Ir 3832 g1, issue 1.

philately and referring to his son, Thomas Byrne TD, as being instrumental in the issue of the internationally-famous marian year stamps in 1954.

In this first edition, philatelic terms were illustrated for those who knew nothing about stamps. The stamp auction programme for the rest of 1954 was revealed. The auctions were to be an all-Ireland affair held in both Dublin and Belfast. The magazine generated huge interest and gave a forum to philatelic interests throughout the country. The Dublin Stamp Society advertised for new members. The society claimed it had introduced philatelic films into Ireland for the first time. The Munster Philatelic Society likewise advertised and so too the Philatelic Society of Ireland (founded 1901). There was no doubt that the Shanahans, and Paul Singer, had discovered an unexploited and potentially lucrative market.

Within an amazing short period of time Shanahan's stamp auctions in Dún Laoghaire had acquired a world-wide reputation. A report of a stamp auction held on 7 August 1954 pointed up the international dimension where the outstanding feature of the afternoon was the large number of postal bids from as far away as Los Angeles, Athens, Copenhagen, Nice and Japan.[20]

The second edition of the magazine revealed the philosophy behind Shanahans' Stamp Auctions. It was to be a fun enterprise. The magazine reflected this philosophy and in presentation was 'light-hearted' and 'consumer friendly'. By that standard alone the magazine was an outstanding success. In the issues that followed, there were reputable articles by authoritative stamp experts. There were articles on 'Stamps as an investment'; 'On being a stamp dealer'; 'How to be president of a stamp society'; 'Where to sell your stamps'; 'A history of stamp auctions', and 'Don't marry a stamp collector, girls'. Women were targeted as potential stamp investors. There was a clever series by an Elsie Purse who wrote about 'A woman in stamp land', and by the end of 1956 the magazine marked the importance of the growing interest of the 'female of the species' in the buying and selling of stamps.

In April 1955 the Shanahan's magazine boasted that they had almost 20,000 customers in sixty-seven countries, most of them postal bidding for stamps at the Shanahan auctions. While postal bidding at auctions was not new, it was fundamental to the Shanahan success. Paul Singer himself, as the in-house authority on stamps, travelled all over the world seeking out and buying, on behalf of the investors, a myriad of stamp collections, and bringing them to Dún Laoghaire and Belfast where higher prices were

20 Ibid., p. 42.

guaranteed at the auctions. In the early days investors made around 25 per cent profit. Word soon spread, and the money poured in. The eighteenth edition of the magazine, in February 1956, confidently declared that *anyone could make a profit from stamps without financial risk.*

Singer had progressive ideas and saw the need to modernise the stamp auctions and move away from 'musty nineteenth-century sales methods to an up-to-date streamlined selling organisation'. One of the first things he did was to establish a mailing list of over 100,000 names of collectors and dealers and developed an 'after-sales service'. In particular, the company gave an absolute guarantee of satisfaction with any large or small collection of stamps.[21] If you didn't like the lot of stamps you bought, you gave it back.

Singer devised ingenious schemes to attract investors. He boasted that the company's 'resale and loan value scheme', was the 'greatest philatelic advance since the penny black'. In this scheme if the client resold his stamps at auction he was guaranteed, at the minimum, his original money outlay. Shanahan's also offered the client an immediate loan of up to 75 per cent of the purchase price of the stamps over a period of six months at a 1 per cent interest rate. Probably the company's most touted scheme was the 'double barrel plan'.[22] This scheme built on the belief that the value of stamps was always on the up and up. The client paid no money for six months, at the end of which he deducted the profit accrued over the period. So for example, given that the average rate of profit was about 15 per cent, if a client invested £100 pounds he only paid £85 six months later.

The operation of the stamp scheme was simplicity itself. Until the company crashed, all investors made money.[23] After a minimum wait of four months, investors could collect a dividend of up to 22 per cent. The company took 10 per cent commission and the rest of the dividend could be cashed or re-invested. The investors came from all over the country and the company employed local agents to collect funds. One agent in Tralee invested £730 for four local people. Commission for the agents was very good. Angela Shanahan was an agent in Cork for the company from March 1958 and conducted business under the name of the Cork Stamp Investment Club. She allegedly received commission of between £2,000 and £3,000.[24] The middle classes and the well-to-do were strongly represented. A doctor from Fitzwilliam Square told the court that he acted as an agent

21 *ISLE* November 1955–December 1957, NLI, Ir 383 S1.
22 *ISLE* January–April 1959, NLI, Ir 383 S 1, vol 4.
23 *Irish Independent*, 19 January 1960.
24 *Irish Independent*, 2 November 1960.

for the firm. He, himself, had invested £600 in 1958 and received a return of over £725 within the year. He cashed his cheque.[25] Other investors re-invested. William Park of Foxrock invested £2,000, received a return of £2,182 and duly re-invested the £2,000.[26] There were big and small investors. One cautious Garda invested £30 to receive a return of 10 per cent. A £100 stg investment was commonplace.[27]

On 3 May 1958, Shanahan's Stamps celebrated its fourth year in existence with a special dinner party.[28] There was a large birthday cake and on it was a map of Ireland in green with a harp. That day the firm had just broken a new record for a single day's sale, over £100,000.[29] The business had moved from 38 Corrig Avenue and now had a staff of fifty equipped with up-to-date heating, lighting and office facilities. At the dinner, Dr Singer paid tribute to Diana, wife of Desmond Shanahan, for her numeracy skills in dealing with almost 10,000 active accounts. This was an important tribute because at his later trial when Singer referred to her accounting abilities within the firm, many thought he was merely attempting to blacken her role in the firm's collapse.

In his concluding words at the dinner, Desmond Shanahan, a sporting enthusiast, referred to the staff as a football team which by doing the right thing in the right place had won 'the triple crown' of the stamp world for Ireland. Finally, Senator Fearon,[30] a distinguished member of Seanad Éireann and professor at Trinity College Dublin, responded on behalf of the guests present. He declared that the people of Dún Laoghaire owed many debts of gratitude to the Shanahan family and Dr Singer for providing much employment locally. They had put Dún Laoghaire on the world stamp map, and in the United States, Dún Laoghaire was now popularly known as 'the place where the stamps came from'. It was the biggest success story in Dublin for many years. Ironically, as the guests toasted, the night mail boat left the harbour town with yet more emigrants destined never to find work in Ireland.

One success led to another and in order that he could purchase stamps abroad at will, the Shanahans signed cheques at Singer's behest, and vast amounts of money were transferred to banks in America (£100,000), Italy

25 *Irish Independent*, 27 November 1959.
26 *Irish Independent*, 4 December 1959.
27 *Irish Independent*, December 1959.
28 *Shanahan's Stamp Auctions*, NLI, Ir 383 S1, vol 2.
29 *Inflation: the value of the pound 1770–2001*.
30 Professor Fearon was Professor of biochemistry at Trinity College Dublin between 1934 and 1959. He also represented the university in Seanad Éireann between 1943 and 1959. He died on 27 December 1959.

19 Fourth anniversary party for staff of Shanahan's Stamp Auctions, 1958.
Paul Singer is mid-way down the table on the right.
Source: Shanahan's promotional bulletin

(£150,000), and Switzerland (£350,000). These sums of money[31] were supposedly used by Singer to buy stamps though no receipts were ever produced in court to validate purchase. Nevertheless, the famous Lombardó–Venezia collection was bought in Milan, while Singer's biggest and final coup was the buying of the British and Netherlands section of the Burrus collection for over £300,000.[32] Burrus, a Swiss resident, furthermore gave Singer the option of buying the other five sections of his collection, worth today the equivalent of over €37 million.[33] Singer was all set to consider it when disaster struck.

The catalyst for the collapse of the business was a mysterious and extraordinary robbery on Friday 8 May 1959. Thieves broke into Shanahans premises and stole the valuable and newly-purchased Lombardó–Venezia

31 'Inflation: the value of the pound' (www.parliament.uk).
32 *Irish Independent*, 1 September 1959.
33 'Inflation: the value of the pound' (www.parliament.uk).

collection of stamps. The stamps were due to be auctioned off the following day. Once news of the robbery spread, rumours abounded that the stamp business itself had gone bust. In microcosm, it was Ireland's belated version of the Wall Street crash. Thousands of investors lost enormous sums of money and there were suicides,[34] giving rise to the popular belief that it was 'the biggest swindle since the South Sea Island Bubble'.[35]

When the crash came in May 1959, public opinion laid the blame for the collapse on Paul Singer's shoulders. He was the public face of Shanahan's Stamp Auctions Ltd. He had 'persuaded thousands of ordinary people – shopkeepers, teachers, policemen, housewives and farmers – to invest their savings in his stamp auctions to the tune of £5 million,[36] and then got clean away with it.'[37] He had not, of course. Over the next two years Singer made numerous court appearances and when his first trial spectacularly collapsed, he was tried a second time.

On Monday morning 12 May 1959, the news of the robbery on the previous Friday night was all over town and the premises were inundated with gardaí under the direction of Garda Inspector Farrell. Initially, it was thought that the stamps were insured. In reality they were not. Financial markets are notoriously fickle and the stamp market was no different. Driven by rumour, harassed-looking investors started appearing at Shanahan's demanding their money back.[38] A fortnight later, the firm could not cope and went into voluntary liquidation as nine thousand investors went in pursuit of their money. The gardaí investigated the robbery and in the light of what they discovered they sent a file to the Attorney General's office (today it would be sent to the office of the Director of Public Prosecutions). On Saturday, 29 May, Jerome Shanahan, his son Desmond, Paul Singer and his wife Irma were arrested and they appeared in the Dublin district court on 1 June 1959.

All four, as directors of Shanahan's Stamp Auctions Ltd, were charged with conspiracy to cheat and defraud. Bail was offered but it was so high it was referred to the high court and there Justice Murnaghan reduced it. However, in the case of Paul Singer the court was unsure about his *bona fides*, and while his bail was reduced, he still couldn't find anyone to go independent surety of £10,000. Subsequently, he was destined to remain in

---

34 *Paul Singer, the stamp of scandal*, RTÉ Library and Archive, 3 November 1996.
35 Brady, *Doctor of millions*, p. 7.
36 'Inflation: the value of the pound' (www.parliament.uk).
37 Brady, *Doctor of Millions*, p. 7.
38 *Irish Independent*, 10 December 1959.

Mountjoy prison until his first trial began in October 1960. Before that, however, there was a court hearing to establish whether in fact there was a case for the four accused to answer. The first hearing took place in September 1959 in the Dublin district court before Justice Cathal O'Flynn and concluded four months later at the end of January 1960.[39] There were thirty-nine charges laid against the four accused and in essence they could be reduced to two.

In the first instance, the ordinary people of Ireland were encouraged to invest in stamps and enter them for auction in the belief that they would return a profit. The majority of investors were Irish, with a third of them investing anything between £500 and £1,000.[40] They were not to be disappointed as the Shanahan firm paid dividends to investors without reference to the prices paid at auction. In other words the Shanahans were 'cooking' the books.

The second charge was that Singer had been putting false valuations on the stamps that he bought, and had initiated a scheme of mythical stamp buyers, the most famous of which was a Mr Zombie.[41] This would-be investor had no first name and no address. His account was opened in January 1959 and he allegedly owed the Shanahans a total of £235,655 for stamps purchased.[42] In the closing months before the crash, other fictitious buyers appeared and were credited with sales in excess of £400,000. These sales appeared in Shanahan's books as money owed to the firm. Yet, at the same time Singer allegedly drew money from the Shanahan's bank account to pay for stamps bought by these fictitious investors. That money had now disappeared into a black hole. It was the prosecution case that the main villain of the piece was the gregarious Dr Singer, and he was aided and abetted in the scheme by his wife Irma, and Jerome and Desmond Shanahan.

At the end of 1958 and early 1959 the accumulation of investors' money far outstripped Singer's ability to secure stamps for auctioning.[43] Just before the burglary occurred, cash was rolling in at over £5 million a year. In the same period, it was alleged that over a million pounds had been transferred from Shanahan's bank account to Singer's bank accounts abroad. Finally, the liquidator came to the witness stand and told the court that when he took

39 *Irish Independent*, 23 January 1960.
40 *Irish Independent*, 15 December 1959.
41 *Irish Independent*, 13 January 1960.
42 *Irish Independent*, 25 January 1960.
43 *Irish Independent*, 15 December 1959.

over the affairs of the company on 25 May 1959 he found £2,671 in cash on the premises with a credit balance in the bank of £5,930. Yet, weeks earlier the firm had a turnover of £5 million. Where had all the money gone? To date the liquidator had only recovered £82,643.[44]

In their defence, counsel for the accused came out fighting. In the case of Irma Singer there was no evidence that she had anything to do with investors' money.[45] There was no evidence in court that £750,000 had been illegally secreted away in foreign banks. The use of fictitious purchasers was a mere book-keeping exercise and no way compromised either Shanahan's or their investors. Ulick O'Connor, then a young barrister and today a celebrated author and member of Aosdána, vigorously defended Desmond Shanahan, saying that his blind trust of Paul Singer in the running affairs of the business meant that he knew little about how the company was run. As for Jerome Shanahan, his counsel painted a picture of the head of the firm as nothing more 'than a handyman around the company'.[46] As far as administration went, Jerome, the head of Shanahan's, knew little or nothing. He never had a key to the premises.[47] He was a temperamental man who often made forays into the office to attack Singer for alleged malpractice but always retired gracefully when Singer put his mind to rest.

On the 23 January 1960, the court, after all the preliminary hearings, decided that there was a case to answer and three of the four were sent for trial to the 'next sitting of the central criminal court' on two charges of conspiracy and thirty-six counts of fraudulent conversion.[48] Jerome Shanahan was dismissed. The judge summed up his role in the affair as nothing more than a 'gofer'.[49] Irma Singer and Desmond Shanahan were allowed bail but Singer himself was stuck in jail. So fraught was his reputation that he couldn't get anyone to go independent surety for him. In fact, over the next two years, Mountjoy prison was home, as he took his case to one court, then another, to obtain reasonable bail conditions and to clear his name of any wrongdoing.

Dr Singer used his time well in prison. He had already studied law in Paris and he had worked out that financially it wasn't going to be possible to engage lawyers over any extended period of time. He decided he would fight the case himself. A resourceful man, he successfully petitioned the

44 Brady, *Doctor of millions*, p. 63.
45 Ibid., p. 66.
46 Ibid., p. 69.
47 *Irish Independent*, 28 August 1959.
48 *Irish Independent*, 25 January 1960.
49 *The Times*, 25 January 1960.

prison authority for a second cell to act as a library for a growing number of law books that he either bought or borrowed from the law library in the Four Courts. At a later date when on trial he complained to the governor of Mountjoy about a weak back that 'couldn't carry the smallest weight'.[50] The governor assured him not to worry but that he would facilitate him in getting his copious law books to and from court. Not a man to keep his light under a bushel, the good doctor also gave free legal counsel to the delighted inmates of Mountjoy, who were detained there on criminal charges.

Early one morning, while in his jail cell browsing the Irish *habeas corpus*[51] legislation, Singer discovered that due process of law had not been followed by his continued detention in Mountjoy. On the 23 January 1960 he had been arraigned to appear at the 'next' sitting of the central criminal court but two sittings of that court had come and gone and his case had not been called. Up to then, no one had ever quibbled over the meaning and significance of the word '*next*' as it appeared in the legislation. According to Singer the law said '*next*' and should be strictly interpreted as '*next*'. Singer argued that he was now in unlawful custody. He should be released forthwith. He immediately appealed to a judge in the high court who granted him a conditional order of *habeas corpus*, and asked the attorney general why Singer should not be released unconditionally. The attorney general responded saying that everything was being done to bring Singer to trial, but as it was such an intricate and complex case the book of evidence was not yet ready. The high court sided with the attorney general and threw out Singer's appeal.[52]

Back in Mountjoy a defiant Singer refused to lie down under the high court ruling. He paced his prison cell with mounting agitation. He sought to get in touch with Seán MacBride, a lawyer with an exceptional legal mind and a founder member of Amnesty International. Would he take his case? MacBride agreed, and on the 11 May 1960 both men appeared in the supreme court. This court, on a split decision, upheld Singer's plea and granted him *habeas corpus*. A delighted Singer returned to Mountjoy to pack his bags. He emerged from prison with two suitcases and a green travelling bag and he was dressed in a gabardine raincoat with a black trilby pulled down over his ears.[53] His anticipation of freedom was bitter-sweet and short-lived. He was no sooner outside the heavy wooden prison door

50 Paul Singer file document, NAI, CCC/39/1960.
51 Joseph Byrne, *Dictionary of Irish local history* (Cork, 2004), p. 145.
52 *The Times*, 30 April 1960.
53 Brady, *Doctor of millions*, p. 83.

sauntering down the avenue when two detectives approached him from nowhere with a warrant for his arrest.[54] That afternoon he appeared in the district court on a new set of charges of fraudulent conversion and he was back in Mountjoy for tea, again unable to secure independent bail.

Whatever Singer thought of the new turn in events, there was huge concern in the Dáil about what was happening in the courts. Lots of ordinary people had lost large amounts of money in the stamps imbroglio and there was a 'great deal of public uneasiness' that the case was not approaching closure. Members of the Dáil were feeling the heat from local constituents.[55] Was the State about to compensate Paul Singer for his period of unlawful custody in Mountjoy? The cost of the case to the state so far came to a conservative estimate of £5,500. There were heated exchanges across the floor of the Oireachtas and talk of 'costly blundering' on the part of the attorney general. It was a golden opportunity for the opposition to embarrass the government and to play up the fact that the highest law officer in the state, the attorney general, was in effect a part-timer with a lucrative private practice. To boot, his brother had married into the family of de Valera, the previous Taoiseach, and that was the reason, alleged the opposition, why he had the prestigious job in the first place.[56]

While it was clear that neither the Dáil nor the Minister for Justice had any power to intervene in the courts of law,[57] a couple of days later, Singer and his wife Irma, and Des Shanahan and his wife Diana, were hastily arrested and brought before the district court. This was Diana's first appearance in court and it represented a new departure for the prosecution. The case against them was the same – they had all conspired to defraud investors of Shanahan's Stamp Auctions. The case was now beginning to become chaotic as a sense of panic appeared to creep into what should have been due legal process. Three of the accused were already awaiting trial in the central criminal court on similar charges. What were they doing before another court? The defence in court did not mince their words – the attorney general was allegedly acting 'like a forensic teddy-boy'.[58]

The upshot of this was that three days later, on 3 June 1960, three of the original accused were brought back to the central criminal court and given the opportunity to be arraigned on the initial charges of company fraud.

54   *The Times*, 26 May 1960.
55   www.historical-debates.gov.ie/D/0182, 21 November 2004.
56   Ibid.
57   Ibid.
58   Brady, *Doctor of millions*, p. 92.

Singer, in a pique of anger, was having none of it. As far as he was concerned he was entitled to be a free man on the strength of a supreme court decision. Not alone that, he believed he was re-arrested on prison grounds and that his detainment was consequently unlawful. He telephoned Seán MacBride who came promptly to the court and argued cogently, yet again, for Singer's unequivocal release. The judge agreed and discharged Singer. But just as Singer stepped triumphantly out of the courtroom, a free man by order of the court, he was immediately re-arrested in the outside corridor and a further new set of charges slapped upon him.

Across the river, in the Dáil, news of the shenanigans in the courts was a source of embarrassment to the government, as the opposition warmed to the task of mischief-making. Much was made of the 'apparent atmosphere of confusion and bewilderment which appears to surround the proceedings in connection with the trial'.[59] William Norton, the Labour leader, declared that 'the state machine did not do anything. Their aim seems to be to make a legendary character out of the chief plucker of the Irish public.'[60]

Back in the courtroom, the case against Irma Singer was put on the back boiler. At this point it would be incautious to proceed against her when there were obvious difficulties getting Singer to trial. Desmond Shanahan was a different story. He was desperately keen to have his day in court. He genuinely believed he had done nothing wrong. He resolutely wanted to distance himself from Singer. Thirty-five years later, Desmond Shanahan, speaking on the record for the first time, described Singer as 'very plausible, convincing, persuasive. He was a master of rhetoric, very acceptable on first appearances, and we were quite impressed with him.'[61] Now, it was different. In court the relationship between the two families was colourfully described as that of 'two goats tethered together, each desperately trying to break free from the other'.[62] That afternoon all three were taken before the district court and MacBride made much of the fact that Singer was now in jeopardy before two courts at the same time for similar charges. Justice Farrell adjourned the case for four days to weigh up the situation. When the case re-commenced on 7 June 1960, the judge decided that while the orders sending Singer for trial at the 'next' sitting of the circuit criminal court were now spent and invalid (Singer's contention all along), he nevertheless

59 www.historical-debates.gov.ie/D/0182, 21 November 2004.
60 *Singer, the stamp of scandal*, RTÉ Library and Archive.
61 Ibid.
62 Brady, *Doctor of millions*, p. 69.

supported the attorney general's directive that Singer had a case to answer and declared that he should be tried in the district court.

Meanwhile, back in the central criminal court the parting of the ways for the main protagonists took a step further when the trial of Desmond Shanahan opened on 27 June 1960.[63] Shanahan was pleased. He had helped the police put their case together in the early stages and now would have his opportunity to put his side of the matter. He pleaded not guilty to twenty-two counts of fraud and fraudulent conversion. The thrust of his defence was that Singer was the 'brains' of the operation and that he and his father did not know what was going on. The Shanahans trusted Singer's judgement in all things. He was the stamp expert, he devised the schemes and syndicates, and he travelled the world buying up stamps. Shanahan was never present at any stamp purchases abroad. Singer told the Shanahans there were no receipts or invoices for these purchases because the trade in stamps was related to income tax evasion and the avoidance of death duties.[64] Desmond Shanahan was paid £50 a week, more than €1,000 in today's values, for his services to the firm, the same salary as Paul Singer himself.[65]

Desmond Shanahan's attempt to distance himself from the activities of Paul Singer failed. After twenty days of trial he was found guilty on sixteen counts of fraud and sentenced to fifteen months' imprisonment on 22 July 1960.[66] He served eleven months of the sentence, and on release moved to England with his family. There, he found employment as a store man on a building site earning just over £600 a year.[67]

Back in Mountjoy, Paul Singer again paced his cell. He kept a sharp eye on the Shanahan trial unfolding in the central criminal court. If Shanahan was convicted, the omens did not favour his release. Seán MacBride got a temporary order from the high court stopping the attorney general from proceeding against Singer in the district court. The response of the attorney general six days later was to bring five new charges against Singer in order to get him into court. In court, Singer was then offered a speedy trial if he agreed to be tried in the central criminal court as was first intended. The wily Singer agreed, provided he was allowed out of prison on his own bail. This was a bridge too far for the court. It was now widely believed that if released on bail, Singer would flee the country. The Desmond Shanahan

63   *Irish Independent*, 28 June 1960.
64   *Irish Independent*, 29 September 1959.
65   *Irish Independent*, 30 December 1959.
66   *Irish Independent*, 23 July 1960.
67   Brady, *Doctor of millions,* p. 122.

trial was coming to an end and Singer's role in the Shanahans' Stamp Auction business was exposed.

On 29 July 1960, the high court delivered its judgment on Singer's third *habeas corpus* request. Three judges agreed that the attorney general was not to blame for Singer's non-appearance in court and that the original order sending him for trial was still valid. Seán MacBride immediately lodged an appeal to the supreme court. Five judges from this court returned from holiday on 4 August to hear the appeal. This was crunch time for Singer. On 9 August 1960 the judges decreed that, notwithstanding that Singer was not brought for trial at the 'next' sitting of the circuit criminal court, the original warrant sending him for trial *in the first place* (author's italics) was valid.[68]

All obstacles, real or otherwise, to the courts pursuing the case against Dr Paul Singer were now overcome and in October 1960, his trial opened at the central criminal court, Green Street, Dublin. Before the court was the most spectacular fraud case in the history of the state. By now the good doctor could ill afford a defence counsel and he proceeded to conduct his own defence. He opened his case with an emotional plea. He argued that, given the amount of previous publicity that attended the Desmond Shanahan trial, he couldn't possibly get a fair trial. He cited the judge who, on the last day of that trial, told the court that Shanahan's firm was 'a criminal machine invented and operated by Paul Singer'.[69]

This emotional plea aside, Singer then got down to setting out his stall as to why Shanahan's Stamp Auctions was a legitimate enterprise. As the trial proceeded he gave a plausible account of all operations. In court he had two blackboards and with diagrams he explained to the jury the finances of his many schemes.[70] He had a transparent explanation as to what the auctions were all about. He explained about syndicates and how they received a dividend, even when their stamp lots went unsold at auction. It was simple. The company, Shanahan's Stamp Auctions Ltd, stepped in and bought up the unsold lots with a view to off-loading them at a future auction. In this way the company underwrote the dividend to investors which would be recouped at a future date, when the company sold the stamps. In this way everyone was a winner. Everything was above board, including the fictitious Mr Zombie and others. They were merely a mechanism for the firm to buy in the unsold lots and pay a dividend to investors.

---

68   *Irish Independent*, 10 August 1960.
69   Brady, *Doctor of millions*, p. 133.
70   *Irish Independent*, 13 October 1960.

He paid tribute to Diana Shanahan, wife of Desmond, who was 'one of the most brilliant women he had ever met'. It was remarked then that Singer, by referring to Diana in this way, was attempting to take the spotlight off himself and unload blame. But two years previously, at the fourth birthday party of Shanahan's Stamp Auctions, when there was nothing at stake, he had equally praised her for her wizardry at figures. She was in charge of the accounts department, with almost half of the eighty-five member staff answerable to her. He completely dismissed the underestimates put on their stamp collections by outside experts like Frank Robson Lowe and others.[71] And he accepted that the panic that set in after the burglary in May 1959 was responsible for the collapse. Investments practically stopped after the burglary.[72]

For four days Singer held the court enraptured. He was an outstanding performer. When he sat down Justice Hough summed up. It wasn't what Singer hoped to hear. His opening remarks dwelt on Shanahan's inventive schemes as 'quite new to the philatelic world and to the auctioneering world'.[73] Such comment could be interpreted either way, but the learned judge went on to say the real problem was that even before the burglary Shanahan's own accountants were saying that their bookkeeping was in a mess.[74] There *were* no profits in Shanahan's stamp enterprise. The nub of the matter was that the money that Shanahan's was paying out as dividends to investors was in effect other investors' money – there was no basis for any dividends to be paid at all. Singer's blackboard exercises were all gobbledy-gook. And what about all that money that was transferred abroad to Singer's bank accounts? Where was it now?

The jury retired on 21 November 1960 and in less than two hours found Singer guilty on nineteen charges of fraud and fraudulent conversion.[75] The judge gave Singer a week to 'consider his position'.[76] At the end of the week if he came back and told the court where all the money was stashed – the £1 million paid into Singer's accounts in banks in Paris, Canada, New Zealand, Zurich and London during the final year of Shanahan's Stamp Auctions – the judge would take it into consideration before passing sentence. Dr Singer thought about it for the week, returned to court but

71 *Irish Independent*, 3 November 1960.
72 *Irish independent*, 16 November 1960.
73 *Irish independent*, 19 November 1960.
74 *Irish Independent*, 22 September 1959.
75 *Irish Independent*, 22 November 1960.
76 Paul Singer file document, NAI, CCC/39/1960.

had nothing to say. The judge wasn't impressed and was annoyed that Singer had not thought fit to respond to his own generosity of spirit. He imposed fourteen years' penal servitude on the good doctor.[77]

What happened next had all the hallmarks of an Hitchcockian court drama. Singer jumped to his feet demanding leave to appeal. To an amazed courtroom, Singer declared that the foreman of the jury was himself a creditor of Shanahan's, with a claim of £375.[78] He was also a member of the firm Craig, Gardner and Company, where the liquidator, Gerard O'Brien, was a senior partner. He would have been privy to all the information that the liquidator might have uncovered. In no way was he an unbiased juryman.[79]

On 11 April 1961 the court of criminal appeal met to consider Singer's application. Two months later, on 23 June 1961, his conviction was struck out and a date for a new trial set. Singer returned to Mountjoy because the bail conditions were as yet too stringent. A couple of weeks later bail was reduced when a Dún Laoghaire publican, a Mr Larkin, arrived at the district court with independent surety of £1,500.[80] Singer was out of prison for the first time in over two years but he would have to wait for three months before his re-trial could begin. In the meantime, he employed the services of Seán MacBride in the supreme court to ward off an attempt by the liquidator to drag him into court to account for Shanahan's finances. It was a move that, if it had succeeded, would have had a detrimental effect on his upcoming trial.

Singer's initial arrest in 1959 and subsequent appearances in the courts received huge publicity. Over a two-year period the affair bemused, confused and enthralled the Irish public. But by the time the second trial came about, Ireland had moved on. The advent of television and Ireland's own TV station saw to that. Ireland, in many ways, was beginning to embrace the wider world. Keynesian thinking and new policies to combat economic stagnation found expression in Whitaker's Programme for Economic Expansion.[81] In religious and cultural affairs the winds of change were already blowing as preparations were well underway for the historic Second Vatican Council.[82] Real drama, not courtroom drama, was now

77 *Irish Independent*, 29 Novemebr 1960.
78 Brady, *Doctor of millions*, p. 158.
79 Paul Singer file document NAI, CCC/39/1960.
80 *Irish Independent*, 10 July 1961.
81 Garvan, *Preventing the future*, p. 115.
82 The Second Vatican Council opened on 11 October 1962.

Dr. Singer gives party for jury men

20 Paul Singer, bearded and smoking a pipe, with some members of the jury after he
was cleared of all charges in the central criminal court in January 1962.
Courtesy of Irish Press Newspapers

sourced in faraway places like the Congo where the crises in West Africa and
Irish troops' involvement in the United Nations became the prime talking
point in the pub and front living room.

In the second trial, no new evidence or revelations were produced by
either side. But the judge, in his summing-up, cut to the nub of the problem.
Incredible as it may now seem – in the light of the investigative tribunals in
the 1990s and early twenty-first century, where fraudulent conversion
required the operation of multiple bank accounts – Shanahan's, despite
their multi-million pound business, operated only one bank account.
Consequently, the judge concluded, it was impossible to distinguish at any
point in time what was investors' money and what was money belonging to
the company.[83] Extraordinarily, the account books of the company and
lodgements to the bank made no distinction between the two. The case for
fraud and fraudulent conversion could not then be proved. On this vital
point, the case against Dr Paul Singer collapsed and the judge instructed the
jury to record a verdict of 'not guilty'.

83   *Irish Independent*, 26 January 1962.

A jubilant Dr Singer ran from the dock, hugged Seán MacBride and, incredibly, signed autographs for some of the jurymen. Minutes later he had warm champagne and some stout sent over to the jury room. He declared that his first priority was to visit his aged mother in Canada who was in failing health. He loved Ireland and he would return. He told waiting reporters that his legal expenses would come to £15,000 and that he had to sell his house in Foxrock for £14,000. He had to defend himself in the first trial because he could not afford lawyers. The state would pay for the second trial.[84]

Over a glass of 'bubbly' he commented on his time in prison. He reminisced on how he chopped wood and made trousers for prisoners in the tailoring shop, earning a penny a day for his efforts. He had his own food brought into prison including fourteen eggs a day.[85] He read law and had access to up to 500 law books. He told everyone present that when everything would be sorted, no one who had invested in Shanahan's Stamp Auctions Ltd would lose money.[86] After lunch he retired with Irma, his wife, to his modest terraced flat in Dún Laoghaire.

Dr Singer was never seen in Ireland again. Police believe he boarded the mail boat at Dún Laoghaire that evening for Holyhead.[87] As he stood on the bridge of the ship watching the lights of Dún Laoghaire fade in the distance, legend has it that he remarked wistfully 'farewell, Treasure Island'. In the following weeks, as the bankruptcy affairs of Shanahan's were wound up, it was like Hamlet without the Prince, and the opposition in the Dáil once again did their utmost to embarrass the government. With Singer gone, the case against Diana Shanahan and Irma Singer was quietly dropped.

Today, Shanahan's Stamp Auctions Ltd is still unfinished business. Singer was found not guilty of fraud but vast amounts of money, millions, went unaccounted for. No one ever knew how much money Singer spent in the buying of stamps and what may have gone to personal aggrandisement but we can be sure that a sum in excess of fifty million euro in today's money was transferred abroad.[88] Desmond Shanahan believed that he had done no wrong and ended up serving eleven months of a fifteen-month prison sentence. The role of Diana Shanahan was never explored. Irma Singer never stood trial and through the courts she managed to have her bail

84 Brady, *Doctor of millions*, p. 167.
85 *Singer, the stamp of scandal*, RTÉ Library and Archive.
86 Brady, p. 167.
87 *Irish Independent*, 6 February 1962.
88 *Singer, the stamp of scandal*, RTÉ Library and Archive.

money (a sum of £10,000 put up by her father) invested and had it returned to her with interest at the end.

On 3 October 1996 Desmond Shanahan and his wife, Diana, spoke to RTÉ for the first time about what happened in those heady days in the late 1950s. Shanahan recalled that when he and Singer were first arrested, brought to the Bridewell and kept overnight, Singer snored the place down without a care in the world, while Shanahan was in bits. Diana was clear: 'I try not to think about him – he blotted out my life.' In the same 1996 interview Ulick O'Connor, the barrister at the centre of the court dramas thirty-five years previously, was more circumspect. With hindsight he thought Singer's fundamentals were sound and legitimate. He felt that Singer was a highly intelligent man who wasn't really dishonest. He wasn't a rogue but 'a clever man who took chances'.

Singer's empire rested on his ability to buy up stocks of stamps world-wide and bring them back to Ireland where they supposedly increased in value at auction. Everything was fine so long as the stamps were there to be sourced. By 1958 huge money was flowing into Shanahan's but Singer was finding it harder and harder to source new stamp collections elsewhere. That was the importance of his buying into the world-famous Burrus collection and the securing of the Lombardó–Venezia stock. When Singer bought the Burrus collection, all the Shanahan staff came out to the airport to greet him and broke into song with 'For he's a jolly good fellow'. Earlier, Singer had confided in his cashier, Hugh Finlay, his concern about the amount of cash being invested in Shanahan's. He wondered what could be done to discourage certain groups from sending in money. Now, in the car on the way back from the airport Singer confided that all their worries were over. With the new stamp collections, the firm could handle all investments.[89] That was the tragedy of the burglary on 8 May 1959. Just as the company was about to go into 'overdrive', investments practically stopped and the firm folded spectacularly overnight.[90]

The legal entanglements that arose out of the collapse of Shanahan's meant that a long and complicated affair ensued. It tested the best legal minds of the day over a three-year period, and made legal history. It also clearly confounded an ambitious young accountant, Charles J. Haughey, who was shortly to become Minister for Justice in the government of the day. Haughey's accountancy firm, Haughey Boland, was asked in the late 1950s to

89 *Irish Independent*, 9 November 1960.
90 *Irish Independent*, 4 Novemebr 1960.

investigate Shanahan's Stamp Auctions. By all reports, it was a very brief arrangement. Singer, being a very dominant character, stonewalled Haughey by not delivering vital information and documentation. He blamed Haughey's firm for lack of results, saying they were too slow. Haughey had to withdraw from the audit, and in his own words, 'was very glad to do so.'[91]

Paul Singer, on leaving Ireland, settled in Canada and died in Toronto on 23 February 1985. He was seventy-three years of age. He left an estate worth seven thousand Canadian dollars and a statement from his wife, lodged with his will, declared that all his debts had been paid.[92]

[91] *Singer, the stamp of scandal,* RTÉ Library and Archive.
[92] Ibid.

Index